THE JEWISH TEACHERS HANDBOOK

Volume III

EDITED BY AUDREY FRIEDMAN MARCUS

Alternatives in Religious Education, Inc.
Denver, Colorado

Published by
Alternatives in Religious Education, Inc.
3945 South Oneida Street
Denver, Colorado 80237

Library of Congress Catalog Number 81-67024
ISBN Number 0-86705-003-9

To Jewish teachers everywhere, dedicated individuals all, and destined to sit at the right hand of God.

TABLE OF CONTENTS

INTRODUCTION

A.R.E. and I are proud to bring to Jewish teachers all over the world the final volume of *The Jewish Teachers Handbook* series. We hope that you will find the contents useful and that your teaching will be enriched by the exposure. Most important, we hope that your abillity to reach and touch the lives of your students will be sharpened and expanded. All of us in Jewish education owe a debt of gratitude to the many outstanding teacher-authors whose willingness to share their expertise and ideas made these volumes possible.

Volume I began the series with chapters on the basics of teaching in a Jewish setting. Volume II continued in the same vein, adding such "extras" as creating community in the classroom, evaluating students, involving parents, working with teen aides, teaching adults and the elderly and using storytelling, dance movement and drama to enrich the classroom. Now Volume III rounds out the picture, featuring as the central focus the teaching of specific subject areas.

We begin with a discussion of the "well dressed classroom" co-authored by Joyce Seglin, who capably directs the Hebrew and Religious School at Temple Emanuel, Beverly Hills, California and Joel Grishaver, one of the most prolific and creative authors on the Jewish educational scene. The chapter points out the importance of designing functional, attractive Jewish learning spaces and includes many suggestions for doing so. Along the same lines, Elyce Azriel draws on her experience as the Director of the Teacher Center in Cincinnati to provide a step-by-step approach to creating effective bulletin boards.

Because so many teachers have inquired about inquiry — what it is and how to use it — I have written a brief overview of this information processing model of teaching. A few examples of inquiry lessons are included.

Rita Kopin, author of the popular book of games, *The Lively Jewish Classroom* (A.R.E.), has contributed an exceptionally useful overview of making and using puppets for Jewish learning. Her talented daughter, Judye, has here, too, provided the illustrations.

Nationally known JESNA consultant Fradle Freidenreich is an expert on teaching Jewish Social Studies. She has authored a challenging chapter on expanding our view of this discipline. Steve and Linda Schaffzin, the imaginative editors of *World Over,* give some excellent pointers on teaching Jewish current events.

Joel Grishaver's *Bible People* workbooks are part of nearly every Jewish child's experiences. Here Joel outlines his approach to teaching Bible, one that involves students in texts and helps them to discover the lessons and intricacies awaiting discovery in every verse of this vast treasury.

Teaching about God is such an awesome challenge that many teachers shy away from it altogether. Sherry Bissell has devoted a decade to developing approaches to this difficult subject and offers some of her ideas here. Her own mini-course for teen-agers, *God: The Eternal Challenge* (A.R.E) puts into practice many of these ideas.

Today death education takes place in secular schools as a matter of course. My chapter in this book on teaching death and dying reiterates the need for death education in religious schools and describes appropriate teaching strategies for every age group.

In their chapter on teaching Jewish prayer, Rabbi Stuart Kelman, Assistant Professor of Jewish Education at Hebrew Union College-Jewish Institute of Religion in Los Angeles and Joel Grishaver describe one model of providing students with both a cognitive background and experiential resource for internalizing the liturgy.

Rabbi Yosi Gordon is Executive Director of the Talmud Torah of St. Paul and a member of the team for an important Hebrew curriculum project. He offers an essay on teaching Hebrew which is both thought provoking and painfully honest. A teacher in Yosi's school, Earl Schwartz, has pioneered a curriculum on moral development based on the Kohlberg model. His chapter represents a condensation of that document.

So often we program primarily for the alienated youngsters who don't care about Jewish learning. Zena Sulkes, Director of Education in Clearwater, Florida and A.R.E. author *(Proud and Jewish)*, makes a case for directing more of our efforts to the gifted among our students.

Dr. Ronald Wolfson, Director of the Educational Program at the University of Judaism in Los Angeles, has developed tools for evaluating and choosing learning materials for the Jewish classroom. His important and comprehensive chapter on the subject seems the natural way to end this volume.

Author Bruce Joyce *(Models of Teaching,* published by Prentice-Hall) has identified over 80 distinct models of teaching — more, he admits, than any teacher could master during a career. Joyce posits that methods make a difference in *what* is learned, as well as *how* it is learned and that different students react differently to any given teaching method. If we take Joyce's stance to heart, we must equip ourselves with a basic variety of models of teaching that we can bring into play for different purposes. It is only by doing so that we can meet the needs of different learners and give our classes variety and depth. Hopefully, this volume and the preceding two will enable you to expand your repertoire of teaching strategies and to think through your approaches to Jewish subject matter in a fresh manner.

DESIGNS FOR JEWISH LEARNING SPACES

by Joel Lurie Grishaver and Joyce Seglin

Every classroom has a wardrobe. It is dressed in its wardrobe (or designed and redesigned) by the teacher every time it is used. The wardrobe can be "store-bought," coordinated and fashionable, or homemade, free flowing and eclectic. It can be custom tailored to maximize potential (and to disguise weaknesses) and it can be up-to-date, influenced by the times and by current styles. It is the responsibility of the teacher to shape the classroom into an inviting space, a place which encourages and enhances Jewish learning in meaningful ways.

While there will always be compromise caused by school regulations and budgetary limitations, every teacher can evolve a teaching space which enhances instruction. This chapter will present some of the possibilities for doing so.

Regardless of how a room starts out, no matter what chairs happen to be in it, no matter how much gum has piled up and no matter what is on the walls, no matter where in the building it is located and no matter how dark, dismal, dungeon-like and dirty it seems, space can be shaped and improved by the teacher. To begin such a transformation, it is necessary to have a vision of what our classroom might become. We need to begin with a sense of the *ideal* place for our class to meet. Then we need to move this ideal into an achievable reality. Few schools, if any, enable us physically to build or rebuild our teaching areas. Indeed, many of us share our spaces, or work in spaces which are not meant to be classrooms at all. Yet all of us can rearrange chairs, pin, tape, tack, staple, hook or otherwise attach objects to the wall. And all of us can buy or make things to beautify our rooms. Thus we begin to outfit our classroom.

The first step in designing an ideal learning space is to collect data on the key elements: the teacher, the subject, the students and the physical space. Below is an outline for a needs assessment. It will provide you with some key areas to consider as you plan your ideal environment.

JEWISH LEARNING ENVIRONMENTS NEEDS ASSESSMENT

First Impressions

Consider first the age and grade of your students, what students are like at this age and the subject of the course. Be aware of the number of students in the class and the number for whom the room is designed. From this basic information you can draw some quick conclusions.

Which of the following statements about instructional needs will be true for you?

My classroom will:

1. be overcrowded
2. have adequate room in which to work
3. be mine alone to do with as I wish
4. be shared with one or two other teachers
5. consist of makeshift space, existing only when the class meets
6. house students for one period at a time
7. house the same students all day for all subjects
8. be the location for the same (or similiar) lessons happening more than once on a given day
9. house the same students for two or three periods each time schools meets

10. be the location for many different types of lessons directed by me
11. change locations from period to period, meaning that my environment has to be carried (or rolled) around
12. be "destroyed" by another class which uses the room
13. contain extremely active students
14. by the middle of the day, be filled with youngsters who will need a change of activity
15. contain munchkins whose bathroom needs have to be considered
16. contain tired, burned out kids who have already been to school, dancing, swimming and/or soccer practice
17. contain not-yet-awake, dragged-out-of-bed kids who refuse to take off their jackets and who try to sleep
18. contain unwashed youngsters who bring the locker room environment with them
19. contain carefully dressed kids who are afraid to get dirty
20. be bothered by all kinds of external distractions
21. have to contend with the effects of climatic conditions (e.g., snow boots, umbrellas, mud, roof leaks and other teaching hazards)
22. need to contain specific resources necessary for my subject
23. need to provide the possibility for use of specific equipment, such as audiovisual hardware.
24. be mysterious to me until I know more
25. be an environment that I can design and manage

Based on what you have learned from these considerations, decide what kind of a room would best suit your needs. Request the ideal space.

Content Needs

The subjects you teach make demands on the classroom environment. Think about the answers to these questions for each subject that you teach:

1. What materials will the students be using in class? (Books, workbooks, worksheets, audiovisual aids, etc.)
2. What kind of working area do these materials demand?
3. What kind of storage will be needed for materials?
4. What kind of possibilities for visual display are needed? (Chalkboards, flip charts, projectors, etc.)
5. What support facilities do these require? (Electrical outlets, window shades for darkness, wall space, etc.)
6. What kind of display space will be needed on an ongoing basis for charts, maps, models, pictures, student projects, etc.?
7. What kinds of access, storage and security will be required?
8. How can you avoid carrying in the needed items each time the class meets?
9. What tools will you and your students need on a regular basis? (Art supplies, writing utensils, various kinds of paper, hole punches, folders, etc.)

The classroom is not only a place to learn; it is also a setting in which to be Jewish. Before continuing, think about the things your classroom needs for you to foster the development of Jewish feelings and actions — e.g., *mezzuzah, Keren Ami* box, an Ark, posters, Israeli flag, etc.

Teacher Needs

On a certain level, a classroom needs to belong to the teacher. It is as personal as an office or a workshop. You have the right to invest some effort in making it a place which reflects your personality and goals and which makes you comfortable. In this regard, you will want to consider the following:

1. What will you want to have in your room to make it yours? (Pictures, coffee mugs, an objet d'art for the desk, posters, etc.)
2. What kinds of privacy needs do you have? Will there be areas that are off limits to students?
3. What teaching styles will you utilize?
   a. Lecture (do not feel guilty — it is a good technique)
   b. Lecture-demonstration
   c. Lecture-discussion (Socratic or free flowing)
   d. Lecture-activity
   e. Media presentations to the whole class (with or without teacher participation)
   f. Worksheets to be gone over by the whole class
   g. Student presentations to the whole class
   h. Games for the whole class directed by the teacher or a proxy
   i. Small group work (each group does the same task)
   j. Small group work (each small group does a piece of the whole)
   k. Small group work (each group rotates

through a progression of tasks)

l. Small group tasks which are competitive or interactive — e.g., debates, games, simulations

m. Small group tasks with motivation or skill level adapted to the specific needs of each group

n. Individualized instruction (each student completes the same material at his/her own pace)

o. Individualized instruction (each student completes similar material with various units added or deleted based on individual needs)

p. Individualized instruction (each student works toward the same objective and chooses the learning tasks that facilitate mastery)

q. Individualized instruction (each student receives a set of materials which have been customized to meet his/her needs and interests)

The teaching styles you use will determine how you organize your room. For each of the styles outlined above, two choices are possible. The student can go to a specific area in the room and complete his or her work there. Or the student can pick up material at a central storage/display area to use at his/her seat. Combinations of these two procedures are possible. Materials can also be passed out by the teacher to each student.

Items (a) through (h) describe frontal teaching, meaning that the attention of the class is focused in one place. Items (i) through (m) describe cluster learning, meaning students are learning in small, interactive groups. Items (n) through (q) describe individualized learning formats in which students are individually paced and directed. Most teachers use a combination of these techniques. Think about the teaching styles you use and estimate the percentage of time you will spend utilizing each. When you design your room, decide which format is the dominant one and to which other styles the room needs to be able to adapt.

Student Needs

While the classroom may "belong" to the teacher, it must also be a setting which supports the students' needs. Things to consider in this area are:

1. How big are your students and what kinds of furniture can they comfortably sit in or on?

2. What kind of energy level can you anticipate? Will you need to contain or arouse?

3. What kinds of classrooms are students used to? How have their weekday schools and their previous religious school rooms been arranged and structured? (You will need to evaluate whether a change will enhance or confuse.)

4. What socialization needs do your students have? Do they socialize in groups of two, three, five or by the roomful? (Here you will have to balance nurturing and restraining student needs.)

5. What time of day do you teach the children — morning, afternoon or evening? Is it before other things they want to do or after important things they have already done?

6. For how many hours will you have a group? Anticipate how many activities it will take to fill that time slot.

7. What are the privacy needs of your students? Are there things you want them to be able to put away during class that neither you nor their peers know anything about? What kind of privacy should they have from other students and from the teacher?

8. Is there a problem child of whom you are aware? How will he or she affect your room?

9. In what way will you allow both the individual students and the group as a whole define the room (and/or portions of the room) as theirs?

Based on the insights that these questions trigger, decide what design factors you want to add to your master plan.

BETWEEN THE REAL AND THE IDEAL

So far, we have been collecting data related to instructional needs. Your answers reflect the kind of place you want your classroom to be. Now envision the room you have been assigned. Visualize the furniture, storage, display areas, chalkboards, bulletin boards, movie screen, electrical outlets, lighting, overall appearance (dark, bright, small, cavernous, cold, etc.), available space and built-in distractions. Analyze the problems you think you might face. Determine the gaps between the real classroom which you inherited and the ideal one you imagined earlier.

Several solutions are possible to the problems you anticipate. Perhaps you can have different furniture brought into you room. You might request additional electrical outlets or other minor alterations. Some of the difficulties may be alleviated by buying or building some items or by changing the wall surfaces with paint, posters or contact paper. If the situation is really untenable, request a different room. It never hurts to try!

GETTING STARTED

The second step, once you have completed your needs assessment, is to obtain a catalogue of classroom supplies. There are available catalogues filled with thousands of useful items — classroom decorations, storage pieces, instructional aids, student awards and items which defy categorization. Remember that any item which was designed for secular education can be adapted to Jewish education. Furthermore, almost all of the expensive items which are pictured (other than the electronic items) were probably first made by a classroom teacher out of shelf paper, cardboard or other scrounge materials. Your challenge will be to figure out how to make or acquire your own version of those items that you feel will enrich your classroom. In the Bibliography at the conclusion of this chapter, you will find lists of companies which sell materials for classrooms, a collection of books which will explain how to make things for your room and a company which specializes in items for the Jewish classroom. If you are fortunate enough to live in a community which has a Jewish Teacher Center (Wilmette, Minneapolis, Silver Spring, St. Louis, Houston, Cincinnati, New York, Los Angeles, Philadelphia, Milwaukee, Toronto and Southfield, Michigan), visit the Center and join the network of caring teachers who share ideas and resources.

In the next section of this chapter, we will examine several elements essential to a well-dressed classroom.

LEARNING CENTERS

A learning center can be a physical location where a student can go (alone or in groups) to work on particular kinds of activities. It can also be a place where students obtain certain types of materials which they utilize or complete in their own work space.

A learning center can be a place for drama. It may be only a pile of cast-off clothes for cos-

tumes, or it may contain scripts or role play cards.

A learning center can be a shoe box filled with objects for students to sort, categorize and identify. The shoe box can also contain items which make up a "historical puzzle." Students are asked to figure out where and when in history the person who used the items lived.

A learning center can be a place to read. It can be any quiet corner of the room — with or without a rug, sofa or pillows — where students can read a specific story, or choose from among a variety of materials. (You might want to supply ear muffs to help make it a quiet place.) Worksheets or activity sheets can provide accountability for the reading that students complete.

A learning center can be a place to listen to tapes and records. It can be stocked with an elaborate headphone system, enabling many students to work at one time, or it can simply contain a small ear plug and a basic cassette recorder. Such a listening center can generate questions, projects and feelings. Directions can be given on a tape recorder. When a second tape recorder is added, students can fill in their own answers. (If you don't have a tape recorder, draft a teenager, a student who needs extra attention or a parent to read.)

A learning center can be a chalkboard. It can be a group writing a story together or in turn. It can be (especially with colored chalk) a place for Hebrew language exercises. And it can be a place where values are expressed.

A learning center can be a window shade which has pockets glued to it. Students sort cards into the correct pockets or take the cards out of the pockets, completing suggested tasks back at their seats.

A learning center can be a collection of art supplies and "scrounge" materials. The materials can be used in an open ended way, or task cards and worksheets can outline instructions for specific projects.

A learning center can be a suitcase or table full of educational games.

A learning center can be a map. Students can use pins to trace routes on wall maps or grease pencils to write on laminated floor maps. Maps can be copied from 3-D models, or 3-D models can be made from maps. Maps can have layers of transparencies. Students can also trace maps on transparencies for their own use.

A learning center can even be just four

sheets of poster board, each with directions for tasks students can complete.

A learning center can be a place for content or interests, required or optional work, scrap paper art, pantomine, music, creative writing, investigation, drills and skills, poetry, programmed materials, construction (as in building), choosing a topic, doing research and writing private journals. Centers can even be places to take tests and quizzes!

A room alive with learning centers becomes an inviting environment in which to learn. In such a room students will be learning in corners, on or under tables, in bookcases, at desks or on the rug. They will be hanging or standing or lying, working in an enriched classroom with a variety of resources including books, worksheets, projectors, computers, art supplies, games, chart stands, flash cards, manipulatives and hands-on materials.

For more on learning centers, see Chapter 4.

BULLETIN BOARDS

A bulletin board is a good way to utilize wall space for display and decoration. Besides the usual cork board, window shades, pegboard, windows, table edges, the back of chalkboards on wheels, cardboard boxes and ceilings can also be used for the same purposes. Bulletin boards can also be interactive, providing opportunities for sorting, ordering and reordering, hanging up answers (and questions) and so on. For more on the subject of bulletin boards, see Chapter 2.

STORAGE AREAS

The way we store our materials can affect a) the way we decorate our classroom, b) the kind of instruction we provide, c) the kinds of things we can keep in our classroom, and d) the kind of freedom our students will have there.

Storage areas can be the most attractive or the most unattractive places in our classrooms. They can be brightly decorated, displaying creative materials and learning possibilities, or they can be cluttered centers of chaos and confusion.

Our storage areas can define the ways we teach. Where we put books, files, paper, pencils, maps, crayons and the like, determines who can get them. If they are accessible to students, then the classwork flows in one manner. If they are managed by the teacher, the classwork will proceed in a different manner.

The kinds of supplies a teacher keeps in the room are determined by budget, space and security. Keeping a tape recorder, a set of reference books, a paper cutter and other similar materials in the classroom necessitates the creation of ways to store them.

Unless they are built into the walls, storage places take up floor space. By placing bookcases, cabinets, cubbies and the like creatively around the room, you can break up the space into subareas and you can enhance or limit movement.

Pencils can be put in tin cans, shoe boxes, pockets on boards, paper cups or even in actual pencil holders.

Papers can be stored in cupboards, drawers, stacking trays, old filefolder boxes, hang-up folders or paper caddies, anything an office uses, a cardboard version of anything an office uses, liquor boxes with sections and dishpans.

Games, materials and other junk can be put away in suitcases, milk crates, any kind of box, ice cream containers (Baskin Robbins gives them away), shelves, file drawers and corners of the room.

Bookcases can be made of boxes, crates, bricks and boards, cardboard cubes, confiscated skateboards. Real bookcases can also be used.

Inventories are stored in the teacher's mind.

SEATING

Chairs, tables, benches, rugs, pillows, mats and counters are meant for sitting. There are many different seating possibilities. Each of these will influence the tone, learning style and management of a room. Some of the books which are included in the Bibliography contain geometric configurations for classroom seating. A few guiding principles, however, will help you more than a graph:

1. Circles are only good if you *really* want your students looking at and talking to each other.
2. The closer to the floor students are, the quieter and more controlled they will be.
3. A classroom can be arranged to support pairs of teaching styles such as these:
   a. Group work and frontal teaching: Furniture is arranged in clusters. All of the clusters face a single focus in the room.
   b. Individual and group learning: Chairs or

desks are clustered in groups of no more than four students per cluster.

c. Lecture and individual work: Chairs and desks are in rows.

(Such arrangements will rarely support a third style of teaching without moving furniture around).

4. If a seating arrangement doesn't work, try another. If one way no longer seems to work, change it. If one way has been working well for a long time, change it just for variety.

TEACHING IN A NON-CLASSROOM

Teaching is most difficult in spaces which are not really meant to be classrooms. Many teachers face their students in hallways, alcoves, sections of social halls and other "creative" spaces. Those of you who work in places like these have a special burden. It is a vital, though difficult task, to make both you and your students comfortable and at home in whatsoever forsaken corner you have been allotted. The three problems you will face in such a situation are distractions, ownership and storage.

Distractions

When you work in "public" space, it is necessary to find ways to cut off the rest of the world. Doing so enables students to focus in on the lesson and the interaction that is taking place. In settings such as these, it is likely that you will have problems with noise from adjoining areas. You may also have problems with visual distractions — people who wander by in the course of the session, classes on their way to music or Hebrew, visiting parents, etc. If the ceiling is high (as it often is in a social hall), you may find students gazing into the vastness while listening to each noise echoing. Additionally, almost every shared environment contains temptations that your students are forbidden to touch, but which they find far more fascinating than anything you have to offer. The following will be helpful when dealing with distractions:

1. Avoid frontal teaching. Have students focus on papers or projects and work in small groups.
2. Work as close to the floor as possible. As mentioned before, the lower a group of students sits, the easier it is to control. They will also feel more together.

3. Limit the space you use even if there is room to spread out. The closer and more limited the working environment, the less distracting outside factors will be. Hold class in a corner made with a folding or rolling partition or construct a natural barrier of tables.
4. A carpet and dividers will draw students together and define the area. The chalkboard should be placed so that it directs your students away from, and not toward, distractions. Thoughtful placement of chairs will also help here.

Ownership

Your students will obviously be aware that yours is not a real classroom. Their first reaction will be to decide that if it is not a real room, then it will probably not be real school. Until they own the space, they won't own the learning process. If, however, students help to create or shape their learning space, they will feel better about being in it and working in it. Some ways of involving your students in the process of ownership are:

1. Roll out sheets of butcher paper and each week let students write, draw, cut, paste, color, paint, etc.
2. Together make a patchwork rug which can become the focal point of your portable room.
3. With your students, decorate the items which regularly roll in or are carried into your temporary classroom (e.g., blackboard, desk, cart, etc.).
4. Ask students to be responsible for carrying in materials and for transforming the space each week.

Storage Again

It is very demoralizing to have to pick up your classroom and put it back into your car trunk after every session. You feel as if you could do a lot more with the class, but that it is just not worth it to drag everything up all those stairs only to bring it back down. Not having one's own closet in the classroom can get the best teacher down. Some of the following suggestions may help:

1. If you don't have a "real" classroom, you nonetheless need, and have the right to have, a permanent storage area for all your materials.
2. Ask your school for a cart, a little red wagon, or for a rolling, folding bookcase.

This will enable you to have both a drawer and a closet.

3. If your storage unit is inadequate, consider suitcases, milk crates and, even as a last resort, boxes from reams of paper. Contact paper helps to make such cardboard containers look nice and the room less tacky.

SNAP SHOTS — A PORTFOLIO

Thus far in this chapter, we have discussed wardrobes and accessories for the classroom. But classroom designs go beyond color coordination. We'll end with a few total concepts. These are a few of our favorite learning places. They are places where the form (the design of the room) really does determine the content (the way the learning takes place). Enjoy these snapshots.

Ralph's Room

Ralph is fifty years old and earns his living as a salesperson. He is the type of guy who can tell you endless stories, most of which you enjoy the first time or two. Ralph loves to teach religious school, and specializes in teaching values to upper junior high school students. He is good at talking with kids about sex, drugs, politics and relationships and tying these to Jewish values. When Ralph taught ninth grade (on a Tuesday evening), he requested the following from his principal: "Put the chairs in a circle. It doesn't matter if they are armchairs or folding chairs. Do not supply desks and make sure there is a chalkboard on which I can write. Put a coffee pot, cups, cream and sugar in the room." When the principal questioned serving coffee to ninth graders, Ralph explained, "They won't drink it. We'll sacrifice a pot of coffee every session, but they'll feel like adults — and our conversations will go better."

Gila's Room

Gila teaches in a double room. Half of it is a "formal classroom" with desks in rows that face her desk and the chalkboard. The back half of the room has pillows and milk crates and a carpet. In the front half of the room, Gila gives lectures and tests and has the students work in workbooks. In the back half, the students stretch out and do their reading assignments. Here they also gather to do group projects. They frequently present plays and act things out. Gila also keeps a costume box in her room.

Once she was working with some students doing research on the rug. They were looking at some maps. She found herself chalking some additional maps onto the floor as she explained things. The following week her students were busy using the floor tiles as a grid on which multi-colored fabric tape was forming a huge world map. Once the class had finished the map, it served as the basis for a number of lectures and a variety of games. The room became an ongoing play-research area, symbolizing the interaction of teacher and student in the learning process.

David's Room

The first week of school David sends a note home to parents telling them that the shirts and ties and dresses the children are used to wearing to religious school will not be appropriate for his class. The following Sunday the kids arrive in torn jeans and overalls. David arrives with hammers, saws, wood and lots of tri-wall cardboard (the material out of which refrigerator boxes are made). The students build a box-like fort out of the tri-wall. Over the course of the year, that box is transformed into a *sukkah,* a model of the Tabernacle, part of Solomon's Temple, a modern synagogue and a time machine. In David's class, the learning environment is the content.

Nate's Room

Nate teaches in a basement room. It is the one he wanted. He had often gotten in trouble for the amount of noise generated by his class. Nate's room has track lighting, a bunch of milk crates, some clipboards, a large area rug and some risers. Nate doesn't teach in any one particular way. He uses every technique from group games to lectures, raps to role play. What he does is to shape, with his students, an intense emotional environment every week. Nate's empty state classroom is the perfect place for him to create the multiple realities through which his students learn.

Conclusion

By now you have seen the connections between the environment and the learning process. You have probably thought of dozens of ways to improve and enrich the environment in which you teach. Be sure to begin with a careful assessment of the physical surroundings, the content of the course, your needs and those of your students. Send for catalogues which will provide the necessary materials and resources. Then organize your room into learning centers, solve your storage problems and decide on methods for display and decoration. The care you take to dress your classroom well will pay off in increased learning and student involvement.

BIBLIOGRAPHY

BIBLIOGRAPHY

Breyfogle, Ethel; Nelson, Sue; Pitts, Carol; and Santich, Pamela. *Creating A Learning Environment.* Santa Monica, CA: Goodyear Publishing Company, Inc., 1976.

Dean, Joan. *Room to Learn: Working Space, Language Arts and A Place to Paint.* New York: Citation Press, 1974.

Greabell, Leon C. and Forseth, Sonia D. "Creating A Stimulating Environment." *Kappa Delta Pi RECORD* (February, 1981), 70-75.

Kaplan, Sandra Nina; Kaplan, Jo Ann Butom; Madsen, Sheila Kunishima; and Gould, Bette Taylor. *A Young Child Experiences.* Santa Monica, CA: Goodyear Publishing Company, Inc., 1975.

Kohl, H. "The Open Classroom." *New York Review, 1969.*

Marshall, Kim. *Opening Your Class With Learning Stations.* Palo Alto, CA: Learning Handbooks, 1975.

Morlan, John E. *Classroom Learning Centers.* Belmont, CA: Fearon Publishers, 1974.

Schrank, Jeffrey. *The Seed Catalogue.* Boston: Beacon Press, 1974.

Trolin, Clif and Putnoi, Johanna. *De-Schooling: De-Conditioning.* Menlo Park, CA: Portola Institute, 1971.

Vander Ryn, Sim, Mimi, Julie, Micah and Ethan, etc. *Farallones Scrapbook.* Point Reyes Station, CA: Farallones Design, Distributed by Random House, 1971.

Whole Earth Catalogue. Menlo Park, CA: Whole Earth Catalogue, 1970.

Yanes, Samuel and Holdorf, Cia. *Big Rock Candy Mountain.* New York: Dell Publishing Co., 1971.

Yanes, Samuel and Holdorf, Cia, etc. *Big Rock Candy Mountain - Winter 1970.* Menlo Park, CA: Portola Institute Inc., 1970.

Catalog for Education Supplies

J.L. Hammett Co., Inc., Box 545, Hammett Place, Braintree, MA 02184.

BULLETIN BOARDS: AN EFFECTIVE TEACHING TOOL

by Elyce Karen Azriel
Illustrated by Joanne Hemmer

Why Bulletin Boards?

There is nothing deadlier than a "dead" bulletin board in a classroom! In an otherwise drab schoolroom, attractive bulletin boards and display areas create a warm atmosphere and complement the learning which goes on there.

Effective bulletin boards are of an even greater value in the Jewish school. Much of the material taught in the Jewish classroom is remote from the students' daily lives; these visual aides help concretize such material.[1] With the use of simple designs and inexpensive materials, even the inexperienced teacher can construct an effective bulletin board.

A successful bulletin board can be created with the slightest amount of time, energy and money. Constructed correctly, it will simply and effectively express the subject or theme to be projected. Almost every subject that can be taught in the religious school can be depicted by means of a bulletin board. The beginning teacher will need the following components of creativity: inspiration, imagination and inventiveness. Possible ideas for bulletin boards are everywhere — in daily conversation, events, holidays, etc. With time and practice, any teacher can become a skillful bulletin board manager.

The bulletin board in the classroom serves to motivate the student, interpret material, reward and recognize student work and supplement lessons and units of study. It is a means of communicating students' and/or teachers' ideas through visual construction. It serves as a beginning to energize the interest of the students. A display of attractive pictures and articles will promote student interest in the subject being taught.

Three Kinds of Bulletin Boards

There are three general types of bulletin boards: 1) teacher-made, 2) student-made, and 3) a combination of both. In the first, the teacher provides the ideas and leadership and carries out the task fully. Less tangible topics such as ethics, law and atonement are usually better managed by the teacher alone. (Example 1)

Example 1 - A teacher-made bulletin board for an ethics unit.

Student-made bulletin boards require student input from the very beginning: — i.e, when the initial design is being visualized.

---

[1]Zalesky, Dr. Moses. *Teacher's Kit No. 10 - The Bulletin Board,* (Cinncinnati, Ohio, Bureau of Jewish Education, 1950), p. 1.

Students are responsible for content and presentation. The teacher allows them a free hand in the construction of the actual bulletin board, even though some of the materials may turn out to be slightly lopsided. In other words, teacher participation is not acceptable, even if it may improve the appearance of the final product. Some feel that the strategy of involving students in this process will result in increased interest in the final product. (Example 2)

Example 2 - A student-made bulletin board for a unit on Israel.

· The third kind of bulletin board is created when the teacher provides the ideas and leadership and, whenever it is appropriate, asks for student involvement. A class discussion is a good stimulus, encouraging the sharing of the entire project and an equal partnership between teacher and student in creating the display. (Example 3)

Example 3 - A combination (teacher/ student) bulletin board. This one is for Tu B'shvat.

Where Do I Begin?

The following represent the five steps necessary in the creation of bulletin boards:

1. Decide upon the purpose and subject.
2. Work out a caption.
3. Make a sketch of the entire bulletin board including locations, lettering and colors.
4. Gather materials.
5. Execute and evaluate.

1. Decide upon the purpose and subject.

Decide on the subject to be headlined and have a clear-cut idea of the purpose. The subject which is presented should include only one thought or idea. Possible topics which can be broadened into bulletin board topics and from which activities can emanate are: holidays and special events, centers of interest, the Jewish and general community, current events, a unit of study. Everything on the bulletin board should accentuate the principal idea that you choose.

2. Work out a caption.

Select or create a caption that is short, captivating and thought provoking. The caption is your selling point; it should tell at a glimpse what the display is about and should begin to generate curiosity and interest. Unusual and exciting captions can do a great deal to create initial interest in the bulletin board. Try using a question: How did Samson do it? Or a pun on words: Israel is real. Or play on a current T.V. show, using "Family Feud" to portray the Joseph story or "The Match Game" to illustrate Noah's ark.

3. Make a sketch.

Begin to make a sketch, keeping in mind the size of the bulletin board. The sketch shows you how the materials can best be placed, and what the overall combination will look like. It will also give you an indication of whether the bulletin board appears overcrowded and if the parts tie together to produce a blended effect. Be careful that the board is not too "busy." A good bulletin board will have an orderly plan of arrangement. The sketch should include wording and location of caption, lettering and colors. Just as a bulletin board must have only one main topic, every display should have a visual area of emphasis, a main point of interest. This can be a large word, a bright color or an unusual shape. Lines or arrows can play up the point of emphasis.

Bulletin boards should communicate their purpose, but it is also good to include a short summary of the purpose. Make it large enough for all to read and put it in a place where it can be read at eye level.

4. Gather materials.

When gathering materials for a display, two main concerns should be variety of materials and color/texture. A variety of materials will maintain interest. It will help to collect and keep a file of all kinds of pictures and prints, as well as three dimensional objects such as pamphlets, models and craft items. When choosing colors, stick with those that are complementary. Choose a color scheme that is stimulating and tasteful, but do not use colors in such a way that parts of the board are competing with one another.

Choose colors which are harmonious. If the colors do not blend well, both the viewer and the message may be lost. In warm weather, "cool" colors should be used: blues, greens, violets, grays, and white. In cold weather, the "warm" colors should predominate: reds, oranges and yellows.

The background must be subordinate to the main display, but at the same time promote interest and vitality for the exhibit. Simple, inexpensive materials work very effectively and can be found easily. Textured materials, as color, should be chosen carefully so as to enhance the display and not to overpower it.

The viewers should be able to see all letters from a distance. Therefore, a sharp contrast between letters and background is desirable. Lettering should be planned along with your art work; it should not be an afterthought.

Always have an eye open for something which can be used in your display. Don't be afraid to ask for what you want. Parents and congregants are more than happy to donate materials which they would otherwise throw out. The variety of materials to be used is practically inexhaustible. Here are a few suggestions for background materials:

Cloth Products

Colored burlap or burlap sacks — Interesting texture, can be found at supermarkets.
Felt
Tablecloth
Colored cheesecloth

Fabric — Can be found in clothing and garment factories. (Try to build up a network of suppliers. Eventually, these people will give *you* ideas for the displays!)[2] Use a dull knife to push raw edges under the frame.
Old sheets — Ask hospitals and linen companies for donations.[3]

Paper Products

Poster Board — Stationery stores, school supply stores, artists' supply dealers.
Construction paper
Tissue paper, crepe paper
Holiday or plain gift wrap
Shelf paper
Wax paper, aluminum foil
Wallpaper samples — Wallpaper or paint stores give away their discontinued stock books.
Newspaper — Gather from doctor's offices or bookstores.
Road maps — Collect from your neighborhood gas stations.

Paint — Cover an old bulleting board with latex paint or spray paint. It's washable and long wearing! Sometimes paint stores sell their returned or mismatched paints inexpensively.

Think of all the different materials that you and your family throw out each day. What about the colorful pages from your favorite magazine? Or the white plastic egg from pantyhose? Why not use all these easily accessible items?

Here are a few suggestions for lettering materials:

Sandpaper	Cut-outs
Pipe cleaners	Chalk letters
Yarn	Graph paper
Rope	Construction paper

5. Execute and evaluate.

As you create your final display, the following guidelines can be helpful.

a. Make the bulletin board express a single idea. If using more than one thought, section the bulletin board.

b. Make neatness in arrangement a governing principle. Don't worry if you're not a great artist!

---

[2]Campbell, Linda. *Library Displays*, (Jefferson, N.C., McFarland and Co., Inc., Pub. 1980), p. 5.

[3]Delores Kohl Education Foundation. *Teacher Centering: Ideas Shared by the Kohl Jewish Teacher Center*, (Wilmette, Illinois, Delores Kohl Education Foundation, 1978), p. 10.

c. Avoid crowding the board with too much material. Confusion does not communicate. Keep away from a scrambled effect.

d. See that the material posted is firmly secured in place.

e. See that the board is changed frequently. In a one to two day a week school, the board should stay up no more than a month.

The following sketch for a bulletin board indicates locations of caption and illustrations, colors, lettering and materials.

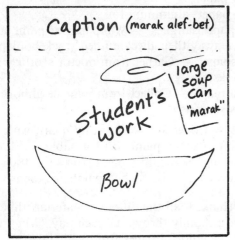

Example 4 - Soup Can - Foil
Bowl - Yellow Construction Paper
Background - Red Burlap
Caption Letters - Yellow and Orange Fabric

In evaluating your display, some of the best suggestions come from your own pupils and other teachers. Take note of the comments made when you first display the board. Then, when you no longer want the materials on display, take a close look and evaluate. Ask yourself these questions:

Does the bulletin board have eye appeal?
Does it attract attention?
Are all elements well thought out?
Is the board neat, orderly and uncluttered?
Are the captions short, concise, easy to read and properly spaced?
Does the board draw reactions from pupils?
Is the material relevant, accurate and up-to-date?

Is the theme apparent at a glance?
Is the display in good taste both in design and material?[4]

Storage

There is no reason why you cannot reuse many materials. The bulletin board itself can be put up each year for different classes. This is especially practical for paper backgrounds, cut-outs, letters and numbers.

Here are a few easy and practical ways for saving displays:

1. Staple two pieces of posterboard together to form folders. File the folders in an upright position. Label. Attach an envelope filled with the letters and small pieces.

2. Use large plastic bags with heavy posterboard in front and in back of all materials. Staple to close. Label.

3. Draw a rough sketch on 3″ x 5″ cards and file by subject. This type of sketch is valuable for the re-creation of the bulletin board at a later date.[5]

4. Place pictures in a large manila folder or large envelope. Label the folders on the tabs and the envelopes in the upper right hand corner.

5. To remember the arrangement and color combinations from year to year, take colored photographs of each completed bulletin board. Attach to stored pieces.

Summary

Either alone or with your students, every teacher can create effective displays for classroom enrichment. Using topics ranging from Torah to Tu B'Shvat, you need only invent a catchy caption and gather eye-catching, diverse materials to bring together one of the most effective learning starters.

The attractive, enriching bulletin board you add to your classroom is well worth the small investment of time and materials.

---

[4]Phillips, Ward and H.O'Lague, John. *Successful Bulletin Boards,* (Dansville, N.Y., F.A. Owen Publishing Co., 1966), p. 14.

[5]Rusk, Alice. *Easy Ways To Displays,* (Baltimore, Maryland, Catholic University of America, Master of Science in Library Science Dissertation, 1958), p. 49.

BIBLIOGRAPHY

Books and Articles

Barnes, Donald L. *How To Make Bulletin Board Designs.* Minneapolis: T.S. Denison and Co., Inc., 1977.

Bullough, Robert V. *Creating Instructional Materials.* Columbus: Charles E. Merrill Pub. Co., 1974.

Campbeil, Linda. *Library Display Ideas.* Jefferson, N.C.: McFarland and Co., Inc. Pub., 1980.

Coplan, Kate. *Poster Ideas and Bulletin Board Techniques: For Libraries and School.* N.Y.: Oceana Publications, Inc., 1962.

Dallman, Martha. *Bulletin Boards.* Darien, Conn.: Teachers Publishing Corporation, 1969.

Dent, Charles and Tiemann, Ernest F. *Bulletin Boards For Teaching.* Texas: Visual Instruction Bureau, University of Texas, 1955.

Dexter, Kerry. *The Display Book.* Wilton, Connecticut: Morehouse-Barlow Co., Inc., 1977.

Fiarotta, Phyllis and Fiarotta, Noel. *Pin It, Hang It, The Big Book of Kids' Bulletin Board Ideas.* N.Y.: Workman Publishing Company, 1975.

Finton, Esther. *Bulletin Boards Should Be More Than Something To Look At.* Carthage, Illinois: Good Apple, Inc., 1979.

Keeter, Georgia and Norris, Carliss. *Successful Bulletin Board Ideas.* Minneapolis: T.S. Denison and Co., Inc., 1964.

Kohl, Dolores, Education Foundation. *Teacher Centering: Ideas Shared By The Kohl Jewish Teacher Center.* Wilmette, Illinois: 1978.

Koskey, Thomas Arthur. *Baited Bulletin Boards: A Handbook For Teachers.* San Jose, CA: Globe Printing Co., 1954.

Phillips, Ward and O'Lague, John. *Successful Bulletin Boards.* Dansville, N.Y.: F.A. Owen Publishing Co., 1966.

Rusk, Alice. *Easy Ways To Displays.* Baltimore, Maryland: Catholic University of America, Master of Science in Library Science, 1958.

Ushijima, Ruth; Leighty, Ruth; and Dahlgren, Cleo. *Trend's Good Work Bulletin Boards.* St. Paul, Minnesota: Trend Enterprises, 1973.

Zalesky, Dr. Moses. *Teachers Kit No. 10 - The Bulletin Board.* Cincinnati, Ohio: Bureau of Jewish Education, 1950.

TEACHING WITH PUPPETS

Rita Kopin
Illustrations by Judye Kopin

WHAT IS A PUPPET?

A puppet is an inanimate object which is brought to life by human effort and used to communicate or dramatize an idea to an audience. Puppets come in many sizes and shapes. They can be as small as a finger or larger than the person operating it. They can represent human or animal characters, objects or abstractions. In the Jewish classroom they can be not only Purim *Shpielers* and Bible heroes/heroines, but also ceremonial objects, history personalities, Hebrew letters, Hebrew speaking children and animals, trees and values. A puppet can be a slow learner trying to learn Hebrew, an interviewer or a singer of Hebrew songs.

Puppets provide a unique and an innovative means of communication, of creative teaching and of making learning pleasurable.

I first used a puppet in the classroom during my early years of teaching Sunday School. It was during the teaching of a unit on scholars to a third grade class, and I was looking for a novel way to introduce the lesson. Filmstrips, storytelling, inquiry method or artifacts had been used in previous lessons. Although I had never tried puppetry before and I was dubious about my ability to carry it through, the idea intrigued me. Saturday night before class, I began to make my puppet. I stuffed the top of a brown paper bag with tissues to make a head and tied a string around the puppet's neck, allowing room for my index finger to fit into the head. In the robe portion of the bag I then cut two slits through which I could insert my thumb and middle finger for the puppet's hands.

Absorbent cotton was used to make hair and a beard, felt odds and ends for features, and burlap scraps for a robe and a hat. Now the puppet was complete. To my delight, the students were pleased with my "Hillel." The paper bag was transformed into a personality. Hillel told about himself and then the students asked him questions. The students were involved, excited and learning. I knew the lesson was a real success when David, a shy boy who rarely spoke up, volunteered to play Hillel and demonstrated that he understood the concepts and ideas being taught.

This chapter will give the "why," "how" and "what" for using puppets in the classroom. Ideas methods and techniques will be shared in the hope that some teachers will be stimulated to try some of the suggestions and will go on to develop their own materials to meet the special needs of their own students.

WHY USE PUPPETS IN THE CLASSROOM?

Puppets are a creative means of communicating and instructing. They encourage imaginative thinking and make learning fun. Puppets are seen on television, in live puppet shows, at zoos, in museums and secular schools. People of all ages are delighted and intrigued by a puppet becoming "alive." Further reasons for using puppets in religious school are:

1. Puppets evoke student interest and reinforce learning. Students listen to puppets attentively.
2. Puppets help students gain self-confidence. Even a shy child loses inhibitions and assumes the identity of the puppet. This is particu-

larly helpful for students who are reticent about using Hebrew or for immigrant children (i.e., Russian, Iranian) who are shy about speaking English. The puppet's errors are more easily tolerated.

3. Puppet productions foster cooperation among students. They integrate different skills and learning activities and encourage the expression of otherwise hidden talents. An important sense of community develops in the classroom.

4. Puppets allow for multi-sensory as well as manipulative experience. They introduce variety in methodology and allow for movement and activity during a sedentary class period.

5. Puppets promote independence and responsibility on the part of students for their learning. Research required to prepare sets, costumes and script can give students a more thorough understanding of a biblical character, hero/heroine, ceremonial object, historical period or Jewish holiday.

6. Puppets can teach Jewish values and help develop positive feelings of Jewish identity.

HOW TO USE PUPPETS IN THE CLASSROOM

Puppets may be used in a variety of ways according to the teacher's preference, the needs and age level of the class and the time which can be devoted to the project. An activity can be structured or unstructured, a teacher strategy or a student performance. Several effective techniques follow.

The Teacher as a Puppeteer

1. The teacher narrates a story and manipulates the puppet. Special puppet voices may or may not be used.

2. The teacher may have a dialogue with a puppet. If the teacher is reticent to use a puppet voice, then the puppet may be depicted as a shy personality who whispers into the teacher's ear. All the communicating is done by the teacher in his/her own voice while the puppet does the acting.

3. The puppet (operated by the teacher) may have a dialogue with the students who ask questions. Interaction is encouraged because the greater the involvement the more effective the learning.

The Student as a Puppeteer

A student may assume any of the teacher roles described above.

Another approach is to provide a puppet learning center within the classroom. Students may use the available puppets in any way they wish. In a more structured format, the students are given a theme like Shabbat, Abraham, *tzedakah,* etc., and are instructed to create a script and to make an informal presentation for the rest of the class.

When teachers think of puppets in the classroom, they often imagine an elaborate student production with stage, sets, puppet-making, script writing, etc., and they dismiss it as too complicated and time-consuming for religious school. The teacher, in preparing a student production, must consider his/her objectives and plan accordingly. When time is very limited, teacher-made or commercially manufactured puppets may be preferred. A teacher or student narrates while the students listen, manipulate the puppets, and/or provide sound effects and background music. This type of performance may fulfill the teacher's objective to reinforce the concepts of a holiday, the contributions of a personality or the requirements of a *tzedakah* project.

For a group of high school students who are studying a particular period in history or a specific Bible personality, the brainstorming and research required to create appropriate costumes, sets, script, etc. may meet the teaching requirements in a very creative and pleasurable way. The production may also evolve into a meaningful *tzedakah* project when it is presented to a group of senior citizens in a nursing home.

More specific teaching stategies and activities using these different formats will be described and examples given.

WHERE TO GET PUPPETS

Puppets may be purchased from stores or mail order firms featuring commercially manufactured puppets, may be produced by the teacher, a paid aide or adult volunteers, or may be made by students as part of a project.

1. Commercially manufactured puppets are readily available and some are relatively inexpensive. They should be inspected to make certain that they are well made, easily manipulated and that the features, especially the

eyes, hair and costume decorations, are not easily damaged or lost.

2. "Teacher-made" puppets can be made by volunteer parents, college students and senior citizens who are enthusiastic about participating in a creative activity which will benefit the education of children.

3. Loan-a-Puppet program. Check to see if your community has such a program. It could be located in your school, library or teacher center.

4. Many students have their own puppets. Encourage the class to bring in their favorite puppet for a class performance, to dramatize a report or to help introduce a book report.

5. Student-made puppets. Creating puppets gives the student a deeper understanding of the personality, dress, setting of the character being developed. Puppets prepared in class should be attractive, simple to make, inexpensive and made of recycled materials. The age and ability of students must be considered.

TYPES OF PUPPETS

There are four basic types of puppets:

1. The hand or fist puppet — controlled by the performer's hand inside the puppet.

2. The rod puppet — controlled by rods and often requiring more than one person to operate.

3. Shadow puppets — flat cutout figures shown as shadows on a screen and illuminated from the rear. Traditionally, these puppets had moving joints which were manipulated by horizontal rods and vertical rods and wires.

4. Marionettes — whole puppets with arms, legs and head moved by strings from above. These are the most complicated to make and operate and are therefore beyond the realm of religious school.

The hand puppet (Fig. 1), a simplified one-rod or stick puppet (Fig. 2), simplified shadow puppetry or overhead shadow puppetry are all recommended for the Jewish classroom.

The hand puppet is one of the easiest puppets to make and one of the most effective in the classroom. Any material into which you can insert an index finger can serve as a head, and a square scarf or other fabric with slits through which your thumb and middle finger can fit, is a puppet with varied movement capability. It can

Figure 1   **Figure 2**

walk, bow, wave good bye, cry, clap hands, etc. Other puppets that are very effective are varieties of the above and include finger puppets (Fig. 3) made of felt, shaped to fit the finger or made from the finger of an old glove.

Figure 3

A story-glove puppet consists of a glove which has velcro sewn on the finger tips. Small felt puppets are stuck onto the velcro or removed as the story progresses.

A "mouth" puppet is moved with the hand inside the head which opens the mouth. Examples of this are a puppet made of a pot holder (Fig. 4) or from a sock. The Spongee designed by Bruce Chesse and described in his book *Puppets From Polyfoam: Spongees* (see Bibliography) is recommended as a quick teacher-made mascot (Fig. 5) for your class. The head is made from polyfoam and contact cement or staples. Add a rod to the arm and you have a "hand and rod" puppet.

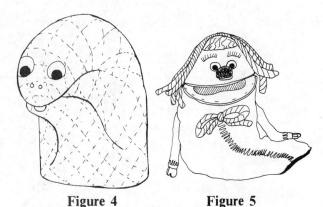

Figure 4   **Figure 5**

A simplified version of shadow puppetry utilizes a cardboard box for a stage with a light source in the rear shining on the screen. After removing the cover of the box, a window is cut in the bottom and covered with translucent fabric or paper. It is then set on its side and looks like a TV. Simple puppets are cut out of poster board and a straw or a dowel attached horizontally. For movable joints, attach the two parts with a paper fastener and add an extra rod.

Shadow puppets may also be provided with light and scenery from an overhead projector.

STUDENT-MADE PUPPETS

Before starting the project, a note should be sent to the parents requesting the donation of items which can be used for making puppets. The list should include felt, fabric, beads, trims, sequins, yarn, scarves, fur scraps and any other objects which will fulfill the requirements of the activity. Items should be sent to the school in a covered box — e.g., a shoe box, marked with the student's name. The following list of supplies is provided to assist you in planning to make puppets.

Basic Equipment and Supplies

Scissors	Elastic bands
Stapler	Pipe cleaner
Needles & Thread	Wire
Hole punch	Pencils
Paint brushes	Markers
White glue	Crayons
Tape	Paint
Sandpaper	Paper fasteners
Poster board	Paper clips
Shirt cardboard	Toothpicks
Tissue paper	Pins
Crepe paper	Tacks
Construction paper	Velcro

For Rods
Dowels
Wire hangers
Tongue depressors
Ice cream stick
Paint stirrer
Tissue paper roll
Bike spoke
Umbrella rib
Chop stick

For Stick/Shadow Puppets
Characters from:
Coloring books
Magazines
Newspapers
Greeting cards

For Tiny Puppets
Plastic spoons
Tongue depressors
Clothes pin
Glove finger

The following items may be used to make:

Bodies and/or Heads	**Heads**
Paper bags	Papier maché
stuffed	Balls, tennis
mouth on flap	ping pong
eyes on flap	rubber
Paper towel rolls	styrofoam
Toilet tissue rolls	Sponges
Paper cup	Fruits
Plastic bottle	Polyfoam
Boxes, e.g. salt	Nylon hose with
egg carton	polyester filling
spaghetti box	Sock
oatmeal box	Pot holder
milk carton	Mitt
match box	Boxes
Paper strip	Paper plates
Ruler	Foil plates
Glove	Envelope
Plastic bottles	Gallon milk jugs
Wooden spoon (Fig. 6)	Large bleach jug
Broom	
Fly swatter	
Spatula	

Eyes
Sequins
Buttons
Felt
Wiggle eyes
Ping pong balls
Pompoms
Beads
Tacks

Nose
Cork
Pompom
Carrot

Figure 6

Costume and Trims

Felt	Bottle caps
Fabric	Sequins
Lace	Trims
Doilies	Ribbon
Wallpaper samples	Velvet
Scarves	Fur fabric
Foil	Feathers
Cellophane	Beads
Tissue	Glitter
Construction paper	Pompoms
Costume jewelry	

Hair

Yarn	Cotton fringe
Fur	Frayed rope
Fake fur	Steel wool
Absorbent cotton	String
Wool fringe	Felt

Remember that some of the most creative and exciting looking puppets are made from household discards and junk.

SIMPLE STAGES

Instructional puppets do not require a stage. The teacher's other arm, a box on the teacher's desk or lap can provide an adequate setting.

When students perform, a simple stage can be constructed by hanging a sheet across a doorway (Fig. 7), by turning a table on its side (Fig. 8) or by using a chart holder (Fig. 9) or a screen.

An appliance carton (Fig. 10) can be converted into an admirable portable theater. The back and top of the carton are removed and a window cutaway in the front section. A curtain may be strung across the top of the stage. One or two "portholes" can be cut in the sides to allow surprise appearances of the puppets. String a curtain across these as well. Place hooks on the inside of the walls to hang puppets.

A large poster board scene may serve as a "stage," e.g., Noah's ark (Fig. 9). Cut out "portholes" in the ark and above deck. Puppets appear through these openings. A map of Israel with openings at key places: Jerusalem, desert, Masada, Dead Sea, etc., can serve as a "stage" as well.

For smaller puppets, a basket (Fig. 11), party hat (Fig. 12), or cereal box (Fig. 13) can

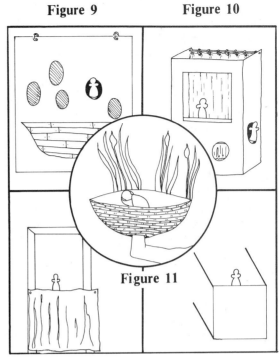

Figure 9   Figure 10

Figure 11

Figure 7   Figure 8

all serve as "stages," with a Moses hand-puppet, Purim jester stick puppet or Hebrew speaking finger puppet as the respective performers.

Figure 12   Figure 13

ABOUT MANIPULATION

Manipulation of the puppets brings them to life, creates the mood and generates interest and excitement for the audience. Even though there is very little time for the students in a religious school to practice, a little time spent on manipulation will considerably improve the results obtained. Students and/or teachers can practice with a partner and then at home in front of a mirror. This is one homework assignment which students will really enjoy!

The following are a few simple rules which will add elegance to a performance.

1. Puppets should be upright and perpendicular to the stage. They should not appear off balance.
2. Puppets should maintain a constant height. They should not be so low that they seem to be sinking or so high that the puppeteer's arm can be seen.
3. The puppet should have a distinct personality. Each puppet should have its own characteristic movements, tempo, idiosyncrasies. The style of movement whether a limp, strut, fast pace, etc., should be consistent throughout the performance.
4. The puppet portrays an impression of life — it is not true to life. Its movements therefore should be exaggerated.
5. In general, only the puppet which is speaking should be moving. The others should be stationery. In this manner, attention is focused on the speaking puppet.
6. To enter the stage, the puppet should seem to climb imaginary stairs — otherwise the puppet seems to be popping up out of the floor.
7. Emphasis should be on the action. All parts of the stage should be used. Puppets may also be brought out in front of the stage.
8. Practice moving the puppet.
   a. Arm for whole body movements: walk, run, jump, limp, dance.
   b. Wrist for trunk or neck movements: nod eyes, turn left and right, sneeze, bow, look for something, pick up object.
   c. Finger for hand movement; wave goodbye, "who me?," play patty cake, cry.

Have students suggest other movements for the class to demonstrate.

Practicing these movements can become a game to learn Hebrew verbs. One student picks a card with a printed verb, and with his or her puppet demonstrates the action. The class must guess the movement using the Hebrew word.

Have the class perform pantomime exercises:

1. Puppet runs, falls, limps off stage.
2. Puppet looks for something, finds it, expresses happiness.
3. One puppet is on stage, a second runs forward, they are happy to see one another, they embrace and walk off together.

ABOUT VOICE AND SOUND

Hearing, as well as seeing the puppet movement, is an integral part of the performance. The following suggestions will help enhance delivery.

1. The voice of the puppet should fit its personality and be consistent and distinct.
2. A characteristic sound such as a cough, sneeze, "ahem" — clearing of throat, etc., before the puppet speaks contributes to giving it a unique identity.
3. With movable mouth puppets, words and lip movements must be synchronized. The lower jaw should be dropped, not the upper jaw lifted, so the eye position does not change.
4. If children are performing behind a stage, be sure they can be heard. Use a microphone, if necessary, or tape record the complete production. For the performance itself, the students should concentrate on listening and manipulating the puppets. The narrator may be up front.
5. Sound effects and recorded or live music enhance the performance and make it more lively and appealing. Encourage students to include these in their presentations. Even preschoolers can create music and sound effects by singing or using rhythm instruments.
6. Practice different voices. Tape record student's voices. Have them listen and try to create greater contrasts. As with manipulation, a little practice and experimentation will go a long way in improving skills and overall performance.

TEACHING STRATEGIES: WHAT CAN THE PUPPET DO?

A Puppet Can Teach Hebrew

1. Uri is a Hebrew speaking puppet who speaks no English. Whenever the teacher brings out this child or animal mascot, the students know that only Hebrew is to be spoken.
2. Students welcome play with *mishpacha* or Hebrew speaking puppets. These can be made of paper plates (Fig. 14) or can be purchased. They are prepared commercially[1] and called "a family of puppets."
3. An American puppet family has just made *aliyah* to Israel. They are having a hard time learning Hebrew. The adults are having the most difficulty. The class must help them learn the language.

[1] Available through Hammett's Educational Supplies.

Figure 14

4. Yossie is having a difficult time learning basic Hebrew even though he is usually very smart. The students help him learn the *Alef Bet,* verbs, etc. He often makes errors. Students have to correct him.

5. The *"Bet Sicha"* (Fig. 13) (adapted Conversation House)[2] is made of a cereal box. The house has two open windows. Two finger puppets or tongue depressor puppets manipulated by two students or the teacher and a student have a conversation in Hebrew.

6. Puppets can sing Hebrew songs. Have a puppet teach the class a Hebrew song or have a student manipulate a puppet which leads the class in song. I know a teacher who taught her class a Hebrew song and then asked her students each to bring in a puppet. (Don't be surprised to find that all the children have puppets! If some don't, provide them.) The puppets enthusiastically sang the song while the students sat behind their chairs manipulating the puppets. The class and the audience loved it.

Puppets Can Teach the Alef Bet and Beginning Sounds

Alef Bet stick puppets (Fig. 15) are made by gluing a tongue depressor to the laminated letter, cut out of bright-colored poster board.

1. Children sit in a circle and are each given an *Alef Bet* puppet. As the teacher says the sound of a letter, the student holding that puppet must display it. If the person is right, all the students pass their letter puppets to the right and the teacher continues.

[2]Judy Sims, *Puppets for Dreaming and Scheming — A Puppet Source Book* (San Francisco: Early Stages Press, 1978).

2. The teacher may play the same game using the name of the letter instead of the sound.

3. After students know the letters of the *Alef Bet,* then teacher proceeds by telling a story about *Alef, Bet* and *Gimel,* etc. Students show their puppet when their letter is mentioned and form words. Some humor can be introduced by having the teacher make an error, by introducing the shy letter *Alef* who keeps dropping out of sight. Don't forget the letter who is always sneezing, the jumpy letter, the slow moving, etc. Students will enjoy carefully listening to the narrator.

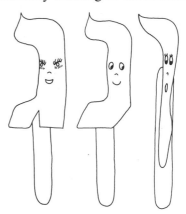

Figure 15

4. Teach the students an *Alef Bet* song. When the student's letter is sung, that puppet must perform a dance or do something in step with the music.

5. Make an *Alef Bet* box by cutting two-inch holes on the large side of a box. Write a different letter of the *Alef Bet* over each hole. When little finger puppet, " עכבר י " appears in the hole, the student must say the letter or sound of the letter. Students may take turns using the mouse puppet (Fig. 16).

Figure 16

6. Make a " כן - לא " box by cutting two two-inch round holes in a box. Write " כן " over one opening and " לא " over the other opening. The mouse appears at one of the openings to show whether or not a Hebrew phrase or sentence is correct. The *"Ken-Lo"* box may be used for any subject. If the student gives the correct response, " עכברי ," appears at " כן "; if the wrong answer, the mouse appears at " לא ."

Holidays/Bible/History

1. An animal or person puppet can tell a Bible story or story of a holiday. A puppet, like Noah, can introduce a story which is completed by the teacher.
2. Puppets can enact one event of the story of a holiday, or puppets can show how the holiday is celebrated.
3. The class can interview the dominant figures of a holiday — e.g., Esther and Haman are interviewed by the students who serve as reporters. This can be used for teaching students how to ask questions which obtain information rather than yes/no answers.
4. Puppets can be interviewers. Students act as the personalities; e.g., students can be Moses, Miriam, Pharaoh, the princess, etc.
5. A puppet can be taught about a holiday. An animal puppet knows nothing about Lag B'Omer. Questions are directed by the puppet to the class to find out more about the holiday.
6. Tree puppets can perform for Tu B'Shvat. See sample lesson.
7. Using the *mishpacha* puppets, students role play the customs and ceremonies of a holiday. (One of my classes added a cat and dog puppet to the family.)
8. Each student is assigned to research one ceremonial object: what it is made of, its shape or form, its use, its history. The student then designs and creates a stick puppet representing the object. The setting or stage may be a Jewish home or a synagogue. The dialogue reflects the knowledge gleaned — it may be in verse, set to music, etc. Students are instructed and helped to present their information in an interesting way.
9. "You were there" format may be used with puppets for Bible, history or a contemporary hero.
10. Life in the *shtetl,* on the Lower East Side, on a *kibbutz* can all be portrayed by puppets (see sample lesson).
11. The JTA puppet (any puppet with JTA on its hat) reports current events about Jewish affairs and Israel. Students will enjoy relaying their news while manipulating this special puppet.
12. Puppets can be part of the class *seder*. As part of our class *seder,* I always have a group of 4-5 students tell (in a creative way) the story of Moses. One year the students prepared the script and used small puppets made of plastic spoons and clothespins. Simple sets were set up on a desk. The students told the story moving the little puppets around to illustrate the different important events in Moses' life.
13. A map of Israel with circles cut out at key cities and other points (e.g., Jerusalem. Tel Aviv, Masada, The Sinai, etc.) is mounted on the outside of the appliance box stage. Have appropriate puppets tell about themselves. A bedouin or a camel in the desert; an Israeli soldier at Masada, etc.
14. Cut out pictures of the builders of Israel. Laminate and make them into stick puppets. Have students develop a script, select music and do a presentation for the class. This is one way of making a report more interesting.
15. Design puppets to accompany cassette taped stories — e.g., Burl Ives, Noah, Creation, etc.

Storytelling

1. A puppet can tell a story — e.g., have Naftali tell one of the I.B. Singer stories.
2. Have K'Ton Ton, a finger puppet, tell or introduce a story.
3. Encourage students to prepare book reports in a creative way. Suggest that they make a puppet of one of the characters who will introduce the report. This can be a project for Jewish Book Month. Make a display of books and their puppets.

Values

More advanced students can design puppets representing values. These can be clever abstract creations.

Behavior and Discipline

1. A puppet can help with behavior problems of young children. The puppet whispers to the teacher about something that upset him — e.g., two children are fighting on the playground or someone knocked down David's blocks. The teacher asks the class what they think about it. A child puppet is sad because no one will play with him. How can the class help?

2. A puppet can teach about *kashrut*. Miss Piggy is interviewed on the subject of *kashrut* (see *World Over* Adar 2/5741 March, 1981). Kermit the Frog can be added also, since he is an ardent proponent of *kashrut*.

Miscellaneous Activities

1. A puppet can open the class and greet the students — *"Shalom yeladim."*
2. A puppet can close the class by leading the students in *"Shalom Chaverim"* or another song.
3. A puppet can relay reminders: "Don't forget your notes for the field trip."
4. A puppet can add interest to a record or casette.

Tzedakah and Learning About the Jewish Community

Students can bring puppets to hospitals, nursing homes, apartments for the elderly, etc. A puppet performance can be part of a *tzedakah* project. At the same time, students receive first-hand knowledge of some Jewish situations in the community.

BEFORE THE PUPPET PROJECT. . .

Before beginning a puppet project, especially with High School students, they should be introduced to puppetry as an art form. Students should be exposed to Bill Baird's *The Art of the Puppet* with its beautiful photographs of puppets through the ages. They should have the opportunity to see museum collections of puppets and to critique puppet shows and report to the class. At present, there is a traveling exhibit of charming puppets made by Simcha Schwartz and Marc Chagall which were used in the Yiddish puppet theater in Paris. The stories combine elements of folklore, Bible stories, and Chasidic dance and music.

A videotape of a performance in Yiddish is available and shown at the exhibit. Children and adults are fascinated even if they do not understand the Yiddish.

PUPPETS TEACH ABOUT THE SHTETL

This unit is designed as an integrated Social Studies unit for Junior and Senior High students which requires them to brainstorm, research and learn the subject content. The wide variety of activities involved allows each individual to participate in those skill areas which are most attractive because of the person's special abilities or interests. This is an opportunity for independent study as well as sharing information in a creative way.

The students have already had a introduction to the *shtetl*. They have had several reading assignments and have seen a filmstrip on the subject. Most of the students have seen "Fiddler on the Roof" and "Hester Street." This is visually reinforced in the minds of the students by a class bulletin board entitled "The *Shtetl*: Soul of a People" which has been prepared by the teacher and/or students using pictures by Ezekiel Shloss from a folio by the same name.

Procedure

1. Brainstorming: the teacher and students prepare a flow chart of all aspects of *shtetl* life which can be portrayed in a puppet production. (For brainstorming about the *shtetl*, see *The Jewish Teacher's Handbook* Volume 1, edited by Audrey Friedman Marcus, page 2.) The students decide which scenes would most effectively convey an understanding of life in the *shtetl*.
2. Research: the students divide into small groups to research and design costumes and sets, to find music and literature, to research the history and to begin planning a script.
3. Creating Materials: the class may regroup if they wish. The script is written, the puppets are made and sets are prepared. Background music, Yiddish songs and special sound effects are taped. The students are encouraged to be original and yet accurate.
4. The Puppets: hand puppets with soft sculpture heads are particularly appropriate. Soft sculpture art is taught in High School and this medium is particularly suitable for

showing the lined faces of *shtetl* inhabitants. Heads made of "instant papier mache" are also suitable and may be produced to be very expressive.

5. The Performance: while brainstorming, planning the research and preparing the materials makes this such a meaningful learning experience, it is the performance and sharing of this knowledge with parents and other students which is the highlight. Furthermore, the students can also use the puppet production to fulfill a *tzedakah* project by presenting it to a group of senior citizens in a nursing home or a hospital.

A TU B'SHVAT PUPPET UNIT

The purpose of this unit is to motivate students to learn about the holiday of Tu B'Shvat and to reinforce the concepts and ideas which have been learned.

Instructional Objectives

1. The students will list the other names and meanings for Tu B'Shvat.
2. They will be able to tell why trees are important, especially in Israel.
3. They will be able to name and identify some of the trees and fruits of Israel.
4. They will be able to tell the story of Honi and the tree.
5. They will be able to recognize biblical quotations relating to trees.
6. They will be able to sing at least four songs about Tu B'Shvat and Israel.

Pre-lessons

Prior to the puppet lesson, the teacher and students will prepare a bulletin board showing a map of Israel and pictures of trees found in Israel. Appropriate biblical quotations relating to the particular tree will be placed beneath its picture. The students will design a chart listing the reasons that trees are important in Israel. They will find or draw pictures to illustrate their chart. They will read stories and learn songs about trees in Israel.

Procedure: Brainstorming

The class and teacher will list possible puppet skits that they can prepare about Tu B'Shvat.

Examples:

1. Importance of trees (in verse if desired)

2. Story of Honi and the tree
3. Customs of planting trees at birth and using branches for *chupah* at wedding
4. Skit which shares Bible quotations with the audience
5. Tu B'Shvat celebration in Israel and North America
6. Puppet show incorporating songs learned
7. Other ideas

Four skits are selected. Two topics may be combined.

Creating Materials

The students divide into four groups according to the skit they select. They write simple original scripts and prepare puppets.

The Puppets

Trees are made of paper towel rolls covered with construction paper or tissue paper. A wide variety of materials are provided for branches (wires, pipe cleaners, tree branch, etc.) and for foliage (construction paper, tissue paper, styrofoam chips, scrap foam rubber, etc.). Students are encouraged to make trees that look authentic but also to introduce some humor by creating trick effects, e.g., pop-up palm tree (Fig. 17).

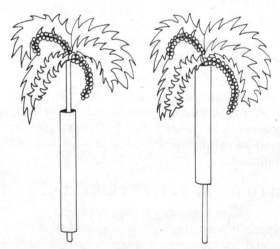

Figure 17

Movable mouths or eyes in the trunks of other trees are produced by inserting a smaller roll into the paper towel roll. An opening is made on the outer roll tube to expose the mouth or eyes drawn on the inner tube. When the tube is moved up, the mouth or eyes close.

People puppets would be simple hand puppets.

The Performance

Each group performs for the rest of the class. Another grade and/or parents may also be invited to a Tu B'Shvat puppet show party. Refreshments would be fruit grown in Israel.

A PURIM UNIT FOR PRE-SCHOOLERS THROUGH GRADE 2

Objectives

1. The children will be able to recognize the characters of the Purim story.
2. They will be able to identify symbols of Purim: *megillah, grogger, hamantash.*
3. They will be able to follow the story of Purim.

The students have already heard the story of Purim and can identify some of the symbols of Purim.

Procedure

The students sit in a circle. The teacher shows the class each puppet and asks the children to identify each personality. When everyone seems to know the characters, children are selected to be puppeteers. They face the rest of the class to whom *groggers* are distributed. The teacher proceeds to tell the story of Purim. Then the name of a character is mentioned, the child holding the puppet has to manipulate it appropriately. When the name Haman is said, all the children respond with their groggers until the teacher indicates stopping by raising a hand.

The puppets are prepared by the teacher, aide or volunteer. Pictures are cut out of a Purim coloring book, pasted to a poster board and cut to shape, laminated and glued to a paint stirrer or tongue depressor (Fig.2). If time permits, preschoolers can make their own puppets. They should be very simple and made from pre-cut materials prepared in advance. For Bible stories and other holiday stories, team each puppeteer with a child playing a rhythm instru-ment. Have puppeteers face the musicians. When a character is mentioned the puppeteer manipulates the puppet and the musician plays the instrument to match the character of the puppet.

This activity sharpens listening skills and reinforces the story.

PUPPET RESOURCE CORNER AND LOAN-A-PUPPET PROGRAM

If your community does not have a puppet resource facility, perhaps you would consider starting one. It may be located at your teacher center, in your school library or in your classroom. The resource corner should be an attractive area which houses and displays puppets, portable stages, patterns and materials for making puppets, suggestions for puppet plays and any available scripts. There should be books and displays on how puppets can be used as an educational tool.

The puppets may be teacher-made or well constructed commercial puppets. They can be displayed on a table, puppet rack, hung on a clothes line or placed in shoe bags or hang-up bags.

The characters represented could be Bible and history personalities, *shtetl* figures, book characters, animals and people, Hebrew letters and ceremonial objects, etc.

Puppets are catalogued for check out. Check out time is for one week.

Teachers should be required to participate in an orientation before being admitted to the Loan-A-Puppet program. Ideally, teachers should also attend a workshop in which they see a demonstration and participate in a hands-on experience showing the correct way of caring for, holding and manipulating puppets, as well as learn techniques for using puppetry in the classroom.

The workshop should also provide an opportunity for each teacher to create a puppet (mascot or other).

BIBLIOGRAPHY

Books available from the Puppetry Store of the Puppeteers of America, Inc.

> Jennifer Ukstins, Director
> 14316 Sturtevant Road
> Silver Spring, MD 20904

Ask for their catalogue for an extensive list of available books.

Baird, Bill. *The Art of the Puppet*. N.Y.: Bonanza Books, 1973.

> Puppets through the ages. Outstanding photographs.

Chesse, Bruce and Armstrong, Beverly. *Puppets from Polyfoam: Sponge-ees*. Walnut Creek, California: Early Stages Publications, 1975.

> Guidelines for creating puppets using polyfoam, glue or staples. Quick, easy, mouth puppets.

Engler, L. & Finjan, C. *Making Puppets Come Alive*. N.Y.: Taplinger Publishing Co., Inc., 1973.

> A method of learning and teaching hand puppetry.

Ferguson, Helen. *Bring on the Puppets*. N.Y.: Morehouse Barlow, 1975.

> Description of variety of puppets and patterns for included plays on David and Goliath, Noah's Ark, Hanukkah, etc. Very good ideas and adaptable, but text not always factually accurate.

Fredericks, M. & Segal J. *Creative Puppetry in the Classroom*. New Plays, Books, Trolley Place, Rowayton, Connecticut, 1979.

> Techniques for making and using puppets in the classroom.

Hughes, K.F. *"Puppets" with a Purpose*.

> Inexpensive 24-pages. Pamphlet describing simple puppets from recycle materials.

Sims, Judy. *Puppets for Dreaming and Scheming — A Puppet Source Book*. Early Stages Press, Inc., P.O. Box 31463, San Francisco, California, 1978.

> Excellent ideas and illustrations for making puppets and how to use them. One of the best.

Sterling, Carol. *Puppetry in the Classroom*. Princeton, N.J.: EIC — Central, 1979.

> A manual for integrating puppetry into the elementary classroom. Excellent and inexpensive.

Vandergun, Alison. *Puppets for the Classroom*. Lampoon Puppettheatre, 1974.

> Easy to follow instructions and photographs for making charming paper and odds and ends puppets.

Books Available from Nancy Renfro Studios

> 1117 West 9th Street
> Austin, Texas 78703

Ask for catalogue which includes books, puppets, secular media kits, etc. (Nancy Renfro is a former Educational Consultant for Puppeteers of America.)

Champlin, C. and Renfro N. *Puppetry and Creative Dramatics*. Nancy Renfro Studios, Austin, Texas, 1979.

> Wonderful book emphasing creative storytelling. Quick puppets. Good sections on interview and sequence (biography).

Renfro, Nancy. *Puppetry and the Art of Story Creation*. Austin, Texas: Nancy Renfro Studios, 1979.

> How to create stories and simple puppets. Well illustrated.

Renfro, N. *A Puppet Corner in Every Library*. Austin, Texas: Nancy Renfro Studios, 1978.

> Many ideas adaptable to a puppet corner in the classroom.

Renfro, N. and Armstrong B. *Make Amazing Puppets*. The Learning Works, 1979.

> Clever, easy to make puppets. Excellent illustrations.

OTHER BOOKS

Gabriel, Michelle. *Jewish Plays for Jewish Days: Brief Holiday Plays for Grades 3-6*. Denver: Alternatives in Religious Education, Inc., 1978.

Rembrandt, Elaine. *Heroes, Heroines and Holidays: Plays for Jewish Youth*. Denver: Alternatives in Religious Education, Inc., 1981.

> Some of the plays in these A.R.E. publications can be adapted for puppet performances.

Scharfstein, S. *Hebrew Language Fun Book: Purim*. N.Y.: KTAV Publishing House, 1970.

> Purim stick figures puppets are made by cutting out pictures from this book.

Sharon, Ruth. *Arts and Crafts the Year Round*. N..Y.: United Synagogue of America, 1965.

> Look up sections on "Puppets" and "Costumes."

ARTICLES

"Miss P Speaks Out on Kashrut." *World Over,* March 6, 1981.

> Humorous script. Miss Piggy is the lead character. Interviewer may be a teacher, a student or another puppet.

Sterling, Carol. *Teaching Art at Ramaz Middle and Upper School: Brush and Color*. N.Y.: Board of Jewish Education, November, 1978, 18, pp. 19-24.

> Brief description of puppet units created in a Jewish Day School.

ORGANIZATIONS

Puppeteers of America. National organization with international membership; for the advancement of puppetry. Sponsors an annual conference, puppetry store, magazine and consultant services in all areas of puppetry. One area is education. For information write to: Gayle Schulter, Membership Chairman, #5 Cricklewood Path, Pasadena, California 91107.

Regional Puppetry Guilds: Write to Puppeteers of America for name and address of regional director of the area. News of Regional Guilds is found in *The Puppetry Journal*.

EXPANDING THE JEWISH SOCIAL STUDIES

by Fradle Freidenreich

INTRODUCTION

For the past several decades we have been told that participation in public life is essential to the growth and health of any system of community. In order to insure the continuity and creative future of society, we must educate each successive generation to identify, understand and work effectively to maintain the values of the community as well as solve the many problems that inevitably face a diversified, complex and interdependent world. Effective Social Studies programs are supposed to do what has just been described: educate future citizens for their roles in society.

The above paragraph could easily have been the keynote charge to a conference of principals and teachers of public schools on "Social Studies Teaching." General education has acclaimed the role of Social Studies to be the linking of knowledge and skills with an understanding of and commitment to democratic principles and their applications in a balanced education.[1]

How is it that such definitions of essentials in the world of general education find so little practical application — if indeed philosophical acceptance — in Jewish schools? Certainly, limitations of time (even in the Jewish day schools with its over-programmed double formula) and priorities of Hebrew language, prayer skills and biblical sources present important considerations. Yet, with all the renewed emphasis of late on the Back-to-Basics

movement, we have yet to see students emerge from those Jewish schools that do *not* offer an enriched Social Studies program with a strong sense of Jewish self, a knowledge of the Jewish community past and present and a willingness and commitment to participate in the continuity of Jewish communal life.[2]

Precisely because our supplementary Jewish schools do not provide a reflection of the community in which the American Jewish child lives, an additional burden is placed upon teachers and curriculum: to train students to understand the nature of Jewish Social Studies and their own roles as future citizens — within a relative vacuum. Rarely does the home, and even more rarely does the street environment, reflect and/or reinforce the teachings of the Jewish school. That education which cognitively prepares youngsters to take their effective roles as contributing future members of the Jewish community, emerges from a carefully planned series of courses and activities in the Jewish Social Studies. These must be presented spirally and sequentially over the span of years during which the child attends a Jewish school. Concurrently, these courses must be integrated into the overall curriculum. In this fashion we teach, and more important than that, the student learns the meaning of Jewish values, our cultural heritage, our history and their relevancy and application to other subject areas being

---

[1]Essentials of Education Statement, Washington, D.C., 1980, The National Council for the Social Studies.

[2]The one exception to this is clearly the network of Yeshiva school systems which the Ultra-Orthodox sects provide where there exists a total support system outside of the school. In these instances, school is merely an extension of home and community, and as such, reflects the community's value system, past and present, in a functioning format.

offered. Fine examples of such materials are to be found, among others, in many of the publications of Limud[3] and Melton.[4]

The latest studies of the Jewish elementary supplementary school have shown that there has been virtually no change in the curriculum over the past several decades.[5] This puts Social Studies (or any of its subsumed subject areas) into the lowest place on the curricular ladder, both in time allotted and importance in the overall Jewish education picture.

Understanding why this presents a serious challenge to the future Jewish citizenry is one function of this chapter. Explaining the expansion of the Jewish Social Studies in an integral fashion is another. Addressing these issues to the Jewish supplementary elementary school as primary targets consequently invites examples from this particular school model. It would appear, however, that much of the material (orientation and philosophy embodied herein) has possibilities for transfer to both Day and High School situations. In addition, every effort has been made to keep the suggestions trans-ideational, allowing for application to various denominational as well as communal and independent schools.

As part of a general introduction to this chapter, it would seem in place to define the terms Social Studies, Jewish Social Studies and Integration.

Social Studies deal with the following areas of knowledge:

History and culture of individual nations

Geography - political, physical, economic and cultural

Social Institutions - the society, the community, the group and the individual

Economics - theories, processes and systems

Relationships - interpersonal and intergroup (touching on anthropology, sociology, psychology and archaeology); between and among institutions, nations, races, and cultures, past and present.

Social Studies teach *concepts, generalizations* and *skills* (both thinking and participation). Social Studies programs are supposed to combine the acquisition of knowledge and skills with an understanding of their application to life through personal participation representing an ideal standard — optimally, the will to take part fully in public affairs.

Jewish Social Studies "personalizes" the above definition within the context of Jewish life. To that end, we refer to Jewish history, a study of Jewish communities of the past and present and the problems of Jewish civics. The latter necessarily calls into play the issue of Jewish values vis-a-vis Jewish survival. In order to teach these two areas, we must deal thoroughly with Customs, Ceremonies and Calendar. If general education relies on the three basic R's, then Jewish Social Studies certainly relies on these three basic C's. Of the seven basic disciplines which come under the rubric of Social Studies, history is generally considered the most basic. Oftentimes it is equated or substituted for the broader umbrella term of Social Studies.

Integration, in the interdisciplinary sense, involves the synthesis of subject areas, affording students opportunities to see interweaving and overlapping relationships. The integrative approach provides a facility for transfer, through the placing of interpretations, attitudes and meanings into previously unrelated contexts. This offers a natural continuity of associative learning.

For the purpose of this chapter, integration refers to inter and intra-school functions. Within the Jewish school, the curriculum is viewed as interdisciplinary — e.g., helping students understand the relationship of *Siddur* to *Chumash;* of *Chumash* to history; of history to the development of culture; etc.; and of all these to each other. Between the supplementary Jewish school and its general studies counterpart (public or private), there is great need to help the student integrate bodies of knowledge as well as discrete subjects — i.e., world history and Jewish history should be seen in parallel. In this way students can begin to recognize appropriate chronological facts and understand the relationships of historical implications from various sources.

A 1978 symposium in writing was devoted to the issue "The Place of Social Studies in the Jewish School."[6] In it, seven renowned Jewish

---

[3]Limud Publications - 181 Finchley Road, Montreal, Quebec, Canada H3X 3A6.

[4]Melton Research Center, The Jewish Theological Seminary of America, 3080 Broadway, New York, N.Y. 10027.

[5]Pollak, George: "Inventory of Curricular Subjects in Supplementary Jewish Schools." Research and Information Bulletin #51, New York: JESNA, 1981.

[6]*The Pedagogic Reporter,* Vol. XXIX, No. 2, 1978, pp. 2-9, AAJE, 114 Fifth Avenue, New York, N.Y. 10011.

educators addressed problems of time, integration, methods and materials, and Jewish citizenship in relation to teaching Jewish Social Studies.

They discussed the goals of Jewish Social Studies and how best to achieve them in light of the problems listed above. Whether arguing for inquiry process in teaching Jewish history, or values teaching for participation in communal survival, all agreed that developing a sense of identity and the willingness to act responsibly within the Jewish community and its unique lifestyle, were basic to the definition of Jewish Social Studies.

THE PROBLEM

Statements of broad societal and personal goals in terms of expected student behaviors were in the forefront of the massive revisions of Social Studies curricula which have been ongoing for the past 15 years. There is consequently a new view about the content to be taught. "A major emphasis has been placed on identifying basic concepts, principles, and methods of investigation in history and the social sciences, and then using those elements as a basis around which to organize the curriculum. Student learning is also being reconsidered. Emphasis is shifting from learning as acquisition to learning as utilization; from learning as a process of absorption of givens (from textbooks and teacher) to learning as a process of discovering important relationships and principles inductively; to learning as a way of inquiring and thinking according to the procedures of the social sciences."[7]

Thus, we understand that teaching Social Studies involves consideration of specific subject areas, their interrelationships with other subject areas of the curriculum, their implications for living within our world and the transferability of the learned material, and skills employed, to other subjects and life situations.

Such a charge is an awesome responsibility for any full-time school and teacher; how much more so for the very part-time teacher in a supplementary Jewish school. Here, motivation, activities and methods and materials must all withstand the rigors of such tests as time constraints, competition from sports, TV,

creative arts lessons and extra-curricular activities. In addition, there is a lack of acceptance of the Jewish school as an important given in the child's educational world, and perhaps most detrimental of all, there is no compulsion of consequence from anyone regarding attendance, passing grades, getting into college, earning a living, etc.

In this most difficult of situations, we must not only teach skills, but forge links of identity with peoplehood and community as well.

The recent study by the Jewish Education Service of North America referred to previously, confirmed statements by Shabatay that in schools where "Jewish civics are taught, its boundaries are set around the synagogue and the home, with relatively meager efforts made to branch out into the larger American Jewish community and to include the study of other Jewish communities as well. The instruction of history, which occupies almost the totality of the 'Jewish People' course, is definitely past-oriented and it generally concentrates on factual information, more than the understanding of trends and ideas. Virtually no attempt is made to place Judaism into a larger context, i.e., the American, or Western culture, or even to correlate the curriculum of the Jewish supplementary school with parallel materials taught in its secular counterpart. These realities contradict the announced lofty ideals of the Jewish school . . . . guiding students toward 'maturity as religious integrated personalities rooted in their faith,' preparing them for 'significant roles in the developing Jewish community.'"[8]

This is the problem facing the Jewish Social Studies teacher. What a challenge!

WITHIN THE JEWISH SCHOOL

A working model for all types of supplementary Jewish schools for developing a Social Studies program must be broad in scope. This allows for involving the entire spectrum of defined subject areas which address a Jew's relationship to his or her physical and social environment. Such components would include:

1. Forces in Jewish History - Major personalities, events, movements and their philosophies, periods of history, and institutions which have shaped our past. Examples of each of these areas of history might be:

---

[7]*A Teacher's Handbook to Elementary Social Studies,* Toba, Durkin, Fraenkel and McNaughton, 1971, p. 1.

[8]Yehudah Shabatay, "The Teaching of Jewish Social Studies in the Weekday Afternoon Religious School," unpublished paper, 1975.

Major Personalities   Groups or Individuals

The Minor Prophets	Amos
Great Names in Rabbinic Literature	Ramban
Builders of the State of Israel	Theodor Herzl
Resistance Fighters	Mordecai Anilewicz
American Jewish Leaders	Stephen S. Wise

Major Events

Destruction of the Second Temple
Expulsion from Spain
The Kishinev Pogrom
The Dreyfus Case
The Warsaw Ghetto Uprising

Major Movements

Messianism
Hasidism
Haskalah
Political Zionism
Reconstructionism

Periods of History

The Babylonian Exile
The Golden Age of Spain
The Shtetl
Pre-Holocaust Europe
The Modern Diaspora

Institutions

The Sanhedrin
The Kehillah
The Bund
Central Agencies for Jewish Education
The World Zionist Organization

Issues Affecting Jews

Anti-Semitism
Assimilation
Cults
Ecology
Identity

These topic examples should be structured in units which can be taught as self-contained entities or related to any or all of the other components which follow.

2. Customs, Ceremonies and Calendar - Those rituals, traditions and cultural heritage legacies which punctuate our Jewish lives and lend purpose to our Jewish identification.
3. Current Events and Jewish Civics - Those happenings in the world around us which impinge on our present and future lives as Jews. The study of our own Jewish community — local, regional and national, and those other contemporary Jewish communities existing around the world: the people, institutions and culture which shape their communal being.
4. The Creative Arts - Jewish literature, music and art are forces which have contributed to our heritage and culture and which bind us as a people throughout time.

These four major components can be taught, as they usually are, as discrete subject areas of the Social Studies. However, this chapter recommends teaching them in an integrated fashion, so that the usual bifurcation existing between subjects in the curriculum is diminished and conceptual bridges and associations are built. In such a manner, for example, students can understand the place of Jewish history in relation to world history. Of even greater importance, they can identify the meaning of leadership (or slavery, or developing nationhood) whenever and in whatever context it applies.

Shabatay summarizes the organization of recent Social Studies curricula into three categories of objectives: 1) knowledge (students need to understand); 2) attitudes (students need to become); and 3) skills (students need to learn how).[9]

Supplementary Jewish schools must, of necessity, deal with all three objectives concurrently. It is expedient to forego the teaching of some Social Studies skills (map, discussion, fact organization, data gathering, etc.), hoping that the public and private schools will assume those time consuming tasks for us. On the other hand, oftentimes Social Studies skills have not yet been introduced to elementary grade students, — e.g., the inquiry method, and our teachers may find it necessary to teach those skills as part of the development of a particular unit. Because of this, it is very important to become familiar with the many skills involved in learning (and teaching) Social Studies subjects, regardless of the particular unit. A partial list

---

[9]Ibid.

is offered here as an outline for understanding the overall Social Studies skills framework:

Thinking Skills
- gathering data
- decision making
- comparing
- classifying
- questioning
- reasoning
- drawing conclusions

Participating Skills
- observing
- working in groups; organizing, planning, decision making, consensus reaching, action
- compromising, bargaining, persuading
- evaluating, etc.

Transmitting knowledge, albeit challenging our creativity in methods and materials, is the stuff of which teachers' jobs are made. Having selected a subject, the quest for texts, print and non-print materials and the best methodologies is pursued. There is generally a direct relationship between the amount of effort and care invested into planning and teaching lessons and the amount of knowledge passed on. Numerous articles have appeared recently on both subjects of methods and materials as they pertain to the teaching of Jewish Social Studies, and the substantive thrusts of the following writing is highly recommended: *Guidelines to Jewish History in Social Studies Instructional Material;* each of the chapters in *The Jewish Teachers Handbook,* Vol. I; Chapter 1, 2, 3, 4, 5, 7, 8, 9, 10, 11, 12 and 15 of *Jewish Teachers Handbook,* Vol. II; "The Pedagodic Reporter," Vol. XXIX, No. 2; and the many fine volumes and articles from the world of general education to be found in the bibliography. (Bibliographical details appear at the end of this chapter.)

Of the three categories of Social Studies objectives which are mentioned by Shabatay, the most difficult to teach is attitudes. This, translated loosely for the Jewish school, is values teaching. A word or two is in order about this often misunderstood area.

For many years it was assumed (and perhaps by some still today) that attendance at a Jewish school assures the learning of values, as if such can take place by osmosis. The questions can rightfully be put: Don't all Jewish texts and subjects automatically teach Jewish values? Why should we teach values as a subject when they are inherent parts of all of Jewish education? Would that the answers were as direct and simplistic as the questions. Unfortunately, the problems of living in a series of heterogenous societies strongly affect the young American Jewish child who is subject to the values and lifestyles of each. Often, they are in conflict. More often, although he/she is a nominal member of more than one community, the child relies primarily on one — the local neighborhood and its larger American societal counterpart — for setting standards in regards to beauty, health, morality, education, business and professional ethics, family life, manners, dress, attitudes towards others, etc. The values which Jews have incorporated and developed for centuries, often embodied in concepts of *mentchlechkeit* and *Yiddishkeit,* are not only unpracticed by our American students, but more alarmingly, are unknown to them as Jewish in origin.

Our teens are often shocked to learn that Judaism has long had points of view (consistent with the most "progressive" of current "liberal" thinking) about ecology, the aged and other such "relevant" contemporary "causes." It is this shock which a carefully thought out Social Studies program can lessen. Since the Social Studies aim to educate students about people's relationship to their physical and social environment, values teaching becomes a primary concern. Teaching *about* values is — as with all good teaching — merely the first step toward providing specific knowledge. The more crucial educational measure of success is how well the student integrates that knowledge in his or her own personal life and, when put to the test of life experiences, how that student reacts. It is rather appalling to note the attitude and behavior of students to each other, to their teachers and parents and towards property that is not theirs. Being able to answer questions correctly on an exam is obviously no test of acting on an issue. The Jewish Social Studies curriculum must therefore make provisions for the kinds of learning experiences which will teach, explore, clarify and lend personal meaning to Jewish values.

INTEGRATING THE JEWISH SOCIAL STUDIES

The most basic subject areas taught in the Jewish supplementary school are listed below at the left. At the right is a column of the thirty examples of Social Studies units previously offered.

If each item on the right is used as a possible theme, it is not too difficult to find rela-

tionships, interpretations and direct examples from each area listed on the left. Brainstorming this exercise with faculty or a small group of peers will yield very rich results. Any of the examples (from the right column) could be developed by applying some or all of the items from the left column into a full curriculum for the appropriate age group that could last a month, a semester or a year.

History	The Minor Prophets - Amos
Hebrew language	Rabbinic Literature - Ramban
Holidays	State of Israel - Theodor Herzl
The Jewish Calendar	Resistance Fighters - Mordecai Anilewicz
Prayer and Synagogue Skills	American Jewish Leaders - Stephen S. Wise
Current Events	Destruction of the Second Temple
Bible	Expulsion from Spain
Law	The Kishinev Pogrom
Ritual and Ceremony	The Warsaw Ghetto Uprising
Israel	Messianism
Ethics	Hasidism
Creative Arts:	Haskalah
Music	Political Zionism
Drama	Reconstructionism
Art	The Babylonian Exile
Dance	The Golden Age of Spain
Literature	The Shtetl
American Jewish Community	Pre-Holocaust Europe
Jews Around the World	The Modern Diaspora
Holocaust	The Sanhedrin
	The Kehillah
	The Bund
	Central Agencies for Jewish Education
	The World Zionist Organization
	Anti-Semitism
	Assimilation
	Cults
	Ecology
	Identity

An excellent example of this kind of integration is the *Purim Kit* (Limud Publications) which could easily take a half year to teach completely.[10] In using this kit, one would

certainly cover the major curricular subjects (perhaps not in the "normal sequence") demanded by the most basic curriculum outlines: language, prayer, history, customs, original text materials, Bible, creative arts, literature, values, Jewish communities, etc. It seems relatively simple when someone has already taken the time and trouble to research

[10]Batia Bettman, Phyllis Pinchuk and Sylvia Stipelman, *Purim Kit,* Limud Publications, Education Resource Centre, Montreal, Canada, 1977.

and compile seemingly disparate subject parts into a finished product. But once attuned to the possibilities and great rewards of such an integrative process, it is difficult not to teach seeking interdisciplinary connections. Otherwise the student is not able to synthesize the various bits of knowledge presented. When one goes further, and takes the initiative of relating the material presented to the learning taking place in the counterpart school, the effect is even more stunning and leaves the greatest and most lasting impression.

As simple examples of the above, witness the surprise of students when they learn for the first time that: Jews lived and were part of the French Revolution ("Oh, that can't be, that happened in France not Canaan or Palestine!"); the shared characteristics of leaders such as Moses, Abe Lincoln, Mahatma Ghandi, F.D. Roosevelt and others transcend the very different periods in which they lived and affected each other ("Aw, gee, Moses was from the Bible, millions of years ago — that's ancient stuff."); and other such seemingly unrelated issues.

Developing the ability to see a problem or fact, or concept — out of its specific context — is a particular Social Studies skill which we as Jewish educators must address in presenting the subjects we teach.

ACTIVITIES AND PROJECTS: THE UNIT APPROACH

A unit approach calls for developmental activities, either in groups or with one individual, which are directed toward helping students find answers to questions and problems that have meaning for them. The following considerations are therefore recommended before developing Social Studies units:

1. What relevance does or could the material and content offered in the class have to the present-day life and experience of the children involved?
2. What are the feelings and personal reactions of the children about and to the materials' content?
3. In dealing with procedures in teaching for affective learning, much thought must also still be given to the cognitive skills.
   a. Process skills are clearly important for the learner, but they are a means to an outcome.
   b. Basic learning skills are taught in order to employ content vehicles. The process skills are "learning to learn" skills.
   c. The third set of skills are "self and other awareness skills" which address themselves to affective learning.
   d. Social Studies units — and indeed the curriculum — should therefore reflect: attitudes towards self-acceptance and personal identification, a concern for continuity of the Jewish people and Judaism, knowledge and understanding and skills and attitudes which can be behaviorally translated during childhood, adolescence and adult life.

Once the unit has been introduced, students should be directed to: recognize and identify general problem areas from which specific problems will evolve; work through a process of teacher-pupil planning by discussion and use of resource materials presented; conference with others (both other students and teachers) to test the validity of the solutions, methods and materials; and employ any number of the following techniques, depending on the subject, nature of the process (large or small group or individual), time, materials and resources available. (Many of these suggestions need teacher initiation and/or preparation.)

- Using classroom libraries and school library and/or resource center;
- Using a multi-text approach (taking parallel material from a variety of texts on the same subject);
- creating student-made movies, filmstrips, slides, radio broadcasts, newspapers, dramatic presentations and music and/or art renditions appropriate to the topic;
- writing quizzes;
- developing polls and questionnaires;
- compiling oral histories, time lines, pictoral displays, scrap books and exhibits;
- listing comparisons and differences;
- assembling explanatory material for maps and charts;
- taking a "show on the road" — presentations of whatever form — to other classes and schools;

- forming a guest lecture bureau — students, parents and other community members who are prepared to make presentations on specific topics — with or without audiovisuals;
- focal activities such as festivals, fairs, assembly presentations, etc.;
- preparing a box of realia;
- debates;
- learning centers within the classroom devoted to particular themes with displays, materials, activities, publications, crafts, resources, etc.;
- games and simulations;
- audiovisuals;
- creating "permanent" presentations: building a library of home-made booklets, reports, multi-media presentations, charts, etc. to be used for other classes in the future;
- stamps and coins;
- role plays and sociodramas;
- personality "autobiographies";
- field trips;
- using the current press — both secular newspapers and magazines as well as publications in English on Jewish topics.

In order to implement these units and activites most effectively, there should be:

1. ongoing in-service work and teacher sharing of ideas, materials and critique;
2. communication with parents about the work being conducted with parental feedback;
3. class meetings with full student participation;
4. continual and careful evaluation including record keeping and student-teacher conferences to assess levels, interest and achievement.

Teaching Social Studies strategies which specifically address the Social Studies skills areas areas must include activities for the thinking processes, student research, informational skills, geography skills and time and chronology skills. As previously indicated, these cannot fall readily within the strictures of the supplementary Jewish school, and so they are not explored in this chapter.

Teaching strategies for conceptual and informational learning are, however, the focus of this chapter. Consequently, the foregoing suggestions for teaching/learning strategies utilize activities directed toward dealing with concepts and related factual material.

Since concepts are intellectual abstractions and the creative efforts of human beings, they are subject to changes — to modifications, revisions and new combinations which reflect our growing knowledge.

Concepts exist on various levels of complexity; therefore it is very important to create teaching units that are age level and intellectually appropriate.

Strategies which will help students to make decisions about personal and social problems will provide the greatest long lasting effect, since that is one of the basic goals of Social Studies education. Social inquiry (utilizing facts, concepts, generalizations and theories) based on questioning strategies will offer a practical vehicle for classroom use.[11] (See Chapter 5, "Inquiry Teaching.")

Strategies for teaching Social Studies concepts and facts can be clustered:[12]

1. Experimental (participatory)
2. Demonstrational (outcome is known in advance)
3. Organizational (group and coordinated individual activities)
4. Reinforcing (providing additional examples)
5. Provoking (stimulating thought processes through exchange of ideas)
6. Speculative (inspiring imaginative and creative responses to problems and material)

Strategies, other than those directed at specific skills, should build in social process, human relations, historical culture, cultures other than our own and current events.

One example of such an interdisciplinary Social Studies unit would be a study of the Jewish community of _____ . (Select a country reasonably unfamiliar to the students.) In teaching this unit, one might approach it vertically (throughout history, or a period of time in history) and so touch upon chronology, particularly in relation to the rest of the world, and the majority culture of that country. Customs and ceremonies would certainly be a part of the unit. How are they similar to, or different from, our own? What literature and what other creative arts has this community contributed? A study of their synagogue and prayer life will certainly allow for new learning and/or reinforcement of that already taught.

---

[11]James Banks has excellent suggestions in *Teaching Strategies for the Social Studies*, Chaps. 1, 2 and 3.
[12]For a full discussion of each of these, see *Activities for Today's Social Studies* by Caleb Bucher.

How is the Jewish life cycle celebrated there? How do we react to customs that, although authentically Jewish are different from our own? What is happening today in that country? How does that affect the Jews living there today? the Jewish future? Is there a relationship between that community and our own? If so, what is it? If not, why not? Can we do anything about it? Should we? How?

In presenting this example, particular effort was made to suggest questions and statements which stimulate thinking, invite discussion of Jewish values, teach information, recreate history and allow for personal decision making.

The importance of selecting appropriate questions and materials cannot be over-emphasized. Texts or teacher lectures which present facts and information, only begin (and sometimes end) the educational process. Steps must be taken to prepare teachers who, and materials that will, seek to address themselves to the stated goals.

In an article on "Teaching Teachers to Teach Jewish History,"[13] Karbal and Lewis trace the methods used in a course which dealt with the philosophy of Jewish history, the preparation of specific units of instruction for use in the classroom and the opportunity for utilization of the material in the educational laboratory of the classroom. The lecture sessions provided the historical and philosophical overview to Jewish history and the various approaches to teaching it. These included:

I. Secular Approaches to History and Jewish History
   A. Greek and Roman historians
   B. Church Fathers
   C. Humanist Renaissance historians
   D. Economic and political historians of the nineteenth and twentieth centuries
   E. The Oriental view of history.

II. Jewish Approaches to History and Jewish History
   A. Biblical views
   B. Talmudic views
   C. Medieval Jewish historians
   D. Haskalah views
   E. N. Krochmal and Luzzatto
   F. Heschel, Yavetz, Kook

III. Problems in Presenting History in the Classroom
   A. Undeveloped sense of historicity
   B. Students who do not think historically think hysterically
   C. Need to unify diverse "facts" of history in some holistic way.

IV. Suggestions for Teaching History
   A. Need to view both world and Jewish history as two sides of the same coin
   B. Need to find meaning in Jewish history[14]
   C. Need to emphasize specific survival traits.

The planning steps needed in creating educational materials for a unit of instruction were presented during the lab sessions of the course.

These sessions were directed towards team development of materials, for the sharing, exchange and enrichment of professional efforts. The results of such a process generally redound most beneficially to the students.

In an article on "Trends in the Teaching of Social Studies,"[15] Lewittes outlines these trends as follows: History has been replaced by Social Studies; scope and sequence must be clearly defined; the multimedia approach has replaced the single textbook; inquiry and critical thinking rather than memorization are emphasized; instruction is sometimes organized around small groups and individual research; role playing and dramatization are frequently used in the teaching of Social Studies; Social Studies teaching aims to develop a variety of skills; an interdisciplinary approach has enriched the Social Studies; the development of values and the understanding of basic concepts are important objectives; evaluation helps us to determine whether we have achieved our objectives. The trends provide much food for thought and represent a fine summary of the suggestions made thus far in this chapter.

---

[13]*Pedagogic Reporter*, op. cit., pp. 19-21.

[15]*Pedagogic Reporter*, op. cit., pp. 9-13.

[14]Justin Lewis, "Competency-Based Enrichment Material for the Inquiry Method in Teaching History in Jewish Schools," Southfield, Michigan: United Hebrew Schools Publication, 1975.

THE CONCEPTUAL APPROACH
Developing the Conceptual Approach

In developing the materials for the Social Studies, the curriculum should be based on a conceptual approach. Such an approach:

1. uses the generalizations accepted by specialists of the various Social Studies disciplines. These generalizations are called concepts and variants.
2. organizes these generalizations into a manageable, teachable whole, with a sequence of development of the concept — e.g., a holiday, Israel, the synagogue, the life cycle, etc., through the grade levels.
3. encourages within pupils
   a. an ability to see beyond the facts so that they can recognize the patterns of human behavior and know the relationship of these patterns in time and place.
   b. an ability to think so that they can approach the study of human behavior analytically rather than descriptively.
   c. an ability to act so that they can assimilate the unending mass of specific data with which they are, and will continue to be, faced.

Understanding the Conceptual Approach

In order to implement this conceptual approach, the teacher should understand:

1. *The meaning of the selected concepts and their variants* in terms of their validity on an intellectual level and their significance for Jewish living.
2. *The relationship of subject matter to the teaching of the concepts and their variants.* Generalizations cannot be taught in a vacuum. Examples must be given in order to illustrate their meaning to the student personally (What does giving *tzedakah* mean to me?) as well as their humanistic universality (What happens in the Jewish community when no one cares about other people and institutions?).
3. *The importance of using skills in context.* The skills to be emphasized are those inherent in the individual social science disciplines. Techniques for gathering, organizing, evaluating and presenting data should be identified and used in context. Above all, pupils should be encouraged to use the skill of critical thinking which is the skill of drawing warranted conclusions from reflec-

tive thought supported by valid evidence. (The teaching of skills will be left to the domain of the public school.)
4. *The inductive method* . This method is particularly applicable to the conceptual approach.

Planning for the Conceptual Approach

1. The teacher should first review the concepts and variants he/she wishes to implement for a given topic or area of study. These generalizations become the teaching objectives of the unit and individual lessons. Carefully selected sources will give the proper support to the objectives of the unit and lessons being designed.
2. Once the selection of material has been made, the teacher should then carefully and creatively design different learning experiences geared to having the pupils discover the truths they contain. These experiences do not have to be revolutionary in format. Paragraph and essay writing, debating, committee reports, discussions, role playing, flannelboard stories, etc. are very suitable experiences.
3. In concluding lessons, carefully formulated questions have to be designed to lead the pupils to arrive at generalizations which they can support, given the knowledge acquired earlier.

Teaching the Conceptual Approach

1. A carefully planned unit or lesson can be easily managed as long as the teacher does not lose track of the concepts, variants and the learning objectives.
2. Whenever appropriate, during the initial presentation of material, as well as during the concluding questions, be on the alert to ask the type of concluding questions that will enable the pupil to see "beyond the trees."
3. Teachers must also use ingenuity to build upon pupil answers by formulating additional questions of a generalizing nature.
4. The key to success of the conceptual approach, once the unit or lesson has been carefully planned, is *asking the proper questions at the proper time.*

Resources

The school library, classroom libraries, texts, homemade materials, and audiovisuals must respond to the needs of the subjects and students. The sharing of teacher prepared material should have a high priority.

As an example, let us explore the concept of *Family,* a unit of study in the elementary grades, so important to Jewish life. The family, like more complex social units (a culture, or community, regardless of time period) should be viewed with the many components which maintain and substantiate its existence in mind. By charting these components, we can provide focal points for the variants of the concept according to the various Social Studies disciplines.

COMPONENTS OF A FAMILY (OR COMMUNITY)

1. Size and Composition
2. Shelter
3. Relationships Among:
   Family, Relatives, Neighbors
4. Health and Safety
5. Dress
6. Work
7. Values & Goals
8. Education
9. Transportation
10. Communication
11. Food
12. Social Life: Culture and Recreation

Social Studies Discipline	Concept	Variant
History	I. Change in Jewish life is a part of histoy	1. Family life sometimes differs among various communities around the world. 2. Families of today are different from families of earlier times: e.g., biblical, Middle Ages, *shtetl,* the *kibbutz,* etc. There must be flexibility to survive.
	II. Jewish experience is continuous and interrelated since we are products of our past and influenced by it.	1. Families celebrate holidays to commemorate their Jewish historical heritage. 2. Family customs and traditions are products of the past. They are transmitted from parents to children.
	III. History is a record of events and problems which people have met with varying degrees of success. The Jewish response has frequently resulted in change and adaptability. Over the long period of our existence, this flexibility has proved successful to our continuation as a people.	1. Being a member of a group requires many adjustments. Change may help some and hurt others. 2. Family roles vary from family to family, in time, place and community.
	IV. Acts and events have consequences which vary greatly in different cultures. A knowledge and understanding of our Jewish past is useful in meeting the challenges of our present day Jewish community.	1. What people say and do affects others (responsibility, cooperation, concern for others). 2. Families are affected by what is done and said in the communities and nations in which they live. 3. Individuals and families learn lessons from the past.

	V. People tend to judge or interpret the evidence of the past in light of their own times. So too, the historical record is influenced by the times and culture of the historian.	1. Evidence of the past and ways in which it differs from the present can be found in our homes and all around us. 2. Many parts of the Bible have important parallels in writings of and about other ancient peoples of the Near East.
Anthropology and Sociology	I. Human beings are more alike than different. They have physical characteristics, and basic needs and wants that are similar.	1. People in the same family usually have some similar characteristics. 2. A family of families — e.g., the Jews, also has similarities.
	II. Human beings live in groups. Jews live in groups.	1. The family is the basic social unit in most societies. 2. The family is the basic social unit in most Jewish societies.
	III. People living in groups develop a unique culture.	1. Jews living in the same area usually have similar cultural traits: language, customs, values, lifestyles. 2. Families may interpret these cultural traits in particular ways.
	IV. Jews are in part a product of their culture. In the diaspora, it is a dual heritage.	1. Cultural traits and skills are learned. 2. Jews accomodate to pluralism in particular ways.
	V. Every group tends to develop formal and informal "controls" to lend stability and provide order among its members.	1. Family members have responsibilities to each other. 2. Families have responsibilities to other members of the community.
	VI. Culture change is continuous but takes place at varying rates.	1. People learn new things as they grow older. 2. Changes in the community are a result of this knowledge.
Political Science	I. Every society creates laws commensurate with its customs and values.	1. Families have rules in their homes. 2. Schools have regulations. 3. Communities and neighborhoods have have laws for health and safety.

	II. Governments and voluntary groupings are established to achieve order, actualize power and implement regulations.	1. Rules have reasons. If change is needed, certain processes have to take place for orderly transitions. 2. Jewish communities in various periods of time and in various places have achieved government by a variety of means — e.g., *Kehillah, Bet Din, Sanhedrin,* etc.
	III. Decision making is a fundamental activity of government and the governed.	1. Families arrive at decisions in various ways. 2. Jews working together are usually more effective when the rights and feelings of others are considered, and where their differences are respected.
	IV. The definition of citizenship varies in different cultures. In the Jewish community it ideally involves active participation.	1. Members of a family can agree upon rules that will be beneficial to all. 2. Jews who are active within their Jewish community make decisions of responsibility
	V. All levels of government are interrelated. At the world level, all nations are interdependent. *"Kol Yisrael Arevim Ze Bazeh."*	1. Some authority is divided between family and the outside world. 2. The rules and welfare of the family and its community are mutually dependent.
Geography	I. Each place on earth (area or specific location) is related to all other areas in terms of size, direction, distance and time.	(The variants for the two concepts listed fall more into the area of skills teaching, and are therefore not expanded upon here.)
	II. A region is a mental concept useful in organizing knowledge about the earth and its people. It is an area which in one or more ways has relatively homogeneous characteristics such as physical features, cultural features, occupations, or political affiliations, and is in one or more of these respects different from surrounding areas.	Specific examples of variants for teaching geography concepts for the Jewish supplementary school would be: biblical Canaan and its surrounding neighbors, the *shtetl,* Jews in Arab Lands, modern Israel, etc.
Economics	I. The economic problem is the scarcity of resources relative to human desires. People have exhibited unusual ingenuity in increasing output. Yet, desires continuously outrun the available goods and services. This is because at any moment of time, resources — human beings (land and machines) — are limited, whereas, human desires are limitless.	1. Individuals and families want more than they can have. They are constantly faced with choice. All members of a family are consumers; a limited number are producers of goods and services. 2. Jewish communities have had to exist within the oftentimes restrictive environments of the host countries in which they live.

	II. Basic economic problems have often been answered by many forces and factors that have helped shape the culture of a given society. Among these are its geography, its ethics, its cultural social structure, its political history, the state of its industrial arts and the level of its technical skills.	1. A budget is a form of organization for the efficient use of family income. 2. Jewish communal funding must be appropriated to many needy causes.

For each concept or variant above, stories from Yiddish and Hebrew literature could be used to motivate, and/or to describe and give information, and/ or enrich, and/or review and reinforce. Other creative arts could similarly be called into play. Verbal expressions in Yiddish and Hebrew that reflect Jewish values and life-style can then be introduced.[16] References to appropriate biblical passages and examples from Rabbinic literature will complete the integrated curricular circle.

Following is a list of additional strategies particularly appropriate for enrichment in teaching Jewish Social Studies.

- Mystery map missions - Charting Jewish communities.
- Yellow pages survey and Anglo-Jewish press - To determine what agencies and services are available to the Jewish community.
- What's to see of Jewish interest in our community? - An annotated listing.
- Tracking Words - Inquiring about different Jewish cultures by analyzing language.
- Who remembers when? Researching the community's development through oral history projects.
- Examining the Jewish community services — a local monopoly board.
- Jewish career awareness.
- Dateline and Byline - Writing about important issues and times in the life of the Jews.
- Time Lines that Talk - Expanding time lines vertically by adding stories and art work to the various segments.
- Can you Locate? - Places of interest in Jewish history and geography indicated with some particular designation on maps or globes.

- Studying Statistics - Population, demography, etc.
- Fashions of the period - A research project into a particular period of time.
- Music of the period, Art of the period, Literature of the period.
- In the Good Old Days - Dramatic history with costumes and personal characterizations.
- The Story Stamps Tell.
- Building a Future Society - Simulation of an ideal community developing a Constitution, flag, anthem, government, institutions, etc.
- I'm Applying For - Job descriptions for various Jewish communal responsibilities and qualifications of persons "applying."
- Current Events Reaction Sheets.
- Let's Look at our Prejudices and Biases.
- Working with primary source materials. (For excellent directions, see "How To Use a Document for Social Studies," The Jewish Teacher Center, 1977.)
- Classroom learning centers appropriate for Jewish Social Studies in a supplementary school.

Some suggestions for learning centers are:

Your Local Jewish Community; Israel; Let's "Dig" the Bible; When in Rome; It's Not Greek To Me; Holocaust History; Around the Globe; Anti-Semitism; The Written Word; The Jewish Calendar; The Jewish Life Cycle; The Enlightenment; Zionism; Hasidism; The Golden Age; The Talmud; Commentaries; Once Upon a . . .; Heroes/Heroines of Yesterday; Heroes/Heroines of Today; Immigration to America; Calligraphy Can Show.

The following steps represent the procedure for organizing learning centers:

---

[16]A good reference is the newly published *Your Jewish Lexicon* by Edith Samuels (New York: UAHC, 1982).

1. Determine curricular areas.

2. Only set up as many "corners" as:
   a. you can handle at once
   b. you have time and material for
   c. you can make attractive and relevant.

3. In each corner:
   a. prepare ample *activities* for a number of children to work with simultaneously
   b. make certain *reference materials* are easy to work with and can be identified
   c. provide for a *variety of materials* to
   d. meet *individual differences* in style, rate and interest in subject matter
   e. write instructions for activities in *behavioral objectives* in language the children can easily understand and relate to
   f. make certain there are *evaluation* and *record keeping* systems present.

4. Organize the room so that:
   a. there is *enough space* to allow the students to *work comfortably*
   b. the teacher - and paraprofessionals - can be in a position to get to groups and individuals as they work
   c. several floor plans are possible and *flexibility* is present
   d. equipment serves your needs

5. You will need:
   chairs
   tables
   bookcases or shelves
   bulletin boards
   file cabinets or boxes
   tape recorders
   slide and/or filmstrip projectors
   some crafts equipment
   some rug remnants
   a supplies closet
   some storage space for each "corner."

6. Teacher (and aides) are *Consultants* or *Facilitators* or *Enablers*. They *direct* and *help* students who work individually or in small groups.

7. Goals include:
   a. high standards of work and accomplishment
   b. student involvement in the learning process
   c. identifying contemporary issues affecting the American Jewish child
   d. indicating to the children that these issues are human concerns and social

problems - dealing with *Attitudes - Values - Identity - Continuity*
   e. Social Studies are various disciplines that can be dealt with interdisciplinarily
   f. Social Studies involve the learning and use of skills
   g. Methods include: research, guided inquiry, problem solving and creative efforts on the part of students
   h. Use of small group, large group and individual activities
   i. The Social Studies centers must be stimulating, multi-sensory environments
   j. Careful instructions and group discussion for all activities
   k. Detailed, ongoing evaluation.

8. How to begin:
   a. try out several physical floor plans.
   b. set up the room carefully and attractively.
   c. Acquaint your pupils and parents with the program, the physical arrangements and the record keeping system.
   d. Explain goals and standards.
   e. Describe behavior, guidance and evaluate on.
   f. Discuss care and operation of equipment and clean up procedures.
   g. Make cards or instruction sheets for each center including:
      • What we want you to learn
      • Instructions for activities
      • Activities
      • Time limitations
      • Evaluation procedures.

9. Supplies and materials for centers: maps, globes, charts, tapes, texts, magazines, newspapers, games, writing materials, junk box, file box, reference books, boxes, time lines, pictures, media equipment, subject realia and artifacts, filmstrips, transparencies, crafts supplies.

(For more on learning centers, see Chapter 1.)

MATERIALS

There is no dearth of good materials for the teacher willing to read, evaluate and modify to suit his/her own needs. A rather full listing of recommended reading, bibliographies and material in the field appears at the end of this chapter. In addition, hundreds of documents of unpublished teacher made material are stored at the National Educational Resource Center of the JESNA, 114 Fifth Avenue, New York, NY 10011.

Many references have been made in this chapter (as in many other books and articles for the Jewish teacher) on the necessity and advisability of creating home made materials to augment texts and published works. There are numerous references in the bibliography which offer help in this direction. For additional assistance, see the chapters and bibliographies in *The Jewish Teachers Handbook Volumes I and II.*

CONCLUSION

Within the Jewish Social Studies lie the rich history, culture, lifestyle and ethics of our people. Excitement and personal gratification await the ready teacher and inquisitive student when they explore our past and relate it to the present, study others of our people and understand their relationships to us, and think through the application of our religious and cultural heritage to our daily lives. Let us hope that this stimulus of expanded and enriched Social Studies teaching will augur well for our continuity, as individuals, as families and as a people.

BIBLIOGRAPHY
Prepared with the assistance of Sarah Kammen

Published Books

A Handbook for the Teaching of Social Studies. Association of Teachers of Social Studies in the City of New York. Boston: Allyn and Bacon, Inc., 1977.

Banks, James A. *Teaching Strategies for the Social Studies: Inquiry Valuing and Decision Making.* Reading, MA, 1977.

Making decision on social and personal problems
Rationale objects process of decision making
Inquiry valuing and decision making exercises
Inquiry theories questions and exercises
Interdisciplinary approach to social science disciplines such as history, strategies for teaching sociology, history, anthropology, geography, political science, social action, methods, disciplines, generalizations and exercises.

Bruner, J. *Process of Education.* N.Y.: Vintage Books, 1963.

Suggests teachers have students be historians and discover knowledge through the way others discovered it. Not finished product.

Bucher, Caleb. *Activities for Today's Social Studies.* Dansville, N.Y.: The Instructor Publications, Inc., 1973.

Cogan, John and Litcher, John H. "Social Studies After Curr. Reform: Some Unfinished Business." *The Elementary School Journal,* October, 1974.

Theories, problems, suggestions for improvement of Social Studies. Good theoretical background.

Curwin, Richard L. and Geri, and editors of *Learning Magazine. Developing Values in the Classroom.* Palo Alto, CA: Learning Handbooks, 1974.

Teaching strategies and activities for helping teachers help kids develop values.

Feldman, Martin and Seifman, Eli, ediitors. *The Social Studies Structure, Models and Strategies.* Englewood Cliffs, N.J.: Prentice Hall, 1969.

Ideas/concepts utilizing strategies and models for teaching anthropology, economics, geography, sociology and history.

Fenton, E. *Teaching the New Social Studies in Secondary Schools: An Inductive Approach.* New York: Holt Rinehart and Winston, 1966.

See Chapter 9 on inductive method of inquiry as applied to study of history. Example given in S. Epstein's chapter in Volume II, *The Jewish Teachers Handbook.*

Fraenkel, Jack R. *How to Teach About Values: An Analytic Approach.* Englewood Cliffs, N.J.: Prentice Hall, Inc., 1977.

Values clarification, moral reasoning, variations for teaching values in different approaches.

Gittelson, Abraham and Freidenreich, Fradle. *Interdisciplinary Integration in the Jewish Day School.* CAJE and AAJE, 1979.

The report of a three year model program in two day schools. Includes chapters on: The Project, The Process, In-Service Education, Classroom Application, Continuing Growth and Evaluation. A valuable appendix includes sample materials and forms appropriate for Jewish Social Studies teaching.

Jarolimek, John. "Curriculum Content and the Child in the Elementary School." *Readings for Social Studies in Elementary Education.* N.Y.: Macmillan, 1966.

_____ . *Social Studies in Elementary Education.* New York: Macmillian, 1967.

Very useful. Chart for planning.

Kenworthy, Leonard S. *Social Studies for the 70's.* Lexington, MA: Xerox Publishing Co., Second edition, 1973.

Koppman, Lionel and Postal, Bernard. *Guess Who's Jewish in American History.* The American Library, P.O. Box 999, Bergenfield, N.J. 07621.

Lee, John R. *Teaching Social Studies in the Elementary School.* New York: The Free Press, Division of Collier Macmillan, 1979.

Using curriculum guides innovatively. Quick and easy lesson plans. Using textbooks; units for students; art; music; literature; techniques of dramatic play; games and simulations; role play; film, personal feelings of author.

"Man as a Group Member," *The Social Sciences Concept and Values.* New York: Harcourt Brace, 1972.

"Man's Changing Cultures," *The Social Sciences Concept and Values.* New York: Harcourt Brace, 1972.

"Man in Culture," *The Social Sciences Concepts and Values.* New York: Harcourt Brace, 1972.

"Man as Individual," *The Social Sciences Concepts and Values.* New York: Harcourt Brace, 1972.

Marcus, Audrey Friedman, editor. *The Jewish Teachers Handbook,* Vols. I and II. Denver: Alternatives in Religious Education, Inc., 1980, 1981.

Mehlinger, Howard. *Global Studies for American Schools.* Washington, D.C.: National Education Association, 1979.

O'Conner, John and Goldberg, Robert M. *Unlocking Social Studies Skills.* New York: Globe Publishing Co., 1980.

Rosen, Gladys. *Guidelines to Jewish History in Social Studies Instructional Material.* New York: The American Jewish Committee, 1971.

Ryan, Frank L. *The Social Studies Sourcebook.* Boston: Allyn and Bacon, Inc., 1980.

Taba, Hilda; Durkin, Mary L.; Fraenkel, Jack R.; McNaughton, Anthony H. *A Teacher's Handbook to Elementary Social Studies (An Inductive Approach).* Reading, MA: Addison-Wesley, 1971.

1. Curriculum development
2. Educational Objectives - Thinking, knowledge, values
3. Selection of Organization of content
4. Selection of Learning Activities
5. Teaching strategies
6. Questioning
7. Development of Skills
8. Evaluational Process

Grades 4-12 projects on such topics as: Ethnic Studies, classifying objects, family history, studying gravestones, making a history booklet, effects on customs, etc. Give data, make predictions. Looking at changes in cultural artifacts (posts from Roman period - Canaanite) constructing laws. All these project ideas can be translated to projects with Jewish content — World Jewish history, Israel, Bible, community, study, values, American Jewish history, personal histories.

Youngers, John C. & Aceti, John F. *Simulation Games and Activities for Social Studies.* Dansville, N.Y.: The Instructor Publications, Inc., 1974.

Articles, Bibliographies and Materials

American Association for Jewish Education. *Materials Resource Guide for the Jewish School.* Fradle Freidenreich, editor. N.Y.: 1982. Sections I, II, III, 175 pages, mimeographed.

A complete (to 1981) annotated and graded listing of Jewish Social Studies texts, related fiction and non-fiction and materials or the teacher and leader. Areas covered: American Jewish community, History, Holocaust, Israel, Jews Around the World, Jewish Life (Holidays, Customs, Calendar, Life Cycle) Faith, Belief, Philosophy, Values and Identity. Covers all ages, Early Childhood through Adult.

Banfield, Beryle. *I Too Sing America. Instructor,* February 1981.

Lists Afro-American folktales and spirituals. Good questions for discussion on slavery, freedom, Pharoah, Moses, the parallels, the differences, Jewish involvement and responsibilities to Black community by American Jewish Community.

Chanover, Hyman. *Jews in the Early Settlement of America.* N.Y.: AAJE, August 18, 1971.

Grade 8 unit on settlement in New Amsterdam. Hebraic contribution to Puritanism.

Dawney, Matthew T. *Pictures as Teaching Aids: Using the Pictures in History Textbooks. Social Education,* February 1980.

Methods of observation used in studying pictures, neccessity for background knowledge generating discussion with pictures. Using pictures in a series to show development and change. Using pictures to identify points of view, values and attitudes. Propagandizing through pictures and cartoons.

Dawnton, David. "Discovering History" *Elementary School Journal,* April 1976. pages 406-410.

Describes an on site archaeological dig. The Jewish Museum is setting up a similar program at a camp setting. Description of the site, diary of a day's dig and stories on finds. Students made folders on background material, history, domestic life, living conditions, development of tools, models of building, religious history.

Ehemarin, Jane. "Globe Trotting from the Classroom." *Learning,* November, 1977, pages 92-99.

Preparing for trips. What to take, background information, itinerary, maps, climate, geography, culture, information on getting materials from library and travel agencies.

Epstein, Seymour. *Jewish Models of Teaching.* Doctoral dissertation. Toronto: Ontario Institute of Studies in Education. 1976.

Having students be historians — compare texts of a period through sample historical documents.

Feldheim, Eric. "You and Your Temple." *Roundup, Pedagogic Reporter,* Spring 1973.

Folpe, Joan. "The Hester Street Experience," Teaching Social Studies. *Roundup* 1976-77, *Pedagogic Reporter,* Spring 1978.

Semester study program on Lower East Side life, including lecture-discussion followed by mini-groups on various aspects of life on Hester St. Yiddish theatre, food booths, sweatshops (studied politics), Settlement House, newspaper and synagogue. Families joined in on building. Final program — filmstrip cassette, presentations, "The Dybbuk," union rally. Ended with a service.

Frazer, Bruce M. "Map Skills for the Primary Grades." *Childhood Education,* February - March, 1980.

Sample Lessons

Freidenreich, Fradle. *Expanding the Social Studies.* AAJE March 8, 1978, Baltimore Conference.

Freidenreich, Fradle. Parallel Resource Unit. *How America Became a Nation. How the Jewish Nation Developed in Bible Times.* N.Y.: AAJE, 1975, mimeographed.

Unit problems; objectives; problem solving. Problems, questions, activities, readings, T.V. simulation, films.

Gilbard, Howard, ed. *Teachers Guide for Social Studies Instruction. Focus: Bicentennial: The Jewish Experience in America 1776-1976.* Los Angeles: Bureau of Jewish Education, The Jewish Federation Council of Greater Los Angeles. 1975.

Goals, discussion, springboards, primary sources, values clarification, roleplaying, activities, cartoons, 5-6 Grades and up.

Green, Kathy. "Jewish Early Childhood Education —
A New Curricular Vision, " *Melton Research Newsletter,*
Spring, 1981.

Discussion of curriculum, education philosophy. Integrative holistic attitude. Importance of familiarity with child development. Literature. Piaget's theories influence teaching of history for early childhood by teaching sequencing.

Hessel, Carolyn S. Jewish Social Studies in the Primary Grades. "On Tour." *Pedagogic Reporter,* Winter, 1978, AAJE.

Primary curriculum for studying Israel through fantasy flight to Israel. Geography, food, living conditions, travel brochures, games, historical background.

Hilton, Kenneth. "Are Your Students Prisoners of the Present?" *Instructor,* March 1980. pages 77-82.

Good ideas for history, teaching time lines, time sense experiments, lifetimes as a time concept, personal time lines, calendars, holiday celebrations. Very helpful for teaching Jewish history.

"How to Use a Document for Social Studies." *Jewish Teachers Center,* 1977.

Use of primary documents, ideas, empathy, role play, photos, articles, good ideas.

Hymovitz, Leon. "After the Holocaust: A Primer for Parents and Teachers." *Religious Education,* 1972, pp. 534-544, September-October, 1977.

Questions about facts on the Holocaust — statements on the necessity for teaching it. Activities for primary and junior high levels - Grades 7, 8, 9.

Keach, Evelett T. Jr. "Social Studies Instruction Through Childrens Literature." *Elementary School Journal,* November, 1977. pp 99-102.

Good examples of using literature in teaching Social Studies. Bibliography included.

King, David C. "Social Studies - How to Recognize Good Ones and Survive Bad Ones." *Learning,* January 1977.

Evaluating Social Studies texts.

Lipnick, Bernard. "The Class as a Community." *Moment,* Vol. 4, June, 1979, pp. 53-7.

A description of an experiential program in Jewish education with a *Vav* class.

Levy, Phyllis Saltzman. *Webbing a Curricular Plan.* Ohio State University, Winter 1979.

Lewittes, Mordecai H., ed. "Teaching Jewish Social Studies." *Pedagogic Reporter,* Vol. 24, #2, Winter, 1978.

Marcus, Audrey Friedman; Wolf, Marlys; Zwerin, Rabbi Raymond. *Jews in Spain.* Denver: Alternatives in Religious Education, Inc., 1976. (Out of print. See Chapter 5, this volume.)

Excellent example of integration of disciplines. Grades 7-9.

Miller, Benjamin. "A Selected, Annotated and Graded List of Print/Nonprint Materials for Teaching Jewish History and Social Studies." *Pedagogic Reporter,* Vol. XXIX, #2, Winter 1978.

Moss, Penrod. "Launching the Social Studies Unit on an Intermediate Grade Level," *Jewish Teacher,* February, 1962.

Short article — good starter for first day of class.

Morin, Cynthia and Richard. *Jewish Social Values.* N.Y.: UAHC, 1974.

Individualized learning unit.

Nadel, Max. "Case Studies in Classroom Teaching. Teaching Jewish Social Studies in Religious School." Jewish Educational Committee of N.Y., 1968.

Good model lessons.

National Council of Social Studies. "Statement on Essentials of the Social Studies." Washington, D.C.

New York Times College and School Service, 229 W. 43rd St., N.Y. 10036.

Units on Social Studies and reading newspapers.

Nussbaum, Dr. Aaron M. "The Jewish People." *Pedagogic Reporter,* Vol. 31, No.1.

Deals with philosophy and educational questions; viewpoints of history - philosophy of history.

Podit, Alan H. "Secular Studies and Religious Uniqueness - A View of Hanukkah." *Religious Education,* 71:6, November-December, 1976.

Importance of geopolitical, historical and social contexts for studying Hanukkah.

Rives, Florence. "What to See in Our Town." from Idea Bonanza: *Learning,* December, 1977.

Tour folders for Jewish community. Children develop tour packets and take each other on guided tours.

Saltzgower, Duane. "The Social Studies Centers," *Elementary Teachers Ideas and Materials Workshops.* January, 1972, pp. 9-10.

Explaining and developing use of centers in conjunction with students.

Smith, Page. "Students Don't Study History - They Are History." *Learning,* January, 1977, pp. 32-6.

A good general article on experiencing history.

Stern, Shirley. *Exploring Our Jewish Heritage - A Course of Study for Intermediate Grades.* N.Y.: KTAV.

Learning about the past; written records; archaeology.

Stipelman, Sylvia. *My Family Heritage Part I.* Montreal: Limud Publications, 1972 (experimental edition).

Excellent example of integration.

Stipelman, Sylvia; Pinchuk, Phyllis; Betman, Batia. "Integrated Programs for Jewish Education." *Limud Publications,* 1972, Montreal.

Defines integration - importance of use of model curriculum.

Tannenbaum, Abraham J. *What General Education Might Contribute to Jewish Education.* Cleveland, OH: Cleveland College of Jewish Studies, February 18, 1981.

Trezise, Robert L. "Developing Performance Objectives in Social Studies in Michigan." *Social Education,* January, 1974, pp. 24-29.

Van Camp, Sarah S. "Social Studies for 5 Year Olds." *Childhood Education,* January/February, 1981.

Use of newspaper pictures to discuss social relationships.

Welton, David A. "What We Know About Teaching Elementary Social Studies." *Social Education,* March 1981.

Problems in teaching Social Studies - children's concept of time versus history.

West, Edith. *The Family of Man - A Social Studies Program.* (Kibbutz Family in Israel). Selective Educational Equip., Newton, MA.

Lists tapes, books, filmstrips, teacher's guides and rationale.

Witkin, Pearl. Program of Individual Study, Aleph - Hey. B'nai Emunah Religious School, Montclair, N. J., Social Studies Department.

Wittstein, Joel. "Social Studies Curriculum - Wise Temple Religious School." *Pedagogic Reporter,* Vol. 31 #1, Fall, 1979.

Teaching of values through exercises and experiences.

Woody, Pam. "Informal Drama in Religious Education: An Innovative Approach." *Religious Education* 71:6, November-December, 1976.

INQUIRY TEACHING

by Audrey Friedman Marcus

Educators all talk about it. Many would like to do it. Few understand it. And even fewer make use of it, especially in the religious school classroom. Yet properly understood and judiciously instituted, inquiry can enrich and enliven Jewish learning, whatever the age of the students. It is particularly apropos for that most difficult age level — junior and senior high school. In this chapter, inquiry will be defined and briefly described. The role of the teacher will be outlined and several examples of inquiry lessons will be provided. A Bibliography of books and articles on the subject concludes the chapter.

WHAT IS INQUIRY?

When we teach, we mostly tell our students something that we think is worthwhile and important. We expect them to recall it when we ask them questions about it orally or on a test. We also expect them to accept it as true. We get our help from authoritative sources besides ourselves, from experts, textbooks, traditions, televison programs and films. We dominate the interaction, controlling and manipulating the pace, substance and sequence of what is learned while students remain passive. This is called expository teaching.[1]

Inquiry is learner centered, requiring more of the learner than passive listening. The pace, substance and sequence are regulated by the learner. Often, the problem to be solved is itself arrived at out of the concerns of the students. Students, confronted with a problem or issue, seek out facts, analyze relationships and generate personal ideas of why things happen or happened as they do or did. Inquiry, then, is based on the inductive process of generating and testing ideas. It is also the process of making personal meaning out of learning, as opposed to being told by someone else what the meaning is.[2]

The inquiry model is a humanistic one. It is based on confidence and trust in human beings and in their ability to think independently and solve problems. It gives credit to the learner for being able to discover facts and relationships on his or her own. It recognizes the accumulation of information that each of us — each youngster, too, — possesses, and strives to enable each learner to bring this reservoir of knowledge to bear on a subject matter.

Inquiry is based on the premise that people are naturally motivated to pursue meaning. Further, it is rooted in the belief that until learners manipulate (work with, transform and restate) the material themselves, they will not "own" it — i.e., internalize it. Such manipulation can take the form of artistic expression — writing about it, doing art projects, acting it out, dancing it, etc. Or it can be accomplished by processing the material intellectually through data gathering, theorizing, evaluating, sorting, making decisions and predicting.[3]

[1]Barry K. Beyer, *Inquiry in the Social Studies Classroom* (Columbus, Ohio: Charles E. Merrill Publishing Co., 1971), 1 pp. 10, 11.

[2]John A. McCollum, *Ah Hah! The Inquiry Process of Generating and Testing Knowledge.* (Santa Monica, California: Goodyear Publishing Co., Inc., 1978), p. 72.

[3]I am indebted to Joel Grishaver for this understanding of the inquiry process.

MAKING INQUIRY HAPPEN

Inquiry occurs naturally in the classrooms of all good teachers. These individuals use every opportunity to encourage student growth. They ask probing questions and engage the curiosity of their students. This informal kind of inquiry is very important. The mindset that produces it and many strategies for accomplishing it are discussed throughout this Handbook series. This chapter, however, is devoted to *making* inquiry happen. To do so requires an understanding of the inquiry process and the procedures for implementing it.

Basically, there are five steps in the inquiry process: 1) defining a purpose for inquiring, 2) guessing at a tentative answer (hypothesizing or explaining), 3) testing the hypothesis or explanation, 4) drawing a conclusion and 5) applying the conclusion to new data and generalizing.[4] Different authors and practitioners offer variations on these five steps, but they are essentially the same.

1. Defining a Purpose for Inquiring

Inquiry begins with the need to find something out, either the answer to a puzzling problem, the reasons for a discrepant event or the answer to a difficult and intriguing question. It is during this step that the task is sharply defined so that students know precisely what it is they are looking for.[5] Ideally, students can have a hand in posing problems or situations that interest them. Most often, however, particularly when time is short and sessions infrequent, the problem situation will be created by the teacher. Problems can be drawn from something puzzling in a textbook, a newspaper or magazine articles, a role play situation or a film. They can be originated from unpopular arguments, conflicting opinions, material which is contradictory to student biases or mystery situations which cry out for solutions.[6] An example of an unpopular argument might be: The Jewish Agency should not help Russian immigrants who choose not to go to Israel.

An example of conflicting opinions might be those of Leon Dulzin of the Jewish Agency regarding Russian immigrants and a leader of the Council of Jewish Federations. Other examples are the repetition of verses found in the Bible (see Chapter 7 for examples). When introducing material that is contradictory to student biases, you might circulate the opinions of a variety of individuals on the subject of who is Jewish (see *Identity* by Martin A. Cohen and Jack Zevin). An example of a mystery-type situation is the question: What was golden about the Golden Age of Spain? This is pursued in the mini-course *Jews in Spain*, reproduced later in this chapter.

2. Guessing at a Tentative Answer

A hypothesis is a tentative answer to a problem or question. It is based on data presented for interpretation and on the previous knowledge of the learners. Such data can consist of reference books, text books, films and filmstrips, written reports, statistics, graphs, unfinished case studies, word lists, photographs and paintings or other primary sources such as maps, diaries, songs, newspapers and magazines.

3. Testing the Hypothesis

At this point in the sequence, students gather data, then evaluate and analyze it to see if it supports their hypothesis.

4. Drawing a Conclusion

During this step, students decide if the hypothesis is valid based on their evidence. If the evidence supports the hypothesis, then the original guess can be viewed as much more probable (though not certain). If the evidence does not support the hypothesis, then the process is repeated from step #2 on. A new hypothesis is arrived at and tested and another conclusion drawn.

5. Applying the Conclusion to New Data and Generalizing

Finally, students test their conclusion in the light of new data, represented by other similar situations, to see if the conclusion holds up. At this point the original conclusion is often broadened or modified. It is this

---

[4]Beyer, pp. 21, 22.
[5]Ibid, p. 22.
[6]Ibid, p. 57-60.

step which trains students to generalize when presented with data and thus to be critical thinkers who are able to cope with new problems and situations.

ROLE OF THE TEACHER

Teaching with inquiry requires hard work and a lot of patience. Before the inquiry begins, the teacher selects or puts together the problem situation. It should, of course, be one that will excite and intrigue students and that has meaning for them. The teacher also plans the entire learning experience by creating, structuring and sequencing the activities and collecting and preparing materials.

While the inquiry process is going on, the teacher will act as a referee, accepting students' ideas and helping them to feel that their ideas are valid. He or she will encourage students to test their guesses rather than giving them the right answer. The teacher also paraphrases student responses and summarizes progress as the unit proceeds.[7] At times the teacher may need the unit proceeds.[7] At times the teacher may need to provide additonal information, perhaps a fact sheet or some clues to help students arrive at conclusions. Later, he or she may bring in new situations so that students can see if the conclusions they reached are valid under other conditions. In all cases, the teacher encourages students to interact directly with each other, to state their conclusions and to support them with evidence.

Another vital facet of the teacher's task is to raise questions which help students clarify their thinking and see other ways of looking at problems. The importance of asking higher level questions (beyond simple recall) cannot be overestimated in inquiry teaching. Helpful questions will be those which ask students how they arrived at an answer, which look for personal meaning and which request personal meaning and which request illustrations. Several good references on questioning techniques are mentioned in the Bibliography. Also recommended are the chapters on language sensitivity in *Ah Hah! The Inquiry Process of Generating and Testing Knowledge* by John A. McCollum.

---

[7]Marsha Weil and Bruce Joyce, *Information Processing Models of Teaching* (Englewood Cliffs, New Jersey: Prentice-Hall, 1978), p. 135.

EXAMPLES OF INQUIRY LESSONS

The following represent three very different lessons, all of which can be categorized under the rubric of inquiry. While all of them do not comply exactly with all of the steps outlined above, each contains aspects of these steps. Each demonstrates models for adapting inquiry to your needs. The first, *Letters From Prague,* is a brief introductory experience in inquiry designed by this author for senior high school students or adults. The second, *History is a Mystery,* was created by Natalie Ray of the Board of Jewish Education of Greater New York for students in Grades 8-10. The final example, *Jews in Spain,* was published as a mini-course for Grades 7-9 by Alternatives in Religious Education, Inc. and is now out of print. It is specifically based on Barry K. Beyer's model of inquiry.

Letters From Prague (Senior High and Adult)

In the seventeenth century, on the eve of the Thirty Years War, letters between the Jewish communities of Prague and Vienna were carried back and forth by messenger. On November 22, 1619, the messenger was intercepted on the way to Vienna. The letters were captured and stored by the Austrian authorities in the archives of the Imperial Court of Vienna. Fifty - four of these letters were discovered early in this century. They provide us with an invaluable guide to Jewish and secular life of the time.

Reproduce for students a selection of the letters from Prague from *Letters of Jews Through the Ages,* Volume Two, edited by Franz Kobler (New York: East and West Library, 1952), pages 450-477. Divide students into groups of four to six. Explain what the letters are. Then assign each group a particular aspect of Prague ghetto life to watch for as they read the letters. These aspects can include family life, economics, political conditions, religious practice, values, etc. Groups discuss the reading, listing findings in their area. One member of each group reports to the group as a whole. A composite picture of life in Prague is then drawn up by everyone in the group. If desired, students can do further research on any area that interests them, verifying their initial findings through the use of other source materials.

History is a Mystery (grades 8-10)
by Natalie Ray

This inquiry unit on Jews in Colonial

America can take place in learning centers. It consists of a problem, fifteen documents, several clues and two task cards.

Problem

The first five synagogues in North America were:
1. Shearith Israel, New York
2. Touro Synagogue, Newport, Rhode Island
3. Beth Elohim, Charleston, South Carolina
4. Mikveh Israel, Philadelphia
5. Berakah v'Shalom, Savannah, Georgia

Documents
1. Map of first Jewish settlements in the United States
2. Information on the openness of the Carolinas to settlement by "Jews, heathens and dissenters"
3. Toleration of Jews in Rhode Island
4. Establishment of a Jewish cemetery in Rhode Island
5. Rights granted to aliens in South Carolina
6. Jews arrive in Savannah, Georgia in 1732
7. Jewish settlement in Pennsylvania
8. Letter to Peter Stuyvesant from the Dutch West Indies Company
9. Letter to her family in Germany from a Jewish woman in Petersburg, Virginia
10. Jews and the College of Rhode Island
11. Letter requesting funds from the Kehilah Kadosh of New York for the city of Safed after an earthquake
12. Oration delivered before the Hebrew Orphan Society in Charleston, 1807
13. Sermon preached at the Synagogue in Newport, Rhode Island
14. Letter to the Federal Constitutional Convention from Jonas Phillips on behalf of Jewish rights
15. Report on the debate in 1818 on the bill to grant equal rights to Jews in Maryland ("The Jew Bill")

Documents 1, 2, 3, and 7 are from *A History of the Jews in the United States* by Lee J. Levinger (New York: UAHC, 1949). Numbers 4, 5, 6, 10 and 15 are from *Heroes of American Jewish History* by Deborah Karp (N.Y.: KTAV and ADL, 1972). Items 8, 9, 11 and 14 may be found in *Eyewitnesses to American Jewish History,* Part One, by Azriel Esenberg and Hannah Grad Goodman (N.Y.: UAHC, 1976). Numbers 12 and 13 come from *Beginnings: Early American Judaica 1761-1845* by Abraham

Karp (Philadelphia: Jewish Publication Society).

Clues
(Suggestions to help you solve the problem):
1. Look at the map (Document #1). Are there any clues in the *geography* of the Eastern United States as to why people might settle there?
2. Check Document #2 - 8. What do these tell you about some of the states where these synagogues were built? Why might Jews want to live in these states?
3. Read Documents #9 - 15. What do these tell you about the ways Jews lived, their interests and concerns, their freedoms and restrictions?

Task Cards
1. Choose a partner. One of you is a person who is settled in America. One is a new arrival. What questions would the new arrival ask and what would the other person reply?
2. Write a short paragraph stating why you think Jews settled in these five locations. Write a second paragraph showing how you came to that conclusion from the clues.

JEWS IN SPAIN[8]
STUDENT MANUAL

By
Audrey Friedman Marcus
Marlys Wolf
Rabbi Raymond A. Zwerin

PART 1 — LIFE IN JEWISH COMMUNITIES IN SPAIN

Drawing upon what you already know, what do you think life was like in a Spanish Jewish community in the Middle Ages? In other words, what was golden about the Golden Age of Spain? Your ideas will only be opinions based on a little bit of information, but you will find you know enough to construct hypotheses. A hypothesis is an assumption or guess that needs to be verified by facts. Use individual Hypothesis List 1 to list what you know about life in a medieval Spanish Jewish community.

---

[8]Reprinted from the mini-course of this name, ©Alternatives in Religious Education, Inc. 1976, out of print.

Individual Hypothesis List 1.

1.
2.
3.
4.
5.
6.
7.
8.
9.
10.

PART 2 — WORD LIST

We have found so far that we all know a little something about Spanish Jewish communities in general. However, we probably don't know very much about the Jews who lived in Spain during the period from 700 C.E. to 1492 C.E. If we had a little more information, we could begin to answer the question, "What were the Spanish Jews like?"

Look at the list of Spanish and Ladino words and their English translations which appear below. Then, try answering the questions about Jewish life in Spain on Data Collection List 1 which follows.

Spanish & Ladino	English	Spanish & Ladino	English
Ductor	Doctor	Impuestos	Taxes
Coplas	Kind of Folk Song	Arte Ceremonial	Ceremonial Art
Escola	School	Bushcar	Search
Poesia	Poetry	Edicto	Edict
Filosofia	Philosophy	Excomunion	Excommunication
Estudiar	Study	Miedo	Fear
Rugar/Oracion	Prayer	Civdades	Cities
Romansa	Kind of Folk Song	Rabino	Rabbi
Destierro	Exile	Padre	Father
Moro	Moorish	Comida	Meal
Leyes	Laws	Vida Doble	Double Life
Hazzan	Cantor	Maestro	Teacher
Famia	Family	Marrano	Swine
Un Dio	One God	Mosaicos	Mosaics
La Rosa	The Rose	Empres	Moneylender
dia de Muet	Holiday, Festival	Tzedakah	Charity
Aislamiento	Isolation	Artisanos	Artisans
Negociante	Trader	Diplomatico	Diplomat

Data Collection List 1.

List some of the characteristics of the Spanish Jews:

How do you know these really describe the Spanish Jews? How can you find out?

Archaelogists and historians study man-made objects from the past as well as architecture, clothing, customs, religious life, etc. to get their information. If your hypotheses about Spain are correct, what do you think the historians and archaeologists found from this period? What was the architecture like? How did the people dress? What did they eat? How did they live? What kind of social structure did these people have? Government? Occupations? Select some of your hypotheses and for each, list on this page the kinds of artifacts and pictures you would like to see in order to test the accuracy of these hypotheses.

PART 3 — GATHERING INFORMATION FROM PICTURES

Work in pairs. What do these pictures tell

you about life in Spain? What were the chief concerns of the people? Did they always get along?

Using this list along with the previous list of words, you should be able to make some recommendations to the group regarding which hypotheses are accurate, which appear doubtful, and which are probably wrong. Remember, if an object, manner of dress, or type of building does not appear here, it doesn't mean that it did not exist then. That particular item may be lost to history, or it may be located in another book (do some research). Only when you find evidence which contradicts a hypothesis should you consider changing it. New hypotheses can also be added based on your evidence.

PART 4 — FACTS YOU WILL WANT TO KNOW TO TEST YOUR HYPOTHESES

The following information will help you test your hypotheses for accuracy. Read the pages quietly to yourself, and answer the questions at the end. You may refer to the readings as often as necessary to help you find the answers. Additional reference works are listed on the last page.

HISTORICAL OVERVIEW:

Life was not always the same for the Jews in Spain. From about 700 C.E. to 1250 C.E., most of the Iberian Peninsula, as it was called, was ruled by various Arab peoples. The ruler of each province was called an Emir, while the ruler of all Spain was the Caliph. During this period of time, all went quite well for the Jews. Our children learned, our poets wrote, our scholars thought and taught, our merchants did very well and some of our Jewish leaders even became powerful figures in government, serving in the courts of Emirs, and even in the court of the Caliph himself.

Although it's difficult to assess the actual population of the Jews of Spain, perhaps as many as a million Jews populated the major cities in those days, especially Cordova, Seville and Granada in the south, Toledo and Lucena in south-central Spain. Lucena was a city which was entirely Jewish, having its own walls and public buildings. Non-Jews were allowed in only with permission of the Jewish government.

Most Jews lived together in one section of each town or city. They were not forced to live there. They were free to live wherever they wished throughout the Muslim period. They just preferred to live near their fellow Jews and near the synagogue which was central to their lives. This enabled them to preserve their customs and sense of community.

The synagogue was usually the largest and finest building in the Jewish quarter. It was built in Moorish style, with tiny colored mosaic tiles decorating the facade, while stately columns and archways dominated the inside. Hebrew lettering often decorated the walls of the sanctuary. (The synagogue of Toledo, which is still standing today, has two rows of biblical phrases in Hebrew carved into the stone all around the top of the four walls in a continuous frieze.)

The synagogue was in a courtyard which was beautifully adorned with flowers and shaded with trees. Nearby were other buildings used by Jews — the school, the assembly hall and an inn where travelers could spend the night.

The synagogue was also the court house where Jews tried their own cases according to

Jewish law. The judges were all learned men who were elected or chosen by the community. The rabbi usually acted as the court of appeal and as the final authority in interpretations of *Halacha* — Jewish law. For some cases the Rabbi in Cordova, the capital city, was the highest authority of Jewish law.

Aside from daily and festival worship, the synagogue was also the central meeting place for all Jews. Reports of the Jewish governing council were read aloud there. Decrees of Emir and Caliph were announced there. Lost and found articles were reported and claimed there. The sale of a house or other property was not legal unless it was made public to the community at the synagogue. Gifts made to charity were also publicly acknowledged there.

As leader of the community, the rabbi (often called *Hacham* — wise man — by Sephardic Jews) was most revered and respected. When more than one rabbi lived in a city, the oldest or wisest was considered to be the Chief Rabbi. Rabbis were not paid. As was the case with rabbis of Talmudic times, they earned a living as physicians, artisans, merchants or tutors.

Second in importance to the *Hacham* was the *Hazzan,* or Cantor. He too, was learned in Jewish subjects and, of course, had to sing well. He was also usually a scribe. He may have copied books by hand and sold them to wealthy members of the community. He may have written letters on behalf of the rabbi or the congregation to other cities. The *Hazzan* was paid for his work.

All boys received a solid Jewish education in school. Bible was taught to the young, and Talmud to the older students. If the rabbi was well known, he might have students from far-off lands also studying with him. Such a rabbi would also receive questions regarding Jewish law from other communities. His answers were eagerly awaited. These questions and answers were saved, and a whole Responsa Literature came into being. Often, these answers became an important part of the *Halacha.* We use this Responsa Literature as a way of learning what life was like for the Spanish Jews.

A visitor to the Jewish quarter would notice an inn near the synagogue. This small building served as a hospital, as a place where the poor might get a warm meal, and as a dispenser of clothing and *Tzedaka.* Jewish merchants from all parts of the known world used to frequent such an inn. This inn was supported by the entire community. No one was too poor to set aside time and money to house the stranger, feed the orphan and the widow, or to educate the poor.

One building was missing in the Jewish quarter. There was no jail. A Jewish thief or robber? Unheard of! A person who committed a wrong was brought before the Jewish court. If the judges found him guilty, he was fined or flogged. The most severe punishment was *Herem,* or excommunication. This was usually the fate of one who did not obey the order of the court. Excommunication meant that one was no longer a member of the community. No one could speak to him, or visit him or do business with him. He could not enter the synagogue. He was alone — living among people who could have nothing to do with him. The judges thought long and seriously before they placed a person in *Herem.* In fact, Spanish courts used *Herem* more frequently than any other Jewish courts. It was a dreadful punishment. Certainly, it was more terrible than any punishment decreed by an Emir or the Caliph.

Jews did employ capital punishment. In fact, Spain was the only country in the world at that time to allow Jewish courts to employ capital punishment. The "privilege" was used when necessary. Jews, however, were able to discipline themselves because of the strength of their religious laws and because of their respect for their religious leaders.

Under the Moors, times were generally good. However, persecutions in the 11th and 12th centuries caused some to flee to Christian Spain. During the early *Reconquista,* Christian monarchs used the Jews and treated them well. As the influence of the Jews dwindled, they came to be treated poorly. Christian forces invaded Spain from the north and slowly but surely conquered the Arab rulers. Christian kings replaced Moslem Emirs. The Jews lost, too. They lost their positions of respect and influence in the government. They gradually lost their freedoms. Judaism was a respected religion to the Moslems. To the Christians it was a threat, and hated.

Jews had to pay heavy taxes to the Christian king. Taxes were levied to support the army and the navy and to pay for wars which came so often. Taxes went to buy elegant clothing for the royal family. Taxes went to buy royal estates and crown jewels. Taxes went to build churches and cathedrals. Often, the Jews were forced to be their own tax collectors; they tried not to collect from widows and the poor.

Before the evil days arrived, there had often been time for fun. Rich families had parties and were occasionally invited to the court for dances and sporting events. They wore fine clothes of elegant design and fabric and rich jewels. In their own houses all Jews welcomed the Sabbath and holidays with joy and in worship. An engagement, wedding, Bar Mitzvah or *B'rit Milah* was a feast day for all of the congregation. But the evil days came, and the riches dwindled. The church sought to make Christians of all Jews. No one was exempt.

SPECIAL LAWS FOR JEWS:

In 1415, a papal bull, (an order issued by the Catholic Pope) forbid Jews to study the *Talmud,* to read anti-Christian writings, to build new synagogues or to redecorate old ones. Each community could have only one synagogue. Jews could no longer judge their own cases, nor could they sue non-Jews. They could not hold public offices, nor could they work in the crafts, serve as brokers, marriage agents, physicians or druggists. They were forbidden to bake, sell or give away *matzot.* They could not dispose of non-kosher meat. They could not speak to Christians, nor could they disinherit their baptized children. Jews were required to wear the yellow badge at all times, and three times a year all Jews over twelve were required to listen to a sermon about Jesus.

Conditions became worse. The Inquisition demanded that all Jews convert to Catholicism or die. Of course, some did convert. Some fled the country. Some Jews hid from the Inquisition. These secret Jews, or Marranos, as they were called, pretended to be Christians but practiced Judaism in the confines of their homes.

LIFE OF THE MARRANOS

In order to keep from being detected, Marranos had to attend Catholic masses, and over the years Catholic practices made their inevitable way into Marrano Judaism. For instance, Marranos knelt rather than stood in prayer, and prayers were recited rather than chanted. No prayer books were kept, for they could be used as evidence, and Talmudic doctrine and lore were passed along verbally from one generation to the next. Marranos

generally abstained from pork. They had secret biblical names, which they used only among themselves. Catholic wedding ceremonies were required, and a private Jewish wedding would be held afterward. Elaborate measures were resorted to in order to keep a Marrano's Christian servants from discovering that a Jewish fast day was being kept. Servants might be sent out on sudden errands at mealtime; in their absence, plates were greased and dirtied to make it appear that the meal had taken place. A favorite device was to stage a family quarrel just before mealtime. By pre-arrangement, one member of the family would run out into the street in a feigned fit of rage, and the others would run after him to try to cajole him. When the quarrel was over, everyone would be too emotionally exhausted to eat anything.

The end of Jewish life in Spain came in 1492 with the edict of expulsion. By then, the Inquistion had burned thousands of Jews at the stake and tortured countless others to death. But as Columbus set out for the new world, those who could still get out said goodbye to a land in which our people had spent almost 800 years — some golden, some cruel.

Accountability: Test What You Have Learned

1.   Where did the Jews live in the Spanish cities of the period?

2.   What was the most important building in the Jewish quarter?

3.   Who tried Jewish court cases?

4.   What was one important occupation in which many Jews were involved at that time?

5.   What was the most severe penalty that a Jewish court could impose?

6.   Why do you suppose the Jews paid such a heavy burden of taxes?

7. List four provisions of the bull of 1415
    which were discriminatory against the Jews:

1.   3.
2.   4.

8. What changes do you think this edict made
    in the lives of the Spanish Jews as it was
    portrayed and explained in the reading?

9. What were some of the Jewish customs
    which the Marranos attempted to hide?

10. How did they hide these customs?

11. What modern-day parallels to the persecution
    of the Jews in Spain can you list?

PART 5 — WRITINGS FROM SPAIN

What people say or write about tells us
much about them and the society in which they
live. The following were written by Spanish Jews
of this "Golden Age." Decide how these writings
might help you to add to or correct your ideas
about Spain during this period, and get ready to
answer the questions below Sections 1 and 2.
Record your general impressions of the readings
on Impression List 1. Then answer the questions
with a partner.

Poems of Judah Halevi:

MY HEART IS IN THE EAST

My heart is in the east, and I in the
    uttermost west —
How can I find savour in food? How shall it be
    sweet to me?
How shall I render my vows and my bonds,
    while yet
Zion lieth beneath the fetter of Edom, and I
    in Arab chains?
A light thing would it seem to me to leave all
    the good things of Spain —
Seeing how precious in mine eyes it is to behold
    the dust of the desolate sanctuary.

LONGING FOR JERUSALEM

Oh, city of the world, with sacred splendor blest,
My spirit yearns to Thee from the far-off West.
A stream of love wells forth, when I recall
    Thy day,
Now is Thy temple waste, Thy glory passed
    away.
Had I an eagle's wings, straight would I fly
    to Thee,
Moisten Thy holy dust with wet cheeks
    streaming free.
Oh, how I long for Thee! Although Thy king
    has gone,
Although where balm once flowed, the serpent
    dwells alone.
Could I but kiss Thy dust, I would not mind
    to die,
As sweet as honey then, Thy soil and stones,
    Thy sky.

O Lord, where shall I find Thee?
Hid is Thy lofty place;
And where shall I not find Thee,
Whose glory fills all space?
Who formed this world, abideth
Within man's soul always;
Refuge for them that see Him,
Ransom for them that stray.
Who saith he hath not seen Thee,
Thy heavens refute his word;
Their hosts declare Thy glory,
Though never voice he heard.
That Thou, transcendent, holy,
Joyest in Thy creatures' praise,
And comest where men gather,
To glorify Thy ways.

Questions

1. What do you think are the poet's chief
    concerns?

2. In what kind of a God did Halevi believe?

3. Why do you suppose Halevi longs so for
    Jerusalem? What does he mean by "Thy
    temple waste" and "the desolate sanctuary"?

Maimonides' Eight Categories

The following represent eight categories of those
who give charity by Moses Ben Maimon

(Maimonides or Rambam). The author ranks these in descending order, the highest category being the first one.

- He who helps the poor man to sustain himself by giving him a loan or by taking him into business.
- He who gives to the poor without knowing to whom he gives, while the recipient is also ignorant of the giver.
- He who gives secretly, knowing the recipient, but the latter remains ignorant of the benefactor.
- He who gives, not knowing the recipient, but the recipient knows from whom the gift comes.
- He who gives before it is asked.
- He who gives after having been asked.
- He who gives inadequately, but graciously.
- He who gives ungraciously.

Impression List 1.

Questions

1. What can you learn from these eight categories about the morals and values of the great thinkers of the society we are studying?

2. What does the reading say about their community?

3. What does Maimonides try to tell us about responsibility to one's fellow human beings?

4. Do you think these categories are true today?

PART 6 — MUSIC OF SPAIN

Listen to some modern-day music. How does this music tell us what the culture and society are like today?

Now, listen to music of the Jews of this period in Spain. When it is over, here are some questions to think about and answer on your Impression List 2:

1. How do the literature, the music, and the architecture tie in together?
2. What do they say about the life of the people?
3. Does the music sound happy or sad? Does it express praise, rejoicing, fear? Something else?

Impression List 2

PART 7 — A LOOK AT SPAIN ON FILM

In this section, you will continue to gather evidence to use in testing your hypotheses about life in Spain. As you know, pictures provide much information. For example, if we should see a building with a cross on top, we can be fairly sure it is a Christian church. If the mosaics have Hebrew written on them, we can assume we are looking at a synagogue. In either case, we would be learning something about the life in Spain, the beliefs and values of the people. Even then, we should be careful, though, because it would be difficult to know how deeply people felt about their religion without additional facts. If there were only one small synagogue in a large city, what would that tell you?

The filmstrip "The Jews of Spain" should help you make some decisions about the accuracy of your statements about Spain. In some cases, you may still need more evidence, and we hope you will be interested enough to pursue the subject in more depth on your own.

Be prepared to answer the following questions on Data Collection List 3 after you have seen the filmstrip:

Data Collection List 3

1. What kinds of things did you see most often in the filmstrip?
2. What do they tell you about life in Spain?
3. What additional things did you learn from this filmstrip which you can now add to your hypotheses?
4. Are there hypotheses which you now want to remove, change or finally approve?

PART 8 — CONCLUSION

Through your own efforts of observation and investigation, you have learned a great deal about Jews in Spain during the Middle Ages. As a concluding activity, you have a choice of a writing project or an art project. In either case, you will have a chance to show off all of your newfound information.

You might choose to write the diary of a Spanish Jew who as a student, a poet, a rabbi, a Marrano or a physician (or perhaps a Maimonides-type who was many things at once!). Tell about the person's life as it is lived day to day — the good times, the persecutions, the celebrations, the mourning. (Perhaps you will want to choose your own format; this is just one suggestion.)

If you prefer to draw, there are many media available for you — tempura, chalk, charcoal, crayons, collage equipment, clay, etc. Choose your medium and portray some aspect of Spanish life at that time. Try to convey what you have learned to a viewer who knows nothing about the period.

LEADER GUIDE

General Objectives:

1. Students will be able to reconstruct and relate the history, the living conditions and the positive and negative experiences of the Jews in Spain from 700 C.E. to 1492 C.E.

2. Students will experience the inquiry method of study.

The Inquiry Method:

The inquiry method of teaching does not require a great deal of prior knowledge of the subject matter on the part of the teacher. He or she can discover and learn right along with the students.

In its essence, the inquiry method enables students to use those facts and opinions which they already know, in combination with new facts and opinions, to arrive at conclusions on a particular subject. In the process, students sort out and internalize correct or valid information, and discard faulty or non-valid information.

This kind of teaching facilitates total student involvement. The teacher does not lecture or provide the facts. Rather, the students find the facts for themselves.

It would be of great benefit to teachers using this unit to be familiar and comfortable with the inquiry method. A good source for in-depth coverage of the Inquiry method is *Inquiry in the Social Studies Classroom* by Barry K. Beyer (Columbus, Ohio: Charles E. Merrill Pub-

lishing Company, 1971.) This particular mini-course is easily adaptable for camp weekends, *kallot*, or Conferences.

Strategies:

Part 1: Read the introductory paragraph. After students have followed the directions and written their hypothesis on the Individual Hypothesis List 1 (allow about 15 minutes for this), ask them to volunteer items from their lists. Write these on the board. (This changing list of hypotheses should remain on the board throughout the unit.)

Part 2: Read the instructions to the students and then have them record their answers to the questions on Data Collection List 1. (Allow about 15 minutes for this.) Following this, read the next paragraph to the class. Allow another 15 or 20 minutes for students to list their hypotheses and to state which artifacts and pictures they want to see to test the accuracy of each hypothesis.

Part 3: Read the instructions to the class. Allow about 20 minutes for the students to write down their observations on Data Collection List 2. Return to the blackboard and ask students to discard by erasing any hypothesis that has been proven through facts to be wrong. They should then add any new hypotheses which they feel are also warranted by facts.

Part 4: Read paragraph one. Give the students ample time to read the Historical Overview in class, or assign it as homework. Students then answer the questions. Discuss and correct the answers as a class, so that the students have a body of agreed upon facts with which to work. Repeat the same procedure at the blackboard as you did following Part 2.

Part 5: Read the instructions. Read the poems and the Eight Categories of Charity. Students may be the readers, or the readings may be put on tape and played for the class. Students record their individual impressions of the readings on Impression List 1 and then, with a partner, answer the questions related to each reading.

Part 6: Read the instructions. Play a piece of contemporary music and then some Ladino songs. These may be found on the records, "Ladino Folk Songs" (Collectors Guild) and "Romancero Judeo-Espanol" (Produced in Israel; sung by Yehoram Gaon) and on The

Adventures in Judaism tape, "A Song From Morocco" (UAHC). Students answer the questions on Impression List 2. Repeat the blackboard procedure. At this time, an attempt should be made to organize the hyptheses on the board. Using another blackboard, have the students group the hypotheses into such categories as religious life, political life, family life, cultural life, economic life, etc.

Part 7: Read the instructions. Show the filmstrip, "The Jews of Spain: Glimpses of Their Life and History" (UAHC). Use the script which comes with it or your own narrative. After students answer the questions on Data Collection List 3, do a final check of the newly grouped hypotheses on the board to see if there are any other facts that need to be discarded or added.

Additional Activities:

1. Research the other people living in Spain during this period and compare their lives with those of the Jews.
2   Study Spanish art more extensively.
3. Compare the oppression of this period with the oppression which the Jews suffered during the Holocaust, in the U.S.S.R., etc.
4. Have students rank order the answers to the question: If threatened by the Inquistion, I would: 1) Convert to Christianity but practice Judaism in secret; 2) Continue to live Jewishly despite the danger; 3) Take my own life. Discuss the rankings.
5. Look into which literature of this period has found its way into present day Jewish liturgy.
6. Include work with the materials and documents in *Journey of Fifteen Centuries: The Story of The Jews of Spain* by Robert Sugar (UAHC). A list of other References follows. It is suggested that these be available as additional resources for Part 4, the Historical Overview.
7. Find out about Jews living in Spain today. There have been many articles about this recently. How are their lives like or unlike ours? What are their special difficulties?
8. Trace the journeys of the Jews who were expelled from Spain. Find out where they settled. See if any class members are descended from these Jews.
9. Have students research some interesting personalities of the Golden Age in Spain. Some suggestions are: Hasdai Ibn Shaprut, Samuel HaNagid (Ibn Nagrila), Joseph Ibn Nagrila, Isaac Alfasi, Rabbi David Kamhi, R. Solomon Abulafia, R. Meir Halevi Abulafia, Nachmanides, Ibn Gabirol, Abraham and Moses Ibn Ezra, Judah Al-Harizi, Samuel Abravanel, Bahye Ibn Pakuda and R. Hasdai Crescas. Reports can be made to the rest of the class in the form of radio or television shows such as interviews, quiz programs, "You Are There," "Hollywood Squares," "To Tell The Truth," etc.

Learning Centers

This mini-course is well suited to learning centers. Use the Word List, Gathering Information From Pictures, the filmstrip and the historical background material in primary centers. Students can use the Accountability as a self-check. Following completion of these centers, students can participate in secondary centers consisting of music and poetry. This method provides variety and an excellent way of reinforcing learning.

BIBLIOGRAPHY FOR JEWS IN SPAIN

Ashtor, Eliyahu. *The Jews of Moslem Spain.* Philadelphia: JPS, 1974.

Baer, Yitzhak. *A History of the Jews in Christian Spain* (2 volumes). Philadelphia: JPS, 1971.

Birmingham, Stephen. *The Grandees.* N.Y.: Dell, 1971.

Gamoran, Mamie. *The New Jewish History.* N.Y.: UAHC.

Graetz, H. *History of The Jews* (Vol. 3). N.Y.: Hebrew Publishing Co., 1926.

Kamin, Henry. *The Spanish Inquistion.* N.Y.: New American Library, 1965.

Lazar, Moshe. *The Sephardic Tradition: Ladino & Spanish Literature.* B'nai B'rith Jewish Heritage Classic.

Millgram, Abraham. *An Anthology of Medieval Hebrew Literature.* N.Y.: The Burning Bush Press, 1961.

Roth, Cecil. *The Spanish Inquisition.* N.Y.: W.W. Norton & Co., 1964.

Sugar, Robert. *Focus Kit on the Golden Age of Spain.* N.Y.: UAHC, 1973.

CONCLUSION

Inquiry teaching is hard work — both for teacher and students. But the excitement and learning it generates justify the effort. Like any new skill we learn, it takes time to perfect. Don't be disappointed if your lessons are not as wonderful as you hope the first few times you introduce inquiry. Your students may have no idea what they are supposed to do. You will have to lead them gently into it and give them the confidence to proceed. One more caution — don't use inquiry too frequently. Vary your strategies so that students do not tire of any one of them. When you do use inquiry, you'll find it satisfying and fun. Especially enjoy the opportunity to learn yourself alongside enthusiastic, inquiring students.

BIBLIOGRAPHY

Allen, Rodney, et al, editors. *Inquiry in the Social Studies.* Washington: National Council for the Social Studies, 1968.

Amidon, Edmund and Flanders, Ned. *The Role of the Teacher in the Classroom.* Minneapolis, Minnesota: Association for Productive Teaching, 1967.

Beyer, Barry K. *Inquiry in the Social Studies Classroom: A Strategy for Teaching.* Columbus, Ohio: Charles E. Merrill Publishing Co., 1971.

Bruner, Jerome. *On Knowing.* Cambridge: The Belknap Press of Harvard University, 1963.

_____. *The Process of Education.* Cambridge: Harvard University Press, 1960.

Carin, Arthur A. and Sund, Robert B. *Developing Question Techniques: A Self-Concept Approach.* Columbus, Ohio: Charles E. Merrill Publishing Co., 1971.

Cohen, Martin A. and Zevin, Jack. *Identity* (Book 1) and *Survival* (Book 2) and Teachers Manual. N.Y.: UAHC, 1976.

Fenton, Edward. *Teaching the New Social Studies in Secondary Schools: An Inductive Approach.* . NY.: Holt, Rinehart and Winston, 1966.

Levow, Mordecai. "An Inquiry-Skills Teacher Education Program." *Pedagogic Reporter,* Vol. XXIII, No. 2, pp. 3-6.

Massialas, Byron and Zevin, Jack. *Creative Encounters in the Classroom.* N.Y.: John Wiley & Sons, 1969.

Massialas, Byron and Cox, C. Benjamin. *Inquiry in Social Studies.* N.Y.: McGraw-Hil Book Co., 1966.

McCollum, John A. *Ah Hah! The Inquiry Process of Generating and Testing Knowledge.* Santa Monica, California: Goodyear Publishing Co., Inc., 1978.

Melton Research Center, 3080 Broadway, New York, NY. 10027. (Inquiry Materials on Bible)

Sanders, Norris M. *Classroom Questions: What Kinds?* N.Y.: Harper & Row, 1966.

Suchman, J. Richard. *Inquiry Development Program: Developing Inquiry.* Chicago: Science Research Associates, 1966.

_____ . "Learning Through Inquiry." *Childhood Education 41* (February 1965): 289-291.

Sugar, Robert. *Focus Kit on the Golden Age of Spain.* N.Y.: UAHC, 1973.

Weil, Marsha and Joyce, Bruce. *Information Processing Models of Teaching.* Englewood Cliffs, N.J.: Prentice-Hall, Inc., 1975.

TEACHING JEWISH CURRENT EVENTS

by Linda K. Schaffzin and Stephen Schaffzin

Why teach current events in the Jewish school? After all, the students are probably studying current events in their Social Studies class. Why clutter up an already overcrowded program with yet another subject area? The reasons, we feel, are compelling.

The responsible citizen in a participatory democracy such as ours (and Israel's) is one who is aware of issues and events that concern the community. Reading newspapers and magazines is one way to become informed, and the skills necessary to form a "reading the news" habit should be taught early.

There are Jewish values to be imparted through this exercise. In *Pirke Avot,* we are taught, "Do not separate yourself from the community," or in a current events sense, we should be well informed citizens.

And as Jews we have special concerns: Israel, human rights, energy and conservation, etc. Again, as Jews we feel responsible for one another. And we feel the need to act on behalf of our Jewish community.

Beyond these underlying values are the specific facts, the processes, the history-in-the-making that contribute to our students' Jewish education and their Jewish identification.

So how to begin? We would like to suggest two approaches: The Current Events Period and the Integrated Approach.

The Current Events Period

Most programs set aside a weekly chunk of time for current events. The class will read student publications such as *World Over* or perhaps students will be assigned to bring in a clipping and be prepared to discuss it with the class.

There are problems with this method. It is unlikely that everyone in the class will be able to present his/her article and students may start "gambling" on not being called. Often students do little more than read the article to the class. Instead, try these suggestions: For younger children especially, it might be better for you to pick the topic. Pick a newsworthy personality, a place or an issue such as Soviet Jewry or U.N. Resolution 242. Be specific and make sure it is something that appears in the press currently. Ask students to find out all they can, bring in pictures, poll family members about an issue, etc. as a basis for an in-depth class discussion the following week.

Another idea: duplicate a political cartoon, map, chart or other graphic aid. Ask students to read about the issue for a few days. Then discuss. You may find that the simplest information is the most worthy of your class time: the meaning of AWACS and what they can or can't do; the definition of lobby and who has one; the picture of a personality in the news and his/her specific job.

Have students bring in articles and cut off headlines. The class can guess how headlines relate to the articles. Then bring in only headlines. Ask students what they think the article said. Is headline skimming a good way to find out about what is happening?

If you do set aside a specific Current Events Period, you may want to turn to more than your local press and Anglo-Jewish papers (see below for more resources).

The Integrated Current Events Program

Another way to deal with current events is the Integrated Current Events Program. This means that instead of isolating current events, they are brought into the teaching of all aspects of your curriculum. For example, current issues and concerns fit in with almost every holiday theme throughout the year:

Rosh Hashanah and Yom Kippur - Use this time to survey events in the year that passed, or judge the world just as we are judged at this time of year.

Hanukah - Deal with the theme of the few against the many (Israel among the Arab nations, status of minority groups, especially Jews, in the U.S. and other countries); or use this time to look at Jews in sports (e.g., Maccabiah from Maccabees as your tie-in).

Tu B'Shvat - This holiday lends itself to the themes of ecology, energy and conservation and their effect on U.S. oil policy, especially as they concern Israel.

Purim - Examine the status of Jewish communities all over the world.

Pesach - Through the theme of freedom, lead into a unit on Soviet Jewry (or Iranian, Syrian, Argentinian, Falashan Jewry, etc.). Examine the relationship between Israel and Egypt today.

Yom HaAtzma'ut - Can be a culmination of a project or concentrated study of Israel in the news.

Yom HaShoah - Study current issues, such as the hunt for war criminals, neo-Nazism or the activities and views of revisionist historians concerning the Holocaust.

Shavuot - Discuss law — civil law vs. religious law in Israel, the rights of Jews according to U.S. law. (There are occasional cases of clashes between school systems or companies or the military and observant Jews. For example, consider the case of Susan and Lynn Stein as described in *World Over,* October 10, 1980, in the *Village Voice* and in other papers. The Steins challenged their local school district which insisted on holding graduation exercises on Shabbat. The young women, who were valedictorians, lost their case, but the legal steps they took, the court decisions and the effect of the case on their community are very interesting.)

The above represent just a few suggestions.

The possibilities for this sort of program are endless.

A current events program could also be integrated into the history curriculum. As each event or period is covered, ask students for evidence of current parallels. Or use history to explore an issue in the news. For example, what are the historical events that have led to the formation of the P.L.O. or to the granting of U.S. citizenship to a Swede named Raoul Wallenberg?

Current events might even be taught in Hebrew language class using Hebrew newspapers for children such as *Olam Hadash* or *La-Mishpaha* (see below for addresses). Or they could be taught in connection with a Jewish values course. In this instance, an issue such as capital punishment could be examined from the standpoint of its current political relevance, as well as from the Jewish point of view.

Resources

Whether you designate current events time during each session or decide to integrate current events into all areas of your curriculum, you will need resources. The following is a list of some possibilities:

1. Publications written for children: A student publication such as *World Over* may be your best answer. Chances are it can best be used as a motivator, helping to teach newspaper skills and to raise issues. In a curriculum which places only a minor emphasis on current events, *World Over's* "Etmol" may be the ideal summarizing tool, helping students obtain some basic knowledge of the events that affect their lives as Jews. (Obviously this publication cannot possibly be up-to-date and completely current, since the lead time is two to three months. The editors try to review and deal with issues. Teachers are encouraged to ask students what has happened since the date when the column was written.) *World Over's* news column is generally geared to the upper end of the readership, to 11-13 year olds. Though most "Etmol" columns are surveys, some go into specific issues in depth.

2. The Anglo-Jewish Press, local editions: Generally speaking, your Anglo-Jewish newspaper can be a good resource if it is used properly. Its greatest value is its news about the local Jewish community. Students

should have a sense of that community, its scope and the services it offers. Its columns, editorials, etc. are often syndicated, strongly pro-Israel and pro-Jewish. Your students should understand this. Most Anglo-Jewish papers get their national and world news from the Jewish Telegraphic Agency (see below) or the Seven Arts Syndicate.

3. National Anglo-Jewish press: There is no national press as such. Most national publications are periodicals, magazines or newsletters that appear monthly or less frequently. Most are published by an organization and emphasize issue-related feature articles. Often, however, there are analyses, background features, or articles on personalities that may be of value to you. For a complete (non-annotated) list of these publications see the *Jewish Literary Marketplace: A Directory of the Press, Periodicals, Publishers, and Booksellers,* published by B. Arbit Books (8050 N. Port Washington Rd., Milwaukee, Wisconsin 53217). The first edition, edited by Bruce Arbit and Howard M. Berliant, is dated 1979, so you may want to look for a second edition or double check addresses.

4. General press: In using the general press, the students' job will be to use newspaper skills to assimilate content and check out facts. Students should be taught to read critically. Do not hesitate to have students go to history books to check out facts and figures. Use the letters to the editor column as a reason to check out historical processes and facts. Let students themselves write in to correct faulty statements or counter opposing views.

   Many national news magazines and some local newspapers have special student editions, supplements or teacher's guides and aids. Some offer reduced prices if bought in bulk for a class. If the reading level of your students is not up to *U.S. News and World Report,* but you have 10 or 15 teachers in your school, you may want to order in bulk just for the faculty. The addresses of such weeklies may be found at the conclusion of this chapter. Costs and offers change, so be sure to check on current rates.

5. Press releases: Many organizations routinely send out press releases and they are very interesting. The American Jewish Congress for example, sends out releases about civil suits affecting Jews, such as the case of the Steins mentioned above. The B'nai B'rith Anti-Defamation League monitors the attitudes and actions of non-Jews toward Jews — e.g., synagogue vandalism and incidents that can be characterized as anti-Semitic. Have each student write to an organization and ask to be put on its mailing list for press releases. Keep a "mail corner" set up in your room. Have school stationery and envelopes, stamps and pens on hand. Make it as easy as possible for students to write and mail a letter to an organization, congressperson, embassy, newspaper, etc. A small telephone address book is helpful. Keep updating addresses so there is no delay between student interest and letter writing.

6. Organizational organs: The newspapers, magazines and newsletters that are put out by American Jewish organizations are a good source for news in a given area — e.g., Zionist groups have magazines with fine features on Israel.

7. Jewish Telegraphic Agency or Seven Arts: These are news syndicates that concentrate on national and international Jewish news. A subscription could be purchased for your class or school. It is an excellent way to get all the Jewish news in daily or weekly capsules. While the JTA has a teletype service, their bulletins would be more appropriate for your purposes. There is a daily bulletin, a weekly (which encapsulates the dailies), and a community news reporter which appears weekly and reports local community news such as awards and appointments. The JTA bulletins are written clearly and are organized well, enabling students to use them easily or enabling you to present the news to the students. If you look at by-lines in your local Jewish paper, you will probably see some JTA entries. For addresses see below.

8. *Jerusalem Post:* This English language weekly is an excellent resource for the Jewish school for current events and for features about life in Israel. We recommend it highly. It is probably too expensive for each child to subscribe, but there should be a few for the school, depending upon how large the school is. A tabloid with news on every aspect of Israeli life (from sports to stock quotations, from editorials to entertainment), the articles are written well and most of the news reports

will be understandable to your upper elementary and junior high school students. Editorials and analyses are for older readers.

The Student as Journalist

Youngsters most often understand news best if they are asked to gather and present it themselves. They can see how facts can be fudged or checked out, how imprecise words can be and how powerful the news (and its writers) can seem.

The projects need not be enormous. Here are some suggestions:

1. Let each student individually, or with a partner, follow an issue, once a week handing in an update to be included in a class newsletter. Ditto the newsletter and share it with other classes in the school.
2. Divide the class into groups. Assign each group one period a month to present to the class, grade or school a news roundup or an in-depth news report (a la "60 Minutes" or "Good Morning America," depending on how sophisticated and critical you feel they can be).
3. Use school-wide surveys to stimulate discussion. Choose a "hot" issue and do some background research on it, either as a class or in groups. Devise a survey to see how other people feel about the issue. When the results are in, discuss them. Present the findings to the school. (For a general piece on polls, see *World Over,* Volume 42, No. 1, September 1980.)
4. *World Over* encourages readers to become "WO Stringers," sharing news of their community with others. Urge your students to participate in this program. Additionally, you can foster an understanding of and relationship to your community through the creation of a community newspaper. Write to local organizations (synagogues, Jewish Community Centers, etc.), requesting that they notify you of upcoming events that may be of interest to kids (and their parents). Reproduce your newsletter on a monthly basis on a ditto machine, using colored dittos for headlines. The activity is especially appropriate for younger children.
5. Other techniques for involving students in their community or in local, national and worldwide issues are letter writing (to newspapers, government officials, etc.), debating, interviewing and inviting informed guests to the classroom.

The Goals of a Current Events Program

The goals of any current events program are important:

1. The learning of newspaper skills (reading headlines and text critically, deciphering cartoons, maps, charts, etc.)
2. The establishment of the newspaper habit which should lead to:

   a. a feeling of belonging to a community

   b. a sense of responsibility as a citizen in a participatory democracy

   c. an understanding of history as it affects current news

As Jews we have special problems. A few years ago a particularly disturbing letter appeared on the OP-Ed page of the *New York Times.* It's writer, Andrew Fauld, a member of the British Parliament clearly outlined the United States' position in relation to the oil producing Arab nations and Israel. He maintained that it was not in the country's best interest to continue its strong support of Israel and that eventually the incumbent president (then Jimmy Carter) would recognize this. He twisted a few "facts" and argued his case well. He advised Carter to forget about Jewish votes and worry about the realities of the world.

Fauld's letter, predictably, met with cries of anti-Semitism from a number of letter writers in the days that followed. Yet the letter could have been answered unemotionally, factually and with a strong, rational case for a pro-Israel, U.S. policy. Our goal is to produce students who could do just that — students who could argue the issues, who could call on history with understanding, who could assume their role as Jews facing the constantly changing, often bewildering issues of our complicated world.

SOURCES

Newspapers and Periodicals for the Jewish School

Jewish Telegraphic Agency
165 West 46th Street
New York, NY 10036

The Jerusalem Post, International Edition
110 East 59th Street
New York, NY 19922
(212) 355-4440

La-Mishpaha
Illustrated Hebrew Monthly
1841 Broadway
New York, NY 10023

Olam Hadash
Illustrated Hebrew Magazine for Children and Youth
515 Park Avenue
New York, NY 10022

General Newspaper/Newsmagazines

New York Times School and College Service
(212) 556-1311

For a minimum order of 15 newspapers, you can get a special rate plus the school weekly supplement free.

Newsweek
(800) 631-1040

Student subscription rate available on orders of 15 or more. That bulk order also entitles the teacher to a multimedia package of teaching aids. An order of 10 student copies entitles you to teaching aids including maps, quizzes, work sheets, etc.

U.S. News & World Report
Call collect, (303) 447-9937 or write:
P.O. Box 2628
Boulder, CO 80321

Call or write for folder outlining special student rates and bonus for teachers.

Note: We have not included *Time* because we find their reporting on Israel biased and frequently inaccurate. You may want to bring in some material from *Time* to illustrate that bias and the power of the media.

Organizations for News Releases:

The American Jewish Committee
165 East 56th Street
New York, NY 10022

American Jewish Congress
15 East 84th Street
New York, NY 10028

Anti-Defamation League of B'nai B'rith
823 United Nations Plaza
New York, NY 10017

ARMDI—American Red Mogen David for Israel
888 Seventh Avenue, Suite 403
New York, NY 10019

Civil Rights Update
1121 Vermont Avenue N.W.
Washington, DC 20425

Conference of Presidents of Major American
Jewish Organizations
515 Park Avenue
New York, NY 10022

Consulate General of Israel in N.Y.
800 Second Avenue
New York, NY 10017

Zionist Organization of America
4 East 34th Street
New York, NY 10016

Miscellaneous

Near East Report
44 N. Capital Street N.W.
Washington, DC 20001

Not for kids, but a sophisticated analysis of events and issues in the Middle East, with a decidedly pro-Israel approach. Good for teacher's background.

Teachers Guide to Television
699 Madison Avenue
New York, NY 10021

Produces guides for NBC shows that have educational value. Some may fit into current events area, but in general, a good resource for the Jewish school.

BEYOND BIBLE TALES: TOWARD TEACHING TEXT

by Joel Lurie Grishaver

The central goal of every Bible teacher is to reveal to his/her students that the Holy Scriptures are haunted — that indeed something is lurking behind the words, phrases and metaphors. Every time we open the text, we try to encounter the force which inhabits each ancient phrase. It does not matter whether we are seeking God's true voice, the ghosts of Rabbinic sages past, the secret identities of the "real" authors, or simply the echoes of ancient footsteps. What is important is that we encounter the text itself, that we allow it to conjure — from our past, from ourselves, from its past and from its own reality — a dynamic relationship. What we are seeking is a text with which, and over which, we can talk.

To search for the text's inner voice, we need to know how to probe the text, how to listen for its response. In doing so, it is necessary to go past the story to the *way the story is told.* The depth of the biblical material lies not in the intricacies of plot, but in the complex workings of the words themselves.

The Bible is well suited for this probing. In fact, it demands it of us. Regardless of our vision of the text, be it divine or exquisitely human, we can see that its style is unlike any other great literature. For it is like a marvelous haunted mansion, carefully crafted. It is filled with individual works of art, which are both more beautiful and more puzzling because of their age. It is alive with echoes and glimmering light sources, and its construction is riddled with secret connections and hidden passageways.

In the course of this chapter, we will first examine five patterns which enable us to engage the text in dialogue. (While there are at least five other such patterns,[1] we cannot cover them all here because of space constraints.) Following the analysis of the five patterns, we will discuss the steps necessary in the preparation of good lessons on the Bible.

The kind of biblical investigation we are suggesting is not limited to the adult or to the sophisticated learner. All who like to engage in dialogue and all who are fascinated by mystery can be involved. Students of all ages will be intrigued when exposed to these patterns and when they become aware of their significance. So let us take candle in hand and begin our investigation of some haunted passages.

PATTERN ONE: REPETITION

We open the Bible and start reading. One of our first impressions is that the text frequently repeats itself. We see the same pattern over and over: God tells someone to do something, and then (more or less repeating the same phrases), the narrator tells us that the deed has been done. Or, a character is told to tell someone something, and then (more or less repeating the same phrases), the character delivers the message. Additionally, we find incidents when the narrator describes a character's actions, and then (more or less repeating the same phrases), that same character or another character describes the action. Such is the biblical style — but there is more to it. The narrative portion of the text is basically made up of narration and dialogue. The two are very carefully structured; it is the variation, not the repetition, which is significant. The repetitions focus our

---

[1]The patterns not dealt with in this chapter are Metaphor, Translation, Word Echoes, Surplus Language and *P'shat* and *Drash.*

attention and build our expectations. But the subtle variation in the pattern holds the author's hidden message.

Let us look at some examples. The first consists of two passages about Abram and his family as they leave certain places. One passage describes leaving Haran and going to the land of Canaan; the other describes leaving Egypt and returning to the land of Canaan.

> And Abram took
> Sarai his wife,
> and Lot his brother's son
> and all their substance. . .
>
> (Genesis 12:5)
>
> And Abram went out of Egypt
> He, and his wife
> and all that he had,
> And Lot with him. . .
>
> (Genesis 13:1)

What seems to be the change in Lot's status? (Clue: Lot's position in the description is not the only thing. Look also at what the syntax suggests about collective ownership of property.)

Genesis 13:1 immediately precedes the fight between the shepherds of Lot and Abram which results in their split. What might the narrator be trying to tell us about that incident? What lesson or message can be drawn from this insight?

A second example from the book of Numbers describes Moses turning the leadership of the people over to Joshua. . .

> and the Lord answered Moses, "Single out Joshua, son of Nun, an inspired man, and lay your hand upon him. Have him stand before Eleazar the priest and before the whole community, and commission him in their sight. Invest him with some of your authority. . ."
>
> (Numbers 27:18-20)
>
> Moses did as the Lord commanded him. He took Joshua and had him stand before Eleazar the priest and before the whole community. He laid his hands upon him and commissioned him — as the Lord had spoken through Moses.
>
> (Numbers 27:22-23)

Some questions to ponder: Moses follows God's instructions, but there is one major shift in sequence as the instructions are carried out. The order which Moses uses to carry out the instructions is the logical sequence. Why might

God have inverted the order when instructions were given to Moses? (Clue: What insight into Moses' character might God have acted upon?) What lesson can be drawn from this inversion of the repetition? Explain why Moses decided to add a hand to his installation process. This explanation can be used as the basis of a moral lesson.

Rashi poses this solution to the case of the extra hand (after all, we are exploring a haunted house):

> And he laid his hands — generously — meaning in much greater measure than he had been commanded — he did it with both hands to make him as a vessel which is full to the brim and overflowing, and so he filled him with a generous helping of wisdom.

Rashi, in his own way (as all of us do) distorts the text slightly for his own purpose. Consider this: In the text, what does God tell Moses to use as he invests Joshua? What does Rashi suggest that Moses used? Is there a correlation? Are the two identical? Should they be identical? Can another lesson be drawn, this time from Rashi's comment?

In each of the above examples, we have found that behind the apparent repetition and use of formula in the text, a message is conveyed through that which is not repeated (more or less using the same phrases) and through that which is altered. This kind of analysis is a form of literary criticism, which is technically known as form criticism. It is used by literary scholars, as well as by the commentators Umberto Cassuto (1883-1951) and Benno Jacob (1862-1955). It is also standard procedure for the *Midrash* and for Rashi. In spite of its "scholarly" roots, any of us can participate in this process.

Classroom Applications

Here are a few possibilities for adapting the pattern of repetition to classroom lessons. You can generalize these suggestions to other passages.

1. Using an inquiry format, have your students find the clues in the text by a) providing them with the portions of the text laid out in such a way that they can easily see the variations, b) having them color code their texts with circles and arrows and other markings, or c) having them read the two

versions out loud. As we have done here, emphasize both the finding of the clue and the creation of lessons to be learned.

2. Adapt the childhood exercise, "What is wrong with this picture?" Create (or have students create) pictures which go with each version of the story. Then have the students match phrase and illustration.

3. A standard vaudeville sketch format occurs when the protagonist repeats the dialogue directed by the narrator:
Narrator: And then God said: "Let there be light."
God: Let there be light.
Narrator: And there was light.
Write skits which exploit this device to reflect the changes in the text.

4. The first text dealt with the relationship between Abram (and Sarai) and Lot. Our reading of the text suggested that relations had begun to break down before the shepherds fought. Have your students act out, or creatively write, the scene inside Abram's tent when he and Sarai talk about Lot, and the scene inside Lot's house as he discusses Abram. Use these scenes to evaluate the solution to the conflict arrived at by Abram and Lot.

5. In the text on the installation of Joshua by Moses, we found a significant issue revolved around the laying on of hands. After studying this passage, have the students invent a ceremony during which they grant gifts to each other through the laying on of hands.

6. In Rashi's solution to the text, we saw that there is a question of the relationship between knowledge and authority. Have your students play blackjack (or any other game). Have them adjust the rules so that the dealer (or the leader) has varying amounts of knowledge and authority. Discuss what happens to the game if the dealer gets to see everyone's cards before he or she plays, or what happens to the game if the dealer can decide for each player how many cards they may (or must) take. Then discuss the question in the passage.

PATTERN TWO: TWICE TOLD TALES

Most events in the Bible are told at least twice. Deuteronomy retells many of the accounts in Exodus, Leviticus and Numbers. Chronicles I and II retell a great deal of history, especially what has already been reported in the books of Samuel and Kings. The Prophets and the Psalms echo many of the accounts in the Torah and especially the portions of Genesis which precede Abram. Often, the second version of a story imparts new information.

Consider, for example, the fourth commandment as it appears in the two versions of the Ten Commandments.

Remember the Sabbath day and keep it holy. Six days shall you labor and do all your work, but the seventh day is a Sabbath of the Lord your God: you shall not do any work — you, your son or your daughter, your male or female slave, or your cattle, or the stranger who is within your settlements. For in six days the Lord made heaven and earth and sea, and all that is in them, and He rested on the seventh day; therefore the Lord blessed the Sabbath day and hallowed it.

(Exodus 20:8-11)

Observe the Sabbath day and keep it holy, as the Lord your God has commanded you. Six days you shall labor and do all your work, but the seventh day is a Sabbath of the Lord your God: you shall not do any work — you, your son or your daughter, your male or female slave, your ox or your ass, or any of your cattle, or the stranger in your settlements, so that your male and female slave may rest as you do. Remember that you were a slave in the land of Egypt and the Lord your God freed you from there with a mighty hand and an outstretched arm; therefore the Lord your God has commanded you to observe the Sabbath day.

(Deuteronomy 5:12-15)

Determine which portions of the text are the same in both versions. Which are parallel (more or less the same words in the same place)? The central difference between the two versions of this commandment is in the reasons given for celebrating the Sabbath. The starting words for each of the two commandments (the active verbs) are different. The closing formulas are also different. In Exodus, God is the subject and the Sabbath is the direct object. In Deuteronomy, God is the subject and "you" is the direct object. All of the Exodus version of this commandment is contained in the Deuteronomic version. However, the commandment as found

in Deuteronomy has two major additions as can
be seen in the following lists:

Exodus	Deuteronomy
Remember	Observe
Creation	Exodus (freedom from slavery)
Bless	command
	Extra material on commandments
	Extra material on slaves resting

How are the elements of each list consistent? Do the two versions of this commandment
contradict each other? Do they complement each
other? If so, in what way? What lesson can be
drawn from the fact that the two versions outline different reasons for celebrating Shabbat?

The first verse of *"Lecha Dodi,"* the song
with which we welcome the Shabbat begins:
" 'Observe' and 'Remember' were said together
in one breath. . ." Is the "lesson" of *Lecha
Dodi"* similar to the one drawn above?

Now we look at a second example — the
two versions of the story about sending spies
into the land of Israel in Numbers 13:1-3, 27-32
and Deuteronomy 1:22-28. Unlike other repetition patterns, these two stories confront us with
significant contradictions rather than literary
variations. In Numbers, 1) the Lord instructs
Moses to send spies, 2) the spies are princes of
the tribes, 3) the land is "flowing in milk and
honey," 4) Moses is credited with bringing the
people there, and 5) the spies spread an evil
report — "that the land consumes its inhabitants." In the book of Deuteronomy, 1) the people ask to send spies, 2) the spies are simply
"twelve men," 3) the land is "good," 4) God gave
it, 5) the inhabitants are "greater and taller than
we," and 6) God brought us there because He
"hated us." Now we have to resolve these differences. Here are some "popular solutions."
Consider the evidence for each.

1. The "documentary hypothesis" suggests that
the Bible was assembled by collecting various documents/texts which had been written by different groups, under different
influences, in different time periods. What
evidence is there that these two editions
might indeed be two different accounts
(from different sources) of the same event?
2. Several commentators say that there is no
real contradiction between the two accounts.
Like two news reporters, the writers are
simply choosing to focus on different
details. Can you explain how both versions could be "factual?"
3. A commentator named David Hoffman sug-

gests that the two accounts had different
intents. The account in Numbers was
created to preserve an historical reality,
while the edition of the story found in Deuteronomy was structured to teach a "moral
truth." What is the evidence for this point
of view?
4. The Ramban (Nachmanides) suggested that
the two versions of the story were designed
to fit the needs of two audiences. The first
was written about (and for) the generation
which left Egypt and the second was written
for the generation which was about to enter
the land of Israel. Is there evidence to support this point of view?
5. Why do you think the Bible includes two
separate accounts of this incident? What
are we supposed to learn from the two
accounts? Do you accept one of the above
explanations or a combination of them? Do
you have a different point of view?

Many portions of the biblical text appear
in more than one location. The Bible seems to
preserve multiple testimonies about specific
occurrences and legal concepts. Sometimes these
experiences are nearly identical; at other times
they seem significantly different. In either case,
we are drawn into the material. We find ourselves looking for the "true" version and, like a
good detective, we begin to sort out the various
testimonies and piece together our version of the
truth. Frequently we discover that it is not the
facts of the event that have changed, but the
nature of the conversation. Different people tell
(and retell) stories differently, and different audiences call for different ways of telling. In confronting conflicting accounts, we must realize
that the resolution may never be clear. Often
the presence of two (or more) voices expands
rather than confuses our image of the text; at
other times the ambiguity enhances our involvement in the material. It is as if the Bible is asking us, "Nu, so what do you think?"

Other examples of the pattern of twice told
tales may be found in the accounts of the story
of Saul's death in I Samuel 31 and I Chronicles
10. Look also at Psalm 105 and find the three
stories retold there.

Classroom Applications

Let's explore a few possible lesson formats
for this pattern. Some of these will deal with the
nature of confronting two sources; the remainder
will draw on the insights gained from the passages.

1. As with the repetition pattern, use written or oral inquiry techniques to find clues in the text.

2. A particular professor was famous for staging a "murder" in his class once a semester. At some point, when everyone least expected it, an assistant would burst through the door, shoot the professor and disappear. The class would then be asked to write an account of the incident. Reports varied as to the size, height, age, race and dress of the "murderer." Adapt this (in a less violent format) to your classroom. Use the various reports to talk about the nature of human testimony.

3. Do the same kind of thing with a past event. Analyze a significant occurrence which took place last year or a while ago and compare the results of "historical memory."

4. Bring in two articles about the same news events or two reviews of the same film from sources such as *Time* and *Newsweek*. Use the two accounts to try to reconstruct the "true" event.

5. Do guided imagery with your class. Have students close their eyes and imagine an event you describe. Then have everyone write down a description or draw a picture of their experience. Compare the diverse impressions of a single experience.

6. Have someone tell a story to a group of adults and then to the first grade class. (Videotape this if desired.) Compare the versions of the stories told. Decide if this situation is analagous to the two accounts of the same story found in the texts you have studied.

7. Compare the other differences in the two versions of the Ten Commandments. Also, look at the structure of the Ten Commandments. For background and activities, see *Bible People Book Two*, Workbook and Teacher Guide (Denver: Alternatives in Religious Education, Inc., 1981).

9. That there are two versions of a commandment about Shabbat could serve as the basis for explaining why Shabbat is celebrated with pairs — of candles, *challot*, angels who, in the *midrash*, escort people home. Explore the pairs theme. A good reference is *The Sabbath* by Abraham Joshua Heschel (New York: Harper and Row, 1952).

10. Imagine what Shabbat would be like in the Garden of Eden and what it was like for the slaves in Egypt. Simulate these experiences with your class, then reread the two sets of commandments.

11. Organize a debate on which version of the incident of the spies is most true (or create a "60 Minutes" report on the topic).

12. Two versions of the story of the spies represent an interesting literary format: we are presented with "mixed reports" of the land, from "mixed reports" of spies. Have students respond to the reports from the point of view of Joshua, of one of the spies, of Moses, of an ordinary Israelite, of Moses 30 years later, of an ordinary Israelite 30 years later, of one of the spy's children or grandchildren, of Joshua's mother, of a history teacher 75 years later, etc.

PATTERN THREE: CONVENTIONS[2]

Certain kinds of events seem to characterize the lives of many biblical characters. Biblical women, for instance, have a difficult time getting pregnant. What is more, it sometimes seems that no self-respecting biblical hero is ever born of a mother who got pregnant on the first try. Aliases (and other name changes) run in biblical families. Many good biblical marriages (and many poor ones) began at a well. And, in almost every generation, the wrong child — the one who is qualified by skill but not by order of birth — takes over the leadership of the Jewish family/people.

The idea of standard events (or technically, "type-scenes") is familiar to us. In movies and television shows we are used to certain basic "conventions." Lightning storms at night (especially around castles and abandoned houses) and full moons (accompanied by ominous string music) are certain clues to what will transpire. It is universally accepted that the first place every western hero goes when he gets to town is through the swinging doors into the saloon. We all know that his entry into the saloon will reveal both the degree and style of his machismo.

Whenever we watch a western movie, we have a number of expectations. We expect to meet many of the following types: a good sheriff trying to tame a bad town, a good sheriff

---

[2]Both the insights and many of the metaphors for this section were inspired by *The Art of Biblical Narrative* by Robert Alter (New York: Basic Books, 1981).

fighting bad guys with the people of the town, a bad sheriff and gang controlling a town, the lovable prostitute, a retired gunman who will not pick up a gun, but who somehow does — just in time to resolve the story, an ex-bad guy, gone straight, who is discovered and soon thereafter dies fighting for right (usually in his son's arms) finally having paid his debt to society, the kid who wants to be a gun fighter, lots of cowardly town folk who make their living by walking back and forth across Main Street in period clothing, etc. In poor westerns, these stock incidents become clichés. In a good western, such conventions are used to establish and define the hero. Similar conventions exist in biblical literature. How the characters behave within the type-scenes, and how they live up to or confound our expectations reveals their unique, dynamic personalitites.

Two characters who provide good examples of conventions and expectations are Samson and Isaac. Both are strange biblical heroes. Samson is strange because he does little that is heroic and less which conforms to normative Jewish values. Isaac, "the silent one," according to the Rabbis, is a quiet presence who intensely occupies, but doesn't fill, his portions of the text.

As we compare some key events in the lives of Samson and Isaac, be aware of how the tension between our expectations and what actually happens shapes our insight into the characters' humanity.

1. THE MOTHER'S INABILITY TO GET PREGNANT
Our Expectation - The mother will be unable to get pregnant. She will appeal to God, and because of her merit or piety, God will "open her womb."

Samson - Samson's mother can't get pregnant. She is not named, but identified only as Manoah's wife. There is no statement of merit, and no demonstration of any positive qualities.

Isaac - (See Genesis 12:7, 15:1-7, 16:1-4, 17:1-7, 18:9-15) - In Isaac's case, neither Abram or Sarai ask God for the pregnancy. Abram appears to merit the pregnancy, and not Sarai.

2. ANNUNCIATION AND NAMING
Our Expectation - Either God, an angel or an agent will inform the mother of her "open womb" and project the nature of the child. The child is given a name either when notice is given or at birth. The name reflects the condition of birth and usually projects part of his character.

Samuel - An angel appears twice, because Manoah doubts the credibility of his wife's report and wants to be told "how to act with the child that is born." The angel predicts that the child "shall be the first to deliver Israel from the Philistines." Something else is also foreshadowed in this portion (which is another example of pattern one, repetition). When the angel first speaks to the wife she is given the following three warnings: 1) let no wine touch his lips, 2) don't eat anything unclean, and 3) let no razor touch his head, because he is to be a Nazirite. When she tells the instructions to Manoah and when the angel/man restates them, wine and unclean food are repeated, but the razor is forgotten.

Isaac (See Genesis 17: 21, 18:9-15 and 21: 1-7) - Abram, and not Sarai, is informed of Isaac's impending birth. Yet, it is Sarai's reaction to the news which determines his name.

3. SIBLING RIVALRY
Our Expectation - The younger brother will struggle with the older brother, and eventually take over the key role. The older brother is usually the outdoor type, and the younger more "homespun."

Samson - No example

Isaac (See Genesis 21:9-14) - It is mother Sarai who does Isaac's fighting.

4. LEAVING/FLEEING FROM HOME
Our Expectation - At some point in our hero's development he will leave home (usually because he needs to flee) and will develop his own lifestyle. The break with the family usually reflects the development of the character's own identity.

Samson - Samson is described leaving home (for no particular purpose) and then returning to his parents once he has seen a woman he wishes to marry.

Isaac (See Genesis 24: 1-9) - Isaac remains at home upon the decision of his father. His wife is brought to him.

5. INITIATORY TRIAL

Our Expectation - Our hero, having left home, encounters a challenge which forces him to demonstrate his strength, courage, faith and abilities.

Samson - Samson wrestles the lion and proves his strength for the first time. When it states "the spirit of the Lord gripped him, and he tore (the lion) assunder with his bare hands," the text informs us that Samson lost control. Rather than applying the minimal force necessary, he uses all his strength. The same will be true at his death. The text tell us, "Those who were slain by him in his death outnumbered those who had been slain by him when he lived." When he returns to the "scene of the crime" a year later, the lion's bones become a source of honey. Thus some good does come from his violence.

Isaac (See Genesis 22) - Isaac left home for his trial when he went to Mt. Moriah with his father. But Abraham is really the star of Isaac's trial.

6. THE BETROTHAL AT THE WELL

Our Expectation - Our hero should go to a town well. There he should meet the girl of his future dreams. The two of them interact. He may do something for her. She will draw water for him. Then, straight from the well, they go to her tent to meet the family and arrangements are made.

Samson - Samson's betrothal scene is aborted; the anticipated marriage is never consummated. He sees the girl (presumably at the well) and then, instead of interacting with her, he goes home and has his parents work out the details.

Isaac (See Genesis 24) - Isaac's marriage is arranged by Abraham's servant Eliezer. He meets Rebekah at the well and then interacts with her family.

7. DYING TESTAMENT

Our Expectation - Unlike western heroes, biblical heroes die in bed surrounded by their families. They usually know they are about to die and gather the family for a "closing benediction."

Samson - Samson doesn't have a family. He dies alone, asking God for the strength to take revenge. His closing remark is, "Let me die with the Philistines." This is a rever-sal of the set formula in which the hero usually asks to be buried with the family. Isaac's final benedictions do not go as he wishes them to. Indeed, he has no control over the situation; his wife sets the stage for the blessing. His actual death is reported in a matter-of-fact manner. Esau and Jacob bury him.

We began this comparison with the notion that Samson was less than the ideal biblical hero. Our study has revealed that he consistently fails to fulfill the expected conventions. His annunciation scene foreshadows his fall. His initiatory trial demonstrates the out of control violence which will determine his death, and the aborted betrothal scene defines his alienation both from his people and from most human contact. Samson is the Jewish leader who is born to "deliver Israel from the Philistines," and who dies "among the Philistines." For the biblical narrator, Samson is a tragic hero, who does kill Philistines, but who dwells in the same gulf of human relations which existed between his unnamed mother and his doubting father. He has to die in order to reach peace with his people.[3]

Isaac, on the other hand, was a quiet figure. If we look at the type-scenes which come into play here, we begin to understand why. Others dominate each of Isaac's key moments. His parents are the central focus of the annunciation. His father dominates the story both when Isaac leaves home and when he goes through his initiatory trial. His betrothal is arranged by his father's servant. And his testament is in the hands of his wife and youngest son. This leaves us with an impression of Isaac as a weak individual who has no control over his own life.

Classroom Applications

The analysis of type-scenes and conventions provides us with many possible lessons. Here are a few suggestions:

1. Each of the type-scenes is like a key life cycle moment. We can bridge from the moments to teaching about birth, courtship, marriage, death and other similar events in

[3]For this understanding of Samson, I am indebted to Rabbi Joel Gordon.

the lives of the biblical characters and of
our students.

2. We can look at characters via the type-
   scene. In doing so, we can go beyond comparing Isaac (Eliezer), Samson, Samuel and
   Moses at the well. What, we might ask,
   would John Wayne, Humphrey Bogart and
   Mork from Ork do there? Write or act out
   type-scenes in which non-biblical characters
   experience biblical conventions. These would
   be appropriate to videotape.

3. Imagine biblical characters experiencing
   American conventions — e.g., Moses walks
   into the saloon, etc.

4. Write biblical conventions for characters in
   the Bible who don't experience them — e.g.,
   Abram and Sarai at the well, etc.

5. Create dioramas (shoe box scenes) of various character's type-scenes. Stack them to
   form a 3-D chart of these characteristics.

6. Use the insights gained into the biblical
   characters you study to project other incidents: Abraham fighting with Isaac, Samson talking to his brothers, etc.

PATTERN FOUR: LEADING WORDS

Read the following text:

> When your brother sinks down beside you
> and his hand falters
> beside you
> hold him fast
> sojourner and settler
> let him live
> beside you
> You may not take from him interest
>   or multiplication
> Stand in fear before your God
> your brother shall live beside you
> Do not give him your money on interest
> for multiplication do not give your food
> I am your God
> who brought you out of the land of Egypt
> to give you the land of Canaan
> to be God to you
>
> When your brother sinks down beside you
> and sells himself to you
> you shall not make him serve the service of
>   a serf
> As hired-hand
> as settler
> shall he be beside you
> Until the year of Recall he is to

> serve beside you
> then he is to go out from beside him
> he and his children beside you
> and return to his clan
> to the land plot of his fathers
>   he shall return
> For they are my servants
> whom I brought out of the land of Egypt
> they shall not be sold in servant-selling

Leviticus 25:35-42
Translated by Everett Fox in
Response. Winter 1971-1972.
Reprinted with permission

Think about these questions: What two
laws does this passage teach? What theological
rationale is given for both commandments?
What is the lesson of this passage? Note how
often the phrase "beside you" appears. Noticing
this phrase can affect our understanding of the
passage or our view of the text's lesson.

Let's look at a second text:

> His word was to Yona son of Amittai, saying:
> Arise,
> go to Nineveh, the great city,
> and call out concerning it
> that their evil-doing has come up before my
>   face.
> Yona rose
> to flee to Tarshish, away from His face.
> He went down to Yafo, found a ship traveling
>   to Tarshish, gave (them) the fare,
> and went down aboard it, to travel to Tarshish,
>   away from His face.
> But He hurled a great wind upon the sea,
> so that the ship was on the brink of breaking up.
> The sailors were afraid, they cried out, each
>   man to his god,
> and hurled the implements which were in the
>   ship into the sea, to be lightened from them.
> Now Yona had gone down into the hindmost
>   deck, had lay down and had gone to sleep.
> The captain approached him and said to him:
> How can you sleep!
> Arise, call upon your god!

Jonah 1:1-6
Translated by Everett Fox
Response, Summer 1974
Used with permission

Does the text tell us anything about what Jonah is thinking or feeling? Note each usage of the verbs "to arise" and "to go down." The use of these leading words can give us clues to Jonah's psychology. This example and the previous one have provided us with some understanding of the ways the biblical text uses words.

The *Leitwort* (leading word) is a pattern in biblical style, defined first by Martin Buber. Biblical texts resemble poetry in many ways, especially in their conscious use of words. This amounts to serious punning. In the biblical text, puns form a subliminal guide, an internal commentary on the text.

Classroom Applications

While the pattern of leading words is hard to generalize (and very difficult to recognize in the usual English translations), your students can feel the presence of the leading words and then recognize their role. They do so by working with a passage — understanding what it says and how it feels — then finding out the significance of repeating phrases. Here are a few ways that this pattern can be used with your students:

1. To convey the idea of word obsession, designate a word for the day. Give out a piece of candy, a point or some other reward for each time the word is used in class. Encourage puns, variations and other word plays.
2. Do as Groucho Marx did and hang up a magic bird (duck) with a secret word. Give out play money every time the magic word is said. (Use a cigar and a grease pencil moustache if you have the gumption.)
3. Upward and downward movement is central in the Jonah story. Create a comic book or a calligraphic version of the text which reflects these movements.
4. Give your students a story to tell or write and a leading word to utilize.
5. Compare one of Everett Fox's translations with either one of the Jewish Publication Society translations. See which words emerge.

PATTERN FIVE: MOTIVATION

The pattern of motivation is similar to what happens in detective movies. A crime, or other action, has occurred and our job is to figure out why. We know who did it (usually), we know exactly what was done. The problem is, we

almost never know the motivation. This pattern is a direct outgrowth of the biblical style. As we have noted previously, the biblical text is essentially made up of two components — dialogue and narration. The dialogue is usually minimal; it captures the essence of the story. That which is said out loud is usually the character's central action or concern. The narration is used to establish and define the action, usually describing it while providing few other details. Whatever explanation of motive that is given is usually spoken "in the heart." Let's look at an example:

> Now Aaron's sons, Nadab and Abihu, each took his fire pan, put fire in it, and laid incense on it; and they offered a strange fire before the Lord, which He had not requested of them. And a fire came forth from the Lord and consumed them; thus they died before the Lord.
>
> Then Moses said to Aaron,
> "This is what the Lord meant when He said: Through those near to Me I show Myself holy, And assert My authority before all the people."
> And Aaron was silent.
>
> Leviticus 10:1-3

Notice that most of the passage is narration. We have only one line of dialogue, spoken by Moses to Aaron. The narrator gives us no clues as to the motivation of Nadab, Abihu or Moses, or the reason for Aaron's silence. We are given a behavioral description of the incident; yet we have no insight into the emotions and feelings — the motivation.

First let us establish the facts:

1. Nadab and Abihu offered "strange fire" that was not requested before God. We don't know if the fire is strange because of its timing or because of the kind of fire used.
2. The fire which killed the two men "came forth from the Lord." Notice that we are not told that God "sent forth" the fire. We don't know if their deaths were caused by the conditions of the fire or by God's reaction to the fire.
3. We do know that Moses goes and talks to Aaron. We know that he quotes God. We do not know if God directed Moses to instruct Aaron, or whether this piece of "instruction" is Moses' reaction.

4. We do know what Moses says to Aaron. We do not know if he intended it to mean a) I'm sorry — we all know how hard it is to be a public servant, or b) they got what they deserved: if you misuse power, you pay the price, or c) both responses. The narrator gives no description of Moses' tone of delivery.

5. We know that Aaron's response to Moses is silence; we have no insight into why. It could be shock, grief, anger or even agreement. Given all the above questions, it is time to play detective. Using the Bible, decide which of the following is the true story of this death/homicide:

   a. GOD did it. Nadab and Abihu violated the sanctity of the Tabernacle and so God punished them.
   b. AARON did it. Nadab and Abihu tried to take over his job. They were doing too much exploring of the role, so he rigged the fire pans.
   c. MOSES did it. There was an ongoing tension between Moses and Aaron which goes back to the Golden Calf. Moses was worried that the priests are getting too powerful, so he arranged the accident as a warning.
   d. THE FIRE WAS AN ACCIDENT.

In his solution to this mystery, detective Rashi found a suspicious verse, Leviticus 10:8-9: "And the Lord spoke to Aaron, saying: 'Drink no wine or other intoxicant, you or your sons with you, when you enter the Tent of Meeting, that you may not die . . .'" Based on that verse, this is Rashi's report:

Rabbi Ishmael said: They died because they entered the Sanctuary intoxicated by wine. You may know that this is so, because after their death he admonished those who survived that they should not enter the Sanctuary when intoxicated. . .

Let's look at a second case, this one from Numbers 20. This is the story of why Moses was not permitted to enter the Promised Land. Most people think this occurred "because he hit the rock" — but that's wrong. Previously (Exodus 17:5), God had *ordered* Moses to hit a rock. Others say that it was "because he didn't talk to the rock" — but that's wrong. Moses stood before the rock and said: "Shall we get water

for you out of this rock?" While he didn't talk exclusively to the rock, he did talk about the rock in the rock's presence.

Now let's take a closer look. (Remember, the clues are usually in the dialogue.) From the dialogue we learn that Moses was really "not publicly affirming God's sanctity." Our next question must be: what action(s) or lack of action did not, in God's view, affirm His sanctity?

Here are several possibilities (suggested by the classical commentators):

1. Getting angry at the people and not responding to them even to reprimand them (with respect). Think about what he says to them. (Rambam)
2. Letting the people think that Moses and Aaron, and not God, were bringing them the water. (He says: "Shall *we* bring you forth water?") (Rambam)
3. Missing an opportunity to teach the people. It was not geting angry, hitting the rock, or saying "we," but rather not using this opportunity to show the people that God would take care of them. This situation wasn't like the first time, when the people were coming straight from being slaves in Egypt. This was the new generation who were about to enter the land. (Ibn Ezra)

Classroom Applications

The pattern of motivation is clearly the most fun, and the most accessible of the five we have looked at. It is easy and challenging to play detective and the text provides us with both an abundance of mysteries and a plethora of clues.

Here are a few exciting classroom activities:

1. Use the same kind of inquiry approach described above in the presentation of this pattern.
2. Have your class script and present the Nadab and Abihu story as an episode of "Quincy" or other detective series. Present it live, as a radio play on tape, or videotape it.
3. Develop a new set of cards and play "Clue" with biblical problems.
4. Have a panel discussion between various commentators on a biblical issue.
5. Create (in any number of media) Moses and Aaron questioning God on what they really did wrong.

So far in this chapter, we have considered ways to approach the text through repetition, twice told tales, conventions, leading words and motivation. For each pattern, a number of classroom applications has been included. The remainder of the chapter will be devoted to an examination of how to prepare for teaching the Bible. This next section will include Objectives for Pre-Academic Bible Study, Preparing the Text: The First Reading, Preparing the Text: Reference Work, Organizing Research into a Lesson, and Choosing Activities: Assembling the Lesson.

TERMINAL OBJECTIVES FOR PRE-ACADEMIC BIBLE STUDY

In my view, the center of our efforts in Bible study, even with the youngest students, should be analysis of the text. A complete program of Bible study should also include basic knowledge of the document, as well as ways to help students personally to integrate and to actualize the biblical texts. Most contemporary Bible teaching in non-Hebrew settings has focused on the latter, while ignoring the real inquiry into the text. We generally read (or tell) a Bible story and then establish relevant analogies.

Virtually every Bible lesson (and learning experience) should contain all three of these elements: content, process and the learner. This means that every lesson should somehow touch and interact directly with the text (even if with only one phrase-clause) and should provide the student with a personal opportunity to "manipulate" the text. This model of Bible study is a lifelong process, requiring the commitment and participation of every teacher of Bible in order to provide continuity. We must guard against presenting our students with material that is far too difficult for them; yet it is equally important to avoid an excessively juvenile approach to the text. We must convey to our students that the text represents more than Jewish bedtime stories or cute tales with ethical morals attached. And we must not teach information or conceptions that need to be unlearned at a later date.

In the Introduction to the workbook *Bible People Book One* (Denver: Alternatives in Religious Education, Inc., 1980), I stated:

> The Bible is a big, long, thick book. It is a book that many people talk about and study. The Bible is a book which tells lots of stories about lots of people.

It tells the story of sisters who really loved each other. And it tells the story of kids who lie to their parents. Stories of parents who favored one child. While older brothers picked on younger brothers. Stories of people who do good things. And stories of the same people doing not such good things. The stories of people's dreams. And the stories of people falling in love.

The Bible is full of stories about people. People who cry. People who laugh. People who worry. People who enjoy life. All the experiences and feelings we have, people in the Bible had, too. As we read about their adventures and understand their feelings, we also begin to understand some of the things we feel.

This model of the Bible is appropriate to second or third graders. It is conceptually and experientially within their capacities, while consistent with a far more sophisticated view of the text. It opens doors; it doesn't close them. While that workbook doesn't introduce parataxis, it implies from the start that Bible study is dialogue and that we enter the text to learn *with* it, not just *from* it. It states that this kind of study is both communal and reflexive. Second graders will not be able to understand intellectually or to verbalize this adult model of text study. But they can work within this framework and come to value it. As in many forms of learning, the patterns we develop early in life ultimately influence our adult view.

With all of this in mind, then, let us look at one statement of terminal objectives for essential background in the Bible for Jewish students.

A. DIVISIONS OF THE BIBLE

1. The learner can list the three sections of the Bible (Torah, Prophets and Writings) and can identify with an 80% accuracy in which section a given book is contained.
2. The learner can locate any quotation within the text, given its book, chapter and verse.
3. Given the names of the books of the Bible, the learner can give a one sentence description of their content.

B. FAMILIARIZATION WITH BIBLICAL TEXTS

1. The learner has read the narrative material in Genesis, Exodus, Numbers and Deuteronomy, as well as most of the early

prophets, the five *Megillot* plus Jonah.

2. The learner has read a selection of legal material from the Torah and a basic selection of prophetic documents.

3. The learner has had some exposure to material from Psalms and Proverbs.

C. SPECIFIC KNOWLEDGE OF BIBLICAL DETAIL

1. The learner can identify, order and define the relationship between all major characters in the Torah.

2. The learner can classify characters from the Prophets as either Kings, Prophets, Priests or Judges with 80% accuracy. (He or she will also be able to sequence key Judges and major figures from the books of Samuel.)

3. The learner can identify 80% of key quotations from biblical stories.

4. The learner can locate on the map: 1) the basic geographic features of *Eretz Yisrael,* 2) the major locations indicated in Genesis, Joshua, Samuel and Kings, 3) locations of at least five tribal areas (including Judah, Ephraim and Manasseh), and 4) the borders of David's kingdom and of Judah and Israel.

D. TEXT SKILLS

1. The learner can identify theme and variation from predefined repetition patterns, including multiple repetitions of stories or laws.

2. The learner can identify 1) examples of the expectations of basic type-scenes and 2) appearances of these in the lives of biblical characters.

3. The learner has struggled to define the motivation of key biblical characters in key incidents.

4. The learner can trace some "word-echoes" (themes) through the biblical text.

5. The learner can define *P'shat* and *Drash* and, with 60% accuracy, distinguish between examples of both.

E. LANGUAGE SKILLS

1. The learner can give examples of the problems of studying the biblical text in translation.

2. The learner can give examples of idioms which reflect the Hebrew mind.

3. The learner can describe, identify and analyze some basic Hebrew literary patterns: poetic parallel, parataxis and verb chains.

4. The learner can describe personal associations with some key verses or images from the text.

F. USE OF RABBINIC SOURCES

1. The learner can explain the concept of *Midrash,* including a) the historical context, b) an explanation of its assumptions, c) an identification of its textual problems and d) a description of its style relative to the biblical text.

2. Given ten *midrashim,* the learner can, for at least eight of them, successfully identify a) the textual issues, b) the solution posed in the *midrash,* and c) the message of the text.

3. The learner can identify Rashi, the Ramban, the Rambam, Nehama Leibowitz, Cassuto and several other biblical commentators by name and persona.

4. The learner has participated in comparing conflicting interpretations of a text.

G. PERSONAL VIEWS OF THE TEXT

1. The learner has a history of evolving his/her own interpretations of the text.

2. The learner has a history of correlating the metaphoric material of the text to his/her own experience.

3. The learner has evolved his/her own sense of the importance of Bible study.

PREPARING THE TEXT: THE FIRST READING

The first step for any Bible teacher is to do a first reading of the intended text. The purpose of a first reading is not to decide what to teach or to find deep scholarly insights into the passage. A first reading is a scouting mission. It is a formal introduction or a renewed acquaintance with the text. We are just looking over the terrain, learning the topography, familiarizing ourselves with the characters, the setting and the words.

Begin by *listening* to the text. (Everett Fox, a contemporary Bible scholar, suggests that you read it out loud.) What is the first thing it says to you? Is there a special tone? Is there an overt message? Is there an interesting ambiguity?

Next, consider what you already know about this text. Are there some key insights that you already possess? What are your past associations with the text? (Remember your interests, but don't be afraid to discover something new.) Does the text have external connections which are important (e.g., it is the theme of the congregation's stained glass window, or part of the Friday evening service, etc.)?

Then analyze what bothers you about the text, what calls out to you, "Explain me." Does the text contain echoes of other things you want to identify? Is there anything you want to know more about?

Up to now, you have not yet begun to make decisions regarding the lesson you will teach. Now it is time to come up with answers to the following questions:

1. What is the text I will be teaching? Which verses will I include? If I am going to be telling a story, or reading a story version of the text, how much of it will I use?

2. What textual issue(s) will serve as the focus of the lesson? If I am working from a text, what will students look for in it? If I am telling the story, what portion of the *actual* text will I bring to the students?

3. What information do the students need to know in order to handle this text — e.g., previous incidents, social phenomena, vocabulary or geography?

4. What skills will the students need to handle this text — e.g., how to compare two stories, find extra language, imagine how someone would feel, etc.

5. What information (facts) should the students retain? Is there a line or two (perhaps a passage) which they should know, or almost know, by heart?

6. What will the students "own" from this passage? What will they find interesting in it? What will they believe is important about it?

7. What does my class need right now? What kind of learning experiences are appropriate — more group work, fewer worksheets, a chance to role play, etc.?

8. How can this story relate to past learning and to things students will study next year? If I show them X, will they be able to relate it to Y?

9. What do I want to teach? What is important in the text for me?

PREPARING THE TEXT: REFERENCE WORK

A good working library for serious Bible teachers consists of about 30-35 volumes. These provide the basis for preparing almost any lesson. Ideally these books belong to the teacher. However, a synagogue or community library can be used instead.

To prepare a text, start with a notebook and a photocopy. (The later enables you to mark up the text.) Then complete the following steps:

Step One

Examine three translations of the text — the 1917 and 1962 Jewish Publication Society translations and a translation by a modern scholar such as Everett Fox *(Response* Magazine, Winter 1971-2 and Summer 1974). Compare the translations, noting instances when the translators differ significantly. Locate idioms which capture something important about the biblical mind. Identify patterns in the language which come through in only one or two of the translations. For questions about the meaning of a word or phrase, consult *Notes on the New Translation of the Torah,* edited by Harry M. Orlinsky (Philadelphia: Jewish Publication Society, 1969).

You might also look up the verse in the *Anchor Bible,* a non-sectarian scholarly translation. This work is still in process and volumes do not yet exist for every book in the Bible. The *Anchor Bible* includes an introduction, an original translation and two sets of notes. The first set discusses the text as a whole, defining patterns and focusing on the possible sources which underlie it. The other set consists of line by line notes in the text itself.

You might also wish to look up some geographical locations in a biblical atlas. One excellent atlas is *The Macmillan Bible Atlas* by Yohanan Aharoni and Michael Avi-Yonah (N.Y.: The Macmillan Company, 1977). One further tool is a concordance, a book which lists all the words in the Bible and every instance that each appears. There are many different ones available; the best is in Hebrew. Use the concordance to locate other times when the words from your passage appear.

Step Two

Look at what the traditional commentators have to say about the passage. Start with books by Nehama Leibowitz, an Israeli Bible scholar

who has authored five excellent books on the
Torah: *Studies in Bereshit (Genesis), Studies in
Shemot (Exodus),* etc. These are published by
the World Zionist Organization, Department of
Torah Education and Culture, Jerusalem, 1974-
1980. Leibowitz presents three to eight sermons/
studies on individual issues for each Torah
portion. She focuses on one problem in each,
defining why the issue is an issue, then quoting
a number of commentators and Rabbinic
sources.

Next, turn to Louis Ginzberg. Ginzberg was
an American scholar who collected *midrashim.*
His collection is published in two editions:
Legends of the Bible and *Legends of the Jews*
(Philadelphia: Jewish Publication Society,
1966/1909). *Legends of the Jews* is a six volume
work which collects virtually every *midrash,*
rewritten in a non-textual format. It consists of
four volumes of *midrashim* and two scholarly
volumes filled with notes and indexes. These
include a list of every biblical verse in the
work. Verses can be found in the discussion of
your portion, as well as in *midrashim* from
other texts. *Legends of the Bible* is a one
volume condensation of the larger work without
the scholarly materials. Another excellent source
for *midrashim* is *The Midrash Rabbah,*
translated by Rabbi Dr. H. Freedman and
Maurice Simon (London: The Soncino Press,
1977).

Dr. A.M. Silbermann's translation of Rashi
*Pentateuch with Targum Onkelos, Haphtaroth
and Rashi's Commentary,* translated into English
and annotated by Rev. M. Rosenbaum and Dr.
A.M. Silbermann, published by the Silbermann
family, Jerusalem, is another good source. Here
you can check out which problems in the text
Rashi addresses and the connections he makes.

Finally, you might take a quick look at *The
Rabbis' Bible* (New York: Behrman House, Inc.,
1966-74) to see which *midrashim* it includes.
There are many other collections of *midrashim*
and commentaries, but by now you will
undoubtedly have found something worth
teaching. Out of all this you may have come up
with any or all of the following:

1. Some interesting problems, echoes or
   issues in the text.
2. Some interesting images from the
   midrash
3. Some good *midrashim* you can use in
   class

For each *midrash* you consider, make sure that

you know the textual question from which the
midrash stems, the resolution of that issue and
the moral or lesson the *midrash* is teaching.
Step Three

If you don't feel that you have enough to
go on, you may turn to what might be called
"idea books." These are books about the Bible
and provide ideas for teaching. They will also
expand your facility with the text. Here are some
suggestions of useful books of this type:
Alter, Robert. *The Art of Biblical Narrative.*
New York: Basic Books, 1981.
    This book applies literary tools to the Bible.
    It has chapters on conventions, repetition,
    leading words, motifs and other stylistic
    elements. Contains many examples from texts
    you regularly teach.

Cassuto, Umberto. *A Commentary on the Book
of Exodus, A Commentary on Genesis: From
Adam to Noah and From Noah to Abraham.*
Jersualem: The Magnes Press, The Hebrew
University, 1967-9.
    These books are difficult but helpful. While
    methodical and scholarly, they are written in
    readable English with little jargon. Cassuto
    does an insightful, close reading of the text
    and is the outstanding revealer of patterns,
    echoes, structures and connections within
    the text.

Fishbane, Michael. *Text and Texture: Close
Readings of Selected Biblical Texts.* New
York: Schocken Books, 1979.
    Another language centered look at the text, a
    place to find echoes, patterns and parallels.

Plaut, W. Gunter. *The Torah: A Modern
Commentary.* New York: Union of American
Hebrew Congregations, 1981.
    An interesting collection of all kinds of
    insights into the text.

Step Four

Look now at your collection of teaching
materials. Go through *The Rabbis' Bible* again,
along with its Teacher Guide and Resource
Book. Look at your collection of materials
published by Alternatives in Religious Education, Inc.: *Bible People Book One, Two* and
Three and their accompanying Teacher Guides,
"Bible People Songs," *Sedra Scenes: Skits
for Every Torah Portion* and *The Learning
Center Book of Bible People.*[4] You

---

[4]Consult this book for a comprehensive bibliography which
includes books on the Bible for teachers and students,
atlases, enrichment materials, tapes, records and music
books.

might also go to your synagogue library to consult a reference book or encyclopedia and to check out some historical background, especially if you are teaching from the Prophets.

ORGANIZING RESEARCH
INTO A LESSON

It is likely that you now feel comfortable with the story and have made some basic decisions about what you will teach. You know the text you will teach, how much of it you will use, the textual issue(s) on which you will focus. You have done your research and have the resources to deal with unanticipated questions which might arise. You are now ready to organize your lesson.

At this time you will want to choose one of the patterns to apply to the text, using the examples provided in the early part of this chapter or others you know. Isolate a question or theme for the class to discuss and explore based on what they discover in the text. Carefully formulate how you will encourage each student to manipulate the text and come to "own" it. Sometimes this manipulation will mean that students identify their own solutions to issues in the text. Sometimes it will mean that they evolve their own solutions to issues in the text. And other times it will mean that you foster the creative expression by students of material in the text. The following chart represents some possible formats for designing Bible Lessons:

	Beginning	**Middle**	**End**
I	Study the Text.	Isolate and discuss central issue.	Encourage students to expand their understanding of the material through personal interpretation/expression.
II	Define the central issue.	Find that issue expressed in the text.	Encourage students to interpret/express the material.
III	Have the students isolate a problem or theme from their own experience.	Have the class generalize about the theme/issue based on their collective experience.	Find and explore the same issue in the text.
IV	Same as first step in III	Find the issue in the text.	Clarify and discuss the issue.
V	Introduce and train students in a skill for text study.	Apply the skill to the text.	Draw out the moral found in the issue.
VI	Introduce a text.	Apply a pattern of text study to the passage (e.g., leading word, repetition).	Analyze and discuss what emerges.
VII	Introduce a text.	Use a pattern of text study to identify an issue.	Generalize the skill, practice its application.

The above formats are not the only ones possible, but they are the ones which work most often. It is often effective to include three activities in the course of every session. However, if the material lends itself, you can introduce the three over two, three or more periods or weeks.

The central issues when organizing a Bible lesson is the nature of the text to be studied — its specific difficulties, loadings and context. If the text needs clarification before your students can approach it, or if it needs extension before its "lesson" can be made clear, then the placement of the text in your sequence of instruction is especially critical. If there are issues to which students need to be sensitized, address yourself first to this. If there is a complex skill needed (one that can't be picked up as it is applied), take time to introduce it and drill it. Once the text has been introduced and probed, don't stop there. You want you students to learn by experience that a biblical text always leads us somewhere — to a reflection of human nature, an insight into ethical relations or a further understanding of Jewish tradition. Rather than conclude with the text, end by helping students find a way to make the text their own, through individual interpretation and expression.

CHOOSING ACTIVITIES: ASSEMBLING THE LESSON

With your basic lesson format decided upon, you now begin to select the activities you will use. Some teachers find it helpful to keep a file of 3″ x 5″ cards, each of which contains an idea for a lesson. These can be collected from a variety of sources — from books, other teachers, your students, workbooks, things you have picked up at conferences and idea exchanges, and from workshops and lectures you attend. Ideas can also be borrowed from other disciplines, and even from other religions. (Many good ideas for teaching Bible can be drawn from such Christian resources as *Twenty New Ways of Teaching the Bible* by Donald L. Griggs and *How To Teach Bible Stories for Grades 4-12* by Mary Nelson Keithahn and Marilyn H. Dunshee, both published by Abingdon, and the materials put out by Brethren House Publications, 6301 56th Avenue North, St. Petersburg, Florida 33709.)

To spark your own creativity, here are a few activities from my own card file.

LEARNING THE DIVISIONS OF THE BIBLE

Introductory Activities

1. Give a basic lecture on the divisions of the Bible.
2. Make cards with the names of the books of the Bible on them. Have students sort them into the categories of Torah, Prophets and Writings.
3. See who can locate various books in the Bible first.
4. Let students design their own memory devices. Use these to learn the order of the books.
5. Design a racetrack board game which reflects the order and sequence of the books of the Bible. Design questions which ask where the various books may be found. Students can look at the board to answer.
6. Design a worksheet or chart which students fill in.
7. Have treasure hunt games (finding items inside the text).
8. Give coded messages using the abbreviations for the Bible books.

Application (students demonstrate understanding and competency)

1. Everytime you mention a book in the Bible, have students review where in the Bible it is located.
2. Have students use the correct form for biblical citations at all times.

Individual Expression

1. Have students design charts, posters, games, cards, drills, quiz shows, displays such as a museum of the Bible with each book on exhibit.
2. Have students develop games and coded messages.
3. Have students teach a younger grade how to find passages in the Bible.

FAMILIARIZATION WITH BIBLICAL TEXTS

Introductory Activities

1. Identify characters as they are introduced.
2. Have students keep lists, charts, cards, etc. of the characters.
3. Post a visual record in the room — e.g., charts, posters, timelines, etc.
4. Give examinations on the material; have a "College Bowl" quiz.

Application

1. As characters are introduced, or reintroduced, have students establish their position and relationship.
2. Have students categorize characters by role, personality or position.

Individual Expression

1. Have students design creative review formats — games, posters, etc.
2. Develop quiz formats.
3. Act out (in any medium) various personalities and their relationships.

TEXT SKILLS

Introductory Activities

1. Lecture/introduce the concept.
2. Develop a visual format to enhance the insights. Use a) capital letters or underlines to enhance perception (split the text into parallel columns) b) have students color code the two parts of a document, c) use circles and arrows.
3. Use two or more photographs/pictures and compare them for differences, similar to "What is wrong in this picture?".
4. Use an outside example to introduce the concept, then have students apply it to the text.

Application

1. Use visual displays to study the text — e.g., posters, charts, timelines, etc.
2. Have two students alternate reading. One reads the first version, the second reads the repetition. Identify and analyze the differences.

3. Once a pattern is clearly understood, have students find examples of the pattern on their own.

Individual Expression

1. Draw "lessons" or conclusions from the repetitions and changes in the text.
2. Compare and evaluate traditional insights.
3. Express the themes and variations creatively through art, music, drama, film, etc.
4. Devise extension activities based on the moral of the story, such as a role play, creative writing exercise, etc.
5. When there are conflicting details in repeated stories, have students see if they can a) identify ways of deciding which version is right or b) figure out how both could be correct.

CONCLUSION

In-depth Bible teaching doesn't depend on teachers with years of academic training. Any teacher who is open to growth and willing to invest time can master the skills for exploring texts and transmitting them to his/her students. The developmental process outlined in the second part of this chapter represents a very stuctured series of steps which, when followed, will produce the kind of dynamics outlined in the first section. Feel free to adapt these steps into your own workable form. Using the tools we have suggested for engaging students in textual study will enrich their lives and yours, as well as enhance the interaction that takes place in your classroom.

THE CHALLENGE OF TEACHING ABOUT GOD

by Sherry H. Bissell

INTRODUCTION

The experience of God is the source, the wellspring from which Judaism as a religion and, later as a way of life, grew. The individual's relationship to the idea of God, and the community's response has nurtured, challenged and shaped Jewish history; it continues to do so. While actions are considered more important by Jews than belief, it is the belief which enables the actions to have meaning. Our ability to experience a relationship with the sacred and the divine, our partnership with God, have created the context for Jewish values, ethics, symbols, etc.

Each Jew, therefore, is responsible for confronting his or her beliefs and feelings about God. As teachers in Jewish schools, we have the privilege of facilitating this experience for our students, of creating the context for the exploration and of making available the content. It is also our responsibility to confront our own doubts, questions, feelings and ideas.

An individual's experience of God will change and grow during his or her lifetime. There are many paths to God, each as different and special as the person who is seeking. This chapter will present the terminology needed to teach and discuss God, then will outline some overall approaches to teaching God and finally, will suggest some specific strategies that can be used and adapted in the classroom. These definitions, approaches and techniques, along with the annotated Bibliography at the conclusion of the chapter, will help teachers facilitate their students' exploration of the subject, as well as their own.

No one method of teaching about God is correct, and there are obviously many more ideas than can be included here. Hopefully, this material will provide a starting point and will encourage teachers to create their own approaches and techniques. It is wise to be aware that every student will respond uniquely to the activities teachers choose, an indication of the richness of this area of our tradition, and of the mystery and wonder of God.

TERMINOLOGY: VOCABULARY AND SYMBOLS

As we begin to approach teaching the ideas and concepts connected with God, or the experience of God, one of the gravest difficulties is the problem of words and language. Words are symbols. We must determine whether the words used in our tradition to speak about God still have the same meaning today or whether we must create a new vocabulary to express our "God-talk" (a term coined by John MacQuarrie in his book of that title). Further, we must understand the statements of faith from other eras in the context of modern secular and technological times — perhaps not in exactly the same way, yet language is the tool we use. Because this is so, here is a list of words that the teacher should be able to define or explain:

Belief Systems

Theism - belief in the existence of God
Atheism - a view which denies the existence of a God
Agnosticism - the view that we cannot know whether or not God exists

Monotheism - a belief that there is one God

Pantheism - God is equated with the forces of
    nature; God is in everything

Nature of God

Omniscient - all seeing

Omnipresent - all present, everywhere

Omnipotent - all powerful

Transcendent - above and separate from human
    beings and the earth, a force, a
    power

Immanent - close and personal, immediate, a
    God that cares

Creation - the act of bringing the world into
    existence

Revelation - the act of communication by God
    to human beings, and the content of
    the communication

Redemption - a religious concept expressing a
    striving by human beings for personal
    improvement. When related to God,
    synonyms include saving, salvation,
    etc.

Covenant - in theological terms, a binding
    agreement between God and human
    beings.

Holiness, Sacredness - that which is set apart,
    special or unique, not common,
    imbued with religious meaning
    (Hebrew: *kodesh*)

Overall Approaches to Teaching God

This section will focus on the ramifications of the particular approach a teacher takes toward the subject of God. Often, we convey to students messages about our own values through the importance we attach to a particular area of the curriculum. These messages are reflected in the amount of time spent, the methodology we use and in the overall approach we take to the subject. We also give our students messages from what we do *not* include. Therefore, it is essential to consider carefully how, when and in what way we teach about God in our own classroom and in the school.

In the following section we will consider the impact of each of several possible approaches to teaching about God.

Responding to Questions as They Arise

The subject of God is often left unexplored until a question arises from a student. Then, depending on the point where the teacher is in the lesson or unit, or where the class is, the question may be answered or may be postponed.

It is best to explore questions about God as they occur. One advantage of doing so is the high level of interest which is already present — i.e., the student is ready to explore this question. A disadvantage of this approach is more subtle: often the students do not know what question to ask. They are afraid to seem ignorant, especially when talking about God.

When using this approach, plan experiences that create questions. Try to integrate ideas about God into the teaching of history, prayer, customs and traditions and values. Don't be afraid to mention the word God during the course of discussion. When the ideas and experience of God are introduced as an integral part of all Jewish life, students will be encouraged to talk freely on the subject.

Feelings and Emotions Connected With God

One of the most frequent ways of approaching God is to explore the question of God through the emotions. Emotions such as love, wonder, awe, mystery, security, doubt, and others, provide openings for discussions and experiences connected with God. Jewish literature, especially Psalms and passages from Prophets, can reinforce this type of exploration.

An advantage of this approach is that it is appropriate for many different age groups. Another is that it can instill love of God and demonstrate that feeling and faith are important parts of Jewish life. However, if the teacher is uncomfortable with the emotion, or if the students are too resistant, the students can become silly and the session meaningless. If there is an adequate preparation, both younger and older students can benefit greatly from approaching the subject of God through the emotions.

Historical Approach

For the older students who understand time and conceptual development, a historical approach to the subject of God is appropriate. Source materials can be arranged chronologically. An emphasis on the developing idea of God will encourage students to continue the chain of tradition by adding their own ideas. This approach is primarily cognitive. However, it can be combined with an expression of feelings that will enrich the explorations of the students. It conveys to the students a message that God is present and active in Jewish history whenever we have a relationship with God.

It is not advantageous to use this approach

before students are ready to assimilate the attendant complex intellectual ideas and concepts. It is important to focus on questions and concepts that are specifically geared to the age level you teach.

Theological Approach

An exploration of, and confrontation with, the ideas about and experiences of God by theologians is also appropriate for older students. The ideas of different theologians — e.g., Rambam, Buber, Heschel, etc. are presented to students. This approach reinforces in students the fact that people think deeply about God and then write about their thoughts and experiences. This, too, is a cognitive approach and, in combination with the historical approach, can be very effective.

The centrality of God in Jewish life obliges us to consider carefully how and when we present the subject to our students. Whatever the approach, a decision must be made in advance and only after a great deal of thought and study. Being clear about the overall approach will facilitate the creation of lessons which will accomplish their intended goals and objectives. If a decision is made to integrate the teaching of God into all aspects of the curriculum, students will, in the course of their years in religious school, be able to experience each of the approaches outlined above. Thus the context and content for a variety of experiences related to God will be present and students can carry on their search throughout their adult lives. However, even if a choice is made to answer questions about God as they arise, some forethought about the answers and familiarity with sources, concepts and strategies is necessary.

SOME SPECIFIC STRATEGIES

Below are some examples of strategies which present ideas, concepts and experiences about God. Whenever possible, credit is given to the originator.

Sugar in the Water - Experiences With Props

Using two glasses of water (one plain, and one with some sugar dissolved in the water so that it cannot be seen) have students taste the contents of both glasses. Do they look the same? (Yes.) God is like the sugar in the water. We cannot always see God, but God's presence sweetens the world and our lives.

Ask students how God sweetens their lives.

Analogies: Rabbi Akiva and The Skeptic

A skeptic asked Rabbi Akiva to prove the existence of God. Akiva answered him by asking, "Who made your suit of clothes?" The skeptic answered, "Why, the tailor, of course." Rabbi Akiva asked him to prove it. The result of the discussion was the realization that no proof was necessary, since the suit obviously could not have made itself. Then Akiva pointed out that the universe could not have created itself anymore than could the suit of clothes.

Have the students find other proofs of God's existence that relate to Rabbi Akiva's explanation (love, a tree growing from a seed, etc.).

Essays on Classroom Doors

Stop in the middle of a high school class to ask students to write a 200 word essay about the door of the classroom. Each essay will be different, yet the door exists. Make the analogy that our views of God are different, yet one God exists. (Rabbi Wolli Kaelter)

Cartoons

Using cartoons can be fun and challenging and can result in stimulating, often illuminating, discussions. Peanuts, Woody Allen, Broomhilda, Kelly and Duke and Feiffer are good sources for cartoons. Students can also create and share their own cartoons to express their ideas about God.

Attributes of God

Place six signs around the room, each of which expresses one idea about God:

1. Master of the Universe - God pulls the strings and works miracles.
2. Watchmaker - God put the world together, wound it up, then left it running
3. List Maker - God takes notes on what we do and rewards or punishes us for our acts.
4. Still Small Voice - our conscience, the voice of right and wrong.
5. God is order, gives order - God is nature and scientific rules.
6. Personal God - God is a presence which conforts us and has a personal relationship with us.

Have students choose the idea that best describes their belief about God. In small groups, discuss why they arrived at the choice. Bring the groups together to share. (Shirley Barish)

For a similar exercise, see the beginning of the Leader Guide for the mini-course *God: The Eternal Challenge* by Sherry H. Bissell (Denver: Alternatives in Religious Education, Inc., 1980).

Art Projects

Art projects are one of the best strategies for teaching about God. Have students make collages or use clay or other media to express feelings about God which words cannot describe. Concepts that lend themselves particularly to art projects include Oneness, Creation, Revelation and Holiness. Begin by using shapes and colors in abstract designs. It is also effective to have students draw the ways that they are partners with God.

1. For older Students:
   Share the various names of God with the students. Alone or in small groups pick one of the names and draw it on a small piece of paper. Then take the smaller pieces and create the shape of the number *one,* or place the names together in a circle. This illustrates that all the names of God are part of "One God."
2. Ask students what color or shape they think of when they hear the word God. Using colored crayons and all kinds of shapes, have them create an abstract expression *of their thoughts* about God.
3. Using clay, have the younger students pretend that they were present at creation and partners with God as the world was created. In what ways would they have helped God? How does creation continue each day? How can they help God now?

Music and Poetry

Music and poetry are like two doorways into the beliefs of others about God. Students can begin by reacting to songs, sounds and words. This is often safer than starting with an exploration of one's own beliefs. (Don't forget that many prayers are also poems.) When using these media, be creative yourself. Use music and poetry as triggers, then add dance, art, discussion and other activities.

As a follow-up, have the students create their own songs and their own poetry about God. Both older and younger students can achieve beautiful expressions.

Excellent poems for the older students may be found in the section on God in *A Time To Seek* (U.A.H.C.). Especially appropriate are Jacob Glatstein's poem "Jewish God" and "The Great Sad One" by Robert Mezey. Younger children can find the poetry in *Let's Talk About God* by Dorothy Kripke (Behrman House) to be a stimulus. Also, don't forget to use the Psalms, which through the centuries have provided inspiration to Jews and non-Jews through their poetic imagery and the relationship with God which they express.

There are many beautiful songs about God which can be used appropriately as teaching tools. Some examples are: the album "Sing Unto God" (Debbie Friedman), *"Lo Ira," "Eyli, Eyli"* (in both Hebrew and English) and *"Eleh Chamda Libi."* A teacher of older students may wish to compare Jewish liturgical music with that of other religions — e.g., Gregorian chants or Christmas carols.

Role Play

The enactment of encounters between God and human beings can be an exciting and stimulating strategy. The biblical and *midrashic* stories present a rich source for short plays or role play situations. Updating the incidents to today's world can be especially meaningful. Here is an example of a role play situation:

Enact the argument between Abraham and God about Sodom and Gomorrah. Have students switch roles. Add the private, inner voice of both God and Abraham.

One caution regarding role playing: unless the students are experienced in the technique and unless the stage is carefully set, the group may become silly and the point of the exercise lost. It is also important to ask follow-up questions which will reinforce the goals of the lesson. For example, how did you feel when you played God? Was it difficult to have so much responsibility? How do you think God "feels" when human beings don't follow the laws and commandments?

Fantasy Trips

The use of fantasy can create the mood and the context for an exploration and confrontation with God. Such fantasy trips also help people to learn to pray. Ask students to close their eyes, and then begin to create an experience. It is very important that students learn to accept their fantasies and not to judge responses. Sharing should also be optional. Here is a suggestion for a fantasy:

Close your eyes and go to one of your favorite spots in the whole world — a beach, the mountains, your room, wherever you are comfortable and safe and loved. Picture the place, smell its odors, listen for its sounds. . . . Relax there.

You may invite someone to be with you, or you may be alone. . . .

You feel love and feel loved. . . .

You feel healthy and strong. . . .

You feel safe and happy. . . .

Listen quietly to your breathing — then listen as a voice fills your thoughts: *Sh'ma Yisrael Adonai Eloheynu Adonai Echad.* . . .

You sense the meaning of the Oneness of God. . . Unique, Alone, Special, God. . . .

You may ask any question of God that you wish. . . .

Perhaps you may be answered, perhaps not.

You can say anything you wish to God. . . .

You may ask for something. . . for yourself, for the world, for friends. . . . You may be answered yes or no. . . .

Say your favorite prayer. . . . The feelings about God will leave you in peace and happiness. . . . When you are ready, open your eyes. . . .

Journals

Keeping a journal can be a very important way for students to express their thoughts about God, enabling them to keep a record of their growth. The teacher can structure the nature of the entries, or material can be freely generated by students. A combination of these approaches is best.

To help students begin their journals, ask them to complete such sentences as: I believe in God when _____ . I doubt God when _____ . Have them describe their reactions to poetry or short stories about God or to your lesson. Suggest that students list their doubts, questions, ideas, and feelings.

It is important that each student share his or her journal with you in an ongoing way. Sharing it with others must be up to you and the student. Your written comments and reactions to the journal will foster growth and provoke further thought about the issues raised.

Guest Speakers and Interviews

Interviewing different people with varying views about God can be an exciting and worth-while undertaking. Invite believers, agnostics and atheists to speak to older children. Have students prepare questions for the speakers in advance. Have students interview the Rabbi, their parents, the educator, Cantor, etc. Compile the responses and compare the similarities and differences between the views. Find out with whom the students most agree. Which person differed most from the students' beliefs? What did the class learn from the exercise?

Creating Audiovisual Materials

Create filmstrips or slide shows of your favorite stories about God. Show them to younger classes. Pick music and words that express creation, revelation and redemption and create a sound tape to accompany the slides. Shirley Barish suggests using books by Molly Cone for this activity. (See the Bibliography at the conclusion of this chapter for titles.)

Discussion

The major consideration when conducting discussions is the establishment of a climate of openness to all ideas, concepts and materials. If desired, a Jewish context can be set up for the discussion which includes Torah, Covenant, Israel, etc. However, do not exclude from the discussion the struggles of students as they wrestle with the complexities of the God idea. If a student is resistant during discussion, simply help the student to be aware of his or her resistance. It is important for students to feel that their views are not wrong and to know that Jews have been struggling for centuries with the very same ideas.

Use a continuum to initiate a discussion. Have students stand along a line in the classroom at the point that best represents their views between two poles. Some examples:

God will redeem Israel if we deserve it	God will redeem Israel because God is God, and chose us

God will send a personal messiah	If all human beings are considerate, we will achieve a Messianic Era

God created the world as it says in the Bible	Science will reveal how the world was created

Other topics for discussion:

Primary Grades:

I feel close to God when _____ .

I pray to God when _____ .

I think God should _____ .

I thank God for _____ .

Intermediate Grades:

Why do bad things happen?

How can I let God work in my life?

Why do people believe different things about God?

Upper Grades:

Which of the two, faith or reason, is more important for Jews when trying to understand God?

Has ritual kept us close to God or separated us from God?

Conclusion

To write a brief chapter on strategies for teaching about God may seem presumptuous. People devote their lives to the questions we have dealt with in these few pages. But we must begin somewhere.

While there is no right way to teach about God, we must use every opportunity to encourage our students to reach out for a spiritual dimension in their lives. We hope these ideas will help you begin this vital task. The Bibliography contains an annotated list of books and materials which can reinforce and expand the ideas and suggestions which have been presented.

BIBLIOGRAPHY

ELEMENTARY LEVEL
Jewish

Brichto, Mira. *The God Around Us: A Child's Garden of Prayer.* Illustrated by Clare Romano Ross and John Ross. N.Y.: UAHC, 1958.

This picture book combines lovely poems and accompanying prayers to God. The Hebrew and transliteration are in tiny print and hard to read. The illustrations are colorful and appropriate and the book is well made. One thrust unique to this book is that both life and death are in God's hands. Overall, this is a good book because the message is appreciation. However, it presents only ideas, making no attempt at explanation or interpretation.

Cone, Molly. *About God.* Illustrated by Clare and John Ross. N.Y.: UAHC, 1973. The Shema Storybooks Series, Book 4.

This book uses stories to answer fundamental questions about God. These include: What is God? Why can't I see God? Does God know me? The lovely illustrations, the good paper binding and the large and readable print make the book appealing to children. Values statements are simple and not trite, and the use of Jewish sources from the *T'fillot* make the overall effect honest and exciting. The view that God is personal and caring is put forth without the use of stereotypical answers. Recommended without qualification for primary, and even intermediate, children.

Cone, Molly. *Who Knows Ten: Children's Tales of the Ten Commandments.* Illustrated by Uri Shulevitz. N.Y.: UAHC, 1965. Chapters 1 - 3.

For an older age group than the *Shema* series, this book uses a similar format — stories to make the point. Unfortunately, the author sidesteps the issue of God, dealing with freedom and responsibility in the first commandment, rather than "I am the Lord, Your God." The book is delightful and the illustrations well done in Shulevitz's inimitable style. It can be used as supplementary material, but not to answer questions about God.

Kipper, Morris and Leonore. *God's Wonderful World.* Illustrated by Audrey Komrad. N.Y.: Shengold Publishers, 1968.

Using green and black as the only colors for the subdued but humorous illustrations, this book begins with a letter to readers presenting questions. The answers follow in three short, imaginative stories. The message of the book is the unseen power of God, but the immature nature of the stories causes the answers to be lost, or to seem secondary to the stories themselves. Yet there is a charm here, and many Jewish sources are used. The stories themselves have little Jewish content. As a follow-up text, this book could be utilized by the creative teacher or parent.

Kripke, Dorothy K. *Let's Talk About God.* Illustrated by Bobri. N.Y.: Behrman House, Inc., 1953.

The theme of this book is "God is Good." Most of it is very "usual," almost trite. There were a few exceptional parts, such as Section Nine — "Sometimes We Make Mistakes." The poems at the beginning and end are very nice. Only in part one, "One God," is the Jewish people mentioned along with Abraham; otherwise the book is universal in approach. The style of writing is conversational and draws directly on the family life experiences of the child. The illustrations are simple but appealing in green and black. Overall, a nice book for the primary child.

Bogot, Howard and Syme, Rabbi Daniel. *Prayer is Reaching.* N.Y.: UAHC, 1981.

This beautiful book explores prayer as an approach to the experience of God for the younger child. It is a book which can be used to answer such questions as why pray, or does God answer our prayers. Or it can be used as an integrated part of the curriculum to introduce the idea of God. Illustrated in brown and white, the book is a welcome addition to the materials for elementary age students.

General

Carley, Royal V. *Thank You God for Eyes.* Illustrated by the author. Norwalk, Connecticut: C.R. Gibson Co., 1975.

This is one of a whole series of books about thanking God, all based on the senses or parts of the body. Done in plastic with large, simple illustrations, it is almost too lovely. Yet it is a useful book for primary and preschool children. No real view of God is presented, except for the statement "all things God made" when referring to nature. Serves to draw children closer to God and give them an appreciation for their eyes (or ears, nose, etc.).

Curtis, Cecil. *He Looks This Way.* Illustrated by the author. London, N.Y.: Lothrop, Lee and Shepard, 1965.

A genuinely beautiful story about Nuru, an African boy who loves Africa and yet wonders what God looks like. He dreams and considers God as the animals he knows, the African crafts and also as a great light. His conclusion is that God looks just the way everyone wants Him to look. The book is well written, the illustrations are beautiful and the story and conclusion suited to learning about God and also about Africa. Highly recommended for any child, but especially the intermediate grade student.

Fitch, Florence Mary. *A Book About God.* Illustrated by Leonard Weisgard, N.Y.: Lothrop, Lee and Shepard Co., Inc., 1953.

Lovely illustrations make this a fine picture book for the small child, showing God as a part of nature. The writing is in a simple style, and the book is well produced. I found it to be charming, and would recommend it for the primary child. The one caution I have is that it presents God in and as nature, and has no other questions about God to raise or answer.

Fitch, Florence Mary. *One God: The Ways We Worship Him.* N.Y.: Lothrop, Lee and Shepard Co, Inc., 1944.

An excellent beginning book for comparative religion. Well chosen and documented photographs illustrate the book and the print is large enough to be read by the intermediate age child. The book includes the Jewish and Catholic and Protestant ways of worshiping God. It is a plea for brotherhood and understanding. It does not, however, discuss what God is, or present philosophies of God.

Fitch, Florence Mary. *Their Search for God. Ways of Worship in the Orient.* N.Y.: Lothrop, Lee and Shepard, Co., Inc., 1947.

A book for older children (grades 5 - 7) that shows the ways of worship from a Hindu, Confucian, Shinto, Buddhist, and Taoist view. There is some attempt to explain the basic philosophic and theologic positions of these faiths in simple terms, and it is a good follow-up book to *One God.* The format of the book is similar to the others, easy to read, well laid out.

God's Wonderful World, Activity Book. St. Louis, Missouri: Concordia Publishing House, 1974.

Based on God's making of animals, flowers, rocks, etc. during the creation, this book can be used as a color book and activity book with young children. In one place a minister is mentioned (on the page where God made people). The good variety of activities are fun and not difficult; the values of happy and sad are expressed well. The book presents activities that parents can do with their children and will encourage discussion.

Heide, Florence Parry. *God and Me.* Illustrated by Ted Smith. St. Louis, Missouri: Concordia Publishing House, 1975.

This delightful hardbound book says that there are many things which we cannot see, but know that they are present, such as a flower in its seed, a bird in its egg. God's presence is like that. Its message is done in beautiful, sensitive language with very colorful illustrations. The cross above the bed when the young boy goes to sleep is the only Christian content. Otherwise I think this is one of the finest books for children about God, using syllogistic reasoning in an eloquent, exciting fashion.

Keats, Ezra Jack (compiler and illustrator). *God is in the Mountains.* N.Y.: Holt, Rinehart and Winston, 1966.

Using quotes from most major religions and some early civilizations (Aztec, African, Greek and Egyptian), this beautiful book is not really for young children. The abstract illustrations are beautiful and exciting, but the concepts too hard for them to understand and appreciate. A mature sixth grader and older students, however, will find it a beautiful supplement to views of God and life.

Trent, Robbie. *Always There is God.* Illustrated by Eleanor Blaisdell. Abingdon: Cokesbury Press, 1950.

Using exciting abstract illustrations, this book takes biblical verses and intersperses the creation story showing how even though time passes, God is always present. God's presence in creation doesn't end — it continues today in the rain and sun. Quotations are given in the back of the book. Recommended for both primary and intermediate age children.

Veranos, Sandi. *God Made it Good.* Illustrated by Mina McLean. Elgin, Illinois: David C. Cook Publishing Co., 1972.

This is a small magic picture book (i.e., pictures appear when a pencil is scratched across designated areas). It contains puzzles and pictures as it goes over the creation story emphasizing the wisdom of God in nature. The ecology section comes on the last page — right after the seventh day when God rested. The next moment there are children taking care of the trash. The book is pretty and fun, and a good combination of God and ecology.

SECONDARY AND ADULT

Jewish

Bissell, Sherry; Marcus, Audrey Friedman; and Zwerin, Raymond A. *God: The Eternal Challenge.* Denver: Alternatives in Religious Education, Inc., 1980. Student Manual and Leader Guide.

An experiential mini-course based on students' questions about God. The course, for Grade 7 and up, explores many areas and contains exceptionally fine background material and supplementary strategies in the Leader Guide.

Borowitz, Eugene B. *A New Jewish Theology in the Making.* Philadelphia: Westminster Press, 1968.

Although this book is not meant as a text, it can be utilized as such for juniors and seniors. The print is unfortunately, very small. In Part II of the book, Borowitz examines five major theologians: Baeck, Kaplan, Buber, Heschel and Soloveitchik. The main thrust of the book is the need for developing a position on and a relationship to God. This can be a strong motivational book.

Efron, Benjamin. *The Message of the Torah.* N.Y.: KTAV, 1963.

Chapters One and Two deal directly with God — first God and the Torah, then God and Man. Dealing only with material in the Torah, the book gives the concept, the verse (in both Hebrew and English) and then some explanations. Discussion on the names and characteristics of God is presented and a section on controversy and conversation with God is included. The second chapter explains personification in a very clear manner. This book can be used when introducing the biblical concept of God to young people in the seventh grade and up.

Fackenheim, Emil. *Paths to Jewish Belief: A Systematic Introduction.* Illustrated by Chet Kalm. N.Y.: Behrman House, 1960.

Using what he calls a systematic approach, Fackenheim raises and answers five major questions about God. He doesn't sidestep issues and attempts to provide many points of view (such as agnostic, atheistic, polytheistic). The book is basically a discussion of Fackenheim's ideas about oneness, revelation and moral evils. The stylized black and white illustrations add to the serious mood of the book. The author's writing style is clear and logical. However, his use of words and concepts may need further explanation for the younger secondary student. Good for eighth grade up.

Freehof, Solomon B. *In the House of the Lord.* N.Y.: UACH, 1951, Chapter 6.

In the chapter "To Whom We Pray Sh'ma," Freehof

deals with the God of the Prayerbook, stressing that prayer is the medium through which we most often communicate with God. Freehof's style flows as he discusses God as Creator, Teacher and Redeemer. A fine chapter to introduce God as portrayed in the *Siddur*.

Gertman, Stuart A., editor. *What is the Answer.* N.Y.: UAHC, 1971, Part I, God.

Many articles are brought together here to help parents and teachers answer children's questions about God and teach God concepts. Several articles discuss specific points in Jewish theology. The book is paperbound and typewritten. Sources are provided for further exploration after each article. Information on the stages of children's questions about God, as well as the practical advice and suggestions reflecting many points of view are exceptionally helpful.

Golub, Jacob S. *In the Days of the First Temple.* Cincinnati: UAHC, 1931, Pages 204 - 212.

In one section this book traces the change from the idea of God as physical power and greed to the Jewish ideal of God of mercy and justice. While the information is written in a semi-historical fashion, the book can be used as a supplement for the study of the Jewish God concept. A good index to other references is provided. The writing style is slightly out of date, but the information is not.

Jacobs, Louis. *Jewish Thought Today.* N.Y.: Behrman House, 1970. Chain of Tradition Series, Volume 3 and Teacher's Guide.

Jacobs presents individual theologians and a selection of their work with explanations. While not a creative approach, it does provide an excellent tool for studying God through the writings of Steinberg, Heschel, Buber, Kaplan, Epstein, Baeck, Rubinstein, Fackenheim and Borowitz. The selections are good, although I disagreed somewhat with the order in which they were presented. Highly recommended.

Joseloff, Samuel Hart, editor. *A Time to Seek: An Anthology of Contemporary Jewish American Poets.* N.Y.: UAHC, 1975, Chapter 5.

This paperback anthology contains poems by Karl Shapiro, David Ignatow, Robert Mezey, Hyman Plutznik, Howard Nemerov, Charles Reznikoff, Kadio Molodowsky and Jacob Glatstein. A wide range of feelings is presented, from anger to sadness and from wonder to joy. The views about God demand a response. The book is illustrated sparsely with photographs. Perhaps the editor felt that these would least detract from the poems. I personally wanted more. Done on high quality paper, this book is highly recommended to trigger discussion and creative writing about God for seventh graders and up.

Kripke, Dorothy K.; Levin, Meyer; and Kurzband, Toby K. *God and the Story of Judaism.* Illustrated by Lorence F. Bjorklund. N.Y.: Behrman House, Inc., 1962. Jewish Heritage Series, Unit II.

Even though this text can be used with grades 4 - 6, many seventh graders will find it the easiest to begin with. The pencil-like drawings add to a text characterized by simple language and concepts. Honest answers are provided to such questions as personification and natural disasters. Darker print section headings and a short summary at the end of each chapter make the book easy to use for teachers or parents. Almost every question that a child of this age might ask is given a particularistic Jewish answer. Differing views within Judaism, however, are not included. A fairly good book for the slower or younger student.

Levin, Meyer. *Beginnings in Jewish Philosophy.* N.Y.: Behrman House, Inc., 1971. Jewish Heritage Series.

This is an outstanding source when the topic God is a part of a larger course on philosophy or theology, as the whole book ties together ideas and concepts in a clear, readable, logical form. The book is easy to look at with good print, picture photograph illustrations in a soft brownish tone, and section headings that aid understanding. Levin has built his section on God around such questions as: What do we mean when we say God? How do we know there is a God? Does God punish wrong and reward good? Does God answer prayer? Why do we suffer? The author also uses the developing ideas of God and Judaism throughout. The book ends with statements about the Jewish soul and the abiding guidance of God. Outstanding for the mature eighth grader and up.

Neusner, Jacob, editor. *Understanding Jewish Theology: Classical Issues and Modern Perspectives.* N.Y.: KTAV and Anti-Defamation League of B'nai B'rith, 1973.

Recommended for the junior and senior age student, this paperbound book pulls together articles and parts of other books to help clarify Jewish theology and various views of God. God, Torah and Israel are the focus. The selections are excellent and the book is arranged so that critical issues, differing views and options all have equal importance. The glossary and index are very helpful.

Silverman, William B. *The Still Small Voice.* N.Y.: Behrman House, Inc., 1955. Story of Jewish Ethics, Book One, Chapter 2.

"Is God a magician?" is the beginning question. Tracing the development of God as Master Magician to the God of the still small voice is the object. The content is presented in the form of a teaching lesson to his students by Rabbi Mayer and is further developed with suggested activities and auxiliary questions. The book is easy to read. Its slightly old fashioned approach doesn't detract from the view of God as our still small voice of conscience in ethical situations. It can still be used for mature intermediate or junior high youngsters. The sequel, *Still Small Voice Today,* is appropriate for older students.

General

Blume, Judy. *Are You There God? It's Me, Margaret.* N.Y.: Dell Publishing Co., Inc., 1970. Yearling Book.

This paperback book tells more about what it is like to be a 12 year old girl than about God, but it is a good supplement for a course. The fact that Margaret talks to God and confides in God gives us a nice model for enhancing the experiential personal concept of God. Margaret raises questions (e.g., "Why do I only feel You when I'm alone?") as she rebels, questions and learns about herself and her relationship to God. Recommended as a good trigger for discussion.

Tapes, Scripts, Pamphlets

Borowitz, Eugene. Torah Session, "Current Options in Jewish Theology." Six tape cassettes from CCAR Convention, June 15 - 19, 1975, Cincinnati, Ohio. Aviva Communications Corp., North Hollywood, California, 1975.

Dr. Borowitz is clear and witty. He says some very important things about options in Jewish theology and in God concepts and modern day Jewish problems. These tapes are a fine tool for the junior or senior in high school, or for the very motivated younger high school student. The quality is good, the black plastic package easy to carry and store. One problem is a bit too much leader at the beginning of the second side of each tape. The set can be used to aid the student who prefers aural learning.

Borowitz, Eugene. "Death of the Death of God Movement." Cassette tape. Aviva Communications Corp., North Hollywood, California, 1975.

The first part of this tape is a very fine response to the Death of God movement appropriate for the older student. It is a relaxed, informal and funny talk which makes it easy to listen to. It is packaged in a plastic container. Side two has too much silent leader. The second side is from a question and answer period with other participants. The editing is good, but it sounds disjointed. Recommmended for students who find listening difficult.

Cohon, Samuel S., D.D. *The Jewish Idea of God*. N.Y.: Commission on Interfaith Activities, UAHC, n.d. Popular Studies in Judaism Pamphlet Series.

The pamphlet emphasizes ethical monotheism, a universalistic God concept and the mission of Israel in living up to this ideal. Its point is that belief in God serves as a source of inspiration and regeneration and hope. The pamphlet also develops the Jewish idea of God, uses source materials and presents a lovely sermon, all in 34 pages. It is small and handy as a supplement to other materials for the older student.

Heschel, Abraham J. "Two Conversations with Abraham Joshua Heschel." Parts I, II. Chapters 1077-78, Eternal Light Television Scripts. Jewish Theological Seminary of America, New York, 1972.

In both of these scripts Rabbi Heschel is interviewed by Rabbi Wolfe Kelman. The first is concerned with Prophets and mentions God in relation to these men. The second is more relevant, as Heschel's book *God in Search of Man* is the starting point. While these tapes

give a clear explanation of Heschel's thought, the vocabulary is often difficult. Hence, older students would be more likely to gain from hearing them. Students can take turns as Kelman and Heschel or use the transcript for further study.

Keeping Posted. "Youth in Search of God." Volume 17:4 (January, 1972), N.Y.: UAHC, Teacher's Edition.

The articles in this issue address religion in general more than the ideas and experience of God. However, there are sections which enhance the study of God, such as Bill Novak's article, "Jewish Youth Search for Religious Meaning." Novak explores the question of false gods as well as the relationship between human beings and God in an attempt to define religiosity and faith. The magazine is nicely put together with photographs and cartoons. For older students.

FILMS

"Anyone Around My Base Is It." 28 min., color. Jewish Chautauqua Society, 838 Fifth Ave., New York, NY 10021.

Portrays the story of a man searching for God who tries to tell a boy whose father was killed where God is.

"Clay (Origin of Species)." 8 min., black and white. Contemporary Films McGraw-Hill, Princeton Road, Hightstown, NJ 08520.

A visual variation on Darwin using clay animation.

"The Creation." 15 min., color. The Genesis Project, P.O. Box 37282, Washington, DC 20013.

The first segment of "The New Media Bible," the ambitious project which has set out to make a film version of the entire Hebrew and Christian Bibles.

"Oh, God" and "Oh, God, Book II." Swank Motion Pictures, 201 South Jefferson Ave., St. Louis, MO 63166.

The 1977 film (and sequel) starring George Burns as God who calls upon John Denver, who plays a supermarket employee, to be a prophet. Theology and philosophy are mixed with humor.

FILMSTRIPS

"Byron Bee Looks For God." New Concepts Associates, 169 Selden Hill Drive, West Hartford, CT 06107.

An introduction to the concept of God for primary children which is based on a *midrashic* account.

"Why Pray." Union of American Hebrew Congregations, 838 Fifth Ave., New York, NY 10021.

Teenagers discuss prayer and the spirituality/community they feel worshiping in the camp setting.

TEACHING ABOUT DEATH AND DYING

By Audrey Friedman Marcus

"The world is a beautiful place to be born into," says the poet Lawrence Ferlinghetti, "but then right in the middle of it comes the smiling mortician." Despite the inescapable nature of death to which the poet refers, and the necessity of facing it, we find death hard to discuss and even more difficult to teach. In this chapter, we will analyze the need for death education, learn how to prepare to teach death, discuss what, when and how to teach it and conclude with a list of appropriate resources.

The Need for Death Education

In the past, death education took place in a natural way. People died most frequently at home, surrounded by family and friends. Death was a familiar experience to both young and old alike — infants and mothers died in childbirth, children died of childhood diseases and animals died on the farm. Today, death is shunted away into hospitals, old age facilities and nursing homes. Few of us ever see a dead person. This has made the whole subject of death mysterious and scary.

Also, in the nineteenth century, corpses were taken care of by family and the community. This was always the case for Jews. Today few cultures continue this practice and, despite its revival among some Jewish groups, most of us are far removed from contact with death.

Still another factor which points up the need for death education is the fact that death is so depersonalized in our society. It has become little more than a meaningless actuarial statistic. In wartime, we use the word "waste" instead of kill. Sophisticated weapons are an everyday fact

of our lives. On our television screens actors die and "reappear" next week in another show. Usually it is only the "bad guy" or the enemy who dies. Death appears to children as punishment, not as a fact of life. And they copy their television role models and play "Bang you're dead."

Writers on the subject of attitudes toward death point out that grief and mourning are deritualized today, or short circuited. We admire and praise individuals who, like Jackie Kennedy, keep a stiff upper lip and don't show their real feelings at the time of tragedy. Similarly, some Jews observe only a short period of *shiva,* or none at all, forgoing the opportunity this ritual provides to work through grief and to mourn properly.

Somehow we think of death as an accident or illness which we can avoid, rather than as a natural event. We refer to it euphemistically as passed away, gone, departed this life. We say "I lost my . . . ," "he or she entered eternal rest or went to sleep." We substitute interred for buried, memorial park for graveyard, coach for hearse and remains for corpse. The effects of death are disguised by embalming. Loved ones are placed in a "slumber room." Some funeral parlors even use light blue hearses instead of black. The emphasis we place on youth further contributes to the denial of death.

What is most damaging, however, is our avoidance of the subject of death with children. Not only are young people growing up without experiencing death directly, they are also denied a forum for their questions and their anxieties.

For all these reasons, then, it is apparent

that death education is necessary and that our religious schools must deal with the subject. We must introduce it throughout our curriculum, helping students to view death as a natural occurrence, and providing them and their parents with the attitudes and skills needed to cope with death as a reality. Children need to learn that good guys also die. Doing so will help them grow up into fully developed human beings. It was heartening to watch death "come out of the closet and into the classroom"[1] in the 1970's. We must continue this encouraging trend.

It is possible that one of the reasons that we avoid discussing and teaching death is because most of us haven't yet worked it out for ourselves. Perhaps, too, we don't know the techniques and tools to use. In the remainder of this chapter, we will discuss the goals for teaching death education and how to prepare ourselves to teach about death. This will be followed by some how-to's.

Goals for Teaching Death

The following represent some overall goals for death education. They grow out of the specific needs mentioned above.

1. To help children face the death of a loved one when it happens by presenting the subject early.
2. To make death less fearful and living more enjoyable.
3. To help develop a realistic and accepting attitude toward death.
4. To explain the Jewish rituals surrounding death, burial and mourning, the rationale and wisdom and their observance.
5. To establish a feeling of trust so children will open up and ask questions.
6. To help children develop mentally healthy ways of coping with separation experiences.
7. To help children to reach out to peers who experience death and grief.

Preparing to Teach About Death

Before dealing with the subject of death in the classroom, we must be comfortable ourselves with the topic. Any anxiety we feel will be conveyed to the youngsters we teach. It is essential to deal matter of factly with the students,

answering their questions, relieving their fears and acknowledging difficult areas. It might be helpful to talk over your own feelings with a relative, friend, Rabbi or colleague before beginning to teach about death.

The first step, when getting ready to teach death, is to read the literature on death and death education and to keep current with it. It is also helpful to attend classes and workshops when they are offered in the congregation or community, at a junior college or a medical school. Next, it is important to familiarize yourself with Jewish teachings and customs. Besides the *Encyclopaedia Judaica,* two excellent sources are: *The Jewish Way in Death and Mourning* by Maurice Lamm and *Jewish Reflections on Death* by Jack Reimer. You will also want to read and analyze the available teaching units for Jewish schools and to preview films and filmstrips on the subject. The complete citations for the resources above, as well as many others, and a comprehensive listing of audiovisual aids may be found in the Bibliography at the conclusion of this chapter.

Before beginning a unit on death, it is a wise idea to inform parents of your intentions. This may be done by letter, but is best accomplished at a meeting. Make the arrangements for such a get-together in cooperation with your Director of Education and Rabbi, both of whom should be present. Approach the contact with parents in a positive way, assuming that they will be supportive. For the most part, they will be. Describe the course material and give parents a chance to ask questions and to calm their own anxieties. Suggest ways that they can reinforce the learning at home. Give them a few well chosen references and some excerpts from books by Rabbi Earl A. Grollman. If possible, show his film, "Talking About Death With Children." Stress the importance of keeping the subject open and of answering their childrens' questions truthfully. A course on death can be a significant aid in widening communication between parent and child and in encouraging a frank discussion of death. Parents need to understand their role as a positive force in helping their children adjust to the realities of life.

Later on, if possible, schedule at least one class for parents alone and also include them in a session with their children.

Be aware of, and sensitive to, any problems among class members such as a recent close death. In these cases, talk to a parent or relative

---

[1] Gene Stanford and Deborah Perry, *Death Out Of The Closet.* (N.Y.: Bantam Books, 1976) p. 1.

to see how you can most help the child. Assess how to include the child in the discussions without causing discomfort. The best way to handle such a situation is in conference with the student. Ask if he or she wants to talk about it. Convey a message of care and help the child to face the irreversibility of death and to deal with the guilt or anger that often surrounds the death of a loved one. However, don't probe or insist on responses or participation from *any* member of the class. Let each child determine the level of involvement.

With all students, it may be necessary to create distance between them and the subject and to avoid personalizing the content, as we do in other courses. Be calm yourself and monitor the anxiety level of the group by asking students what is going on for them.[2]

Try to establish a climate of sensitivity to the feelings of others and an atmosphere of trust before you begin teaching about death. Help students learn to listen to each other and to avoid putting each other down (see "Listening Skills, Lecture and Discussion" by Audrey Friedman Marcus in *The Jewish Teachers Handbook*, Volume I). You will find the effort worthwhile to establish a sense of community in the classroom, helping students to be more caring toward their classmates and more understanding of each other's views (for a series of exercises to accomplish this, see "Creating Community in the Classroom" by Ronald Wolfson in Volume II of the Handbook series).

Finally, be accepting and non-judgmental yourself regarding the questions students ask and the opinions they express. It is only by responding in this manner that the necessary climate of openness and trust can be built. Don't hesitate to give your own ideas, but be sure students know that these are your views and that other opinions are just as valid.

Outlining the Course

Once you have decided on the topic and have done your research, decide on the time frame for the course and list age appropriate sub-topics. Let students help you do this by submitting their questions anonymously. Their participation can aid you significantly in formulating the course. Identify resources for the classroom, including books, audiovisual materials,

---

[2]Gene Stanford and Deborah Perry, *Death Out Of The Closet*. (N.Y.: Bantam Books, 1976) pp. 18, 21, 23.

guest speakers (a Rabbi, Minister, psychologist, social worker, funeral director, etc.) and potential field trip sites (cemetery, funeral home, Holocaust memorial, etc.). Then determine your objectives.

The following objectives are reprinted with permission from the Leader Guide for the minicourse *Death, Burial & Mourning in the Jewish Tradition* (Denver: Alternatives in Religious Education, Inc., 1976).

Cognitive Objectives:

Students will be able

1. To describe and explain the Jewish customs relating to death, burial and mourning.
2. To compare Jewish death, burial and mourning rituals and traditions with those of several other cultures.
3. To differentiate between traditional and liberal Jewish practices in regard to death, burial and mourning.
4. To describe the emotions which accompany bereavement — grief, anger and disbelief and guilt.
5. To summarize the Jewish views of life after death.
6. To give examples of the reverence for life that the Jewish tradition espouses.

Affective Objectives:

Students will be able

1. To relate their anxieties about death.
2. To show awareness that death is a natural part of the life cycle.
3. To describe their own experiences with death — pets, nature, friends, relatives.
4. To present in writing and discussion their own feelings about death and dying.
5. To express the humaneness and psychological soundness of the Jewish rituals associated with death, burial and mourning.

The book *Death Out of the Closet* provides an excellent list of objectives for death education in the areas of attitudes toward death, the personal experience of death (survival, the process of dying, grief), death rites and rituals, social and ethical issues, death and the humanities, immortality and the hereafter and death and science. Consult this extensive list if you need help preparing your objectives.

Next, write your course outline, decide on the methods of presentation and on appropriate activities and exercises for each sub-topic. Many excellent activities can be found in the aforementioned book *Death Out of the Closet* and in the next section of this chapter. The introductory activity you choose will set the tone for the course. There are many interesting ways to get into the subject of death. These include asking questions, sharing thoughts and feelings, using a questionnaire, discussing population statistics, reading a quotation or passage from a novel or poem (such as the one quoted at the beginning of this chapter[3]), watching a film, making a collage or lifeline, comparing plant and animal cycles. Or you might discuss what would happen if no one ever died. Or, from a list of words such as loss, pain, evil, joy, beautiful, gone, unexpected, peace, nothingness, etc., ask which words students associate with death. Compare choices, analyze the percentage of positive and negative words chosen, talk about euphemisms for death, etc.

Now you are ready to choose the other readings and materials you will use and to decide on the films and filmstrips. Determine which, if any, guest speakers to invite. Decide if you will include one of the field trips you identified earlier.

Do your time budgeting now. Estimate how long each segment of the course will take and adjust your outline to fit your allotted time frame. Allow plenty of time for open discussion — don't over program. Finally, write good discussion questions, plan lectures and organize student materials. Order films and filmstrips, invite guest speakers. Give a lot of thought to closure. You will want to end on an upbeat note, affirming life and its joys and the beauty of the Jewish tradition.

Finally, decide on a method of evaluation. Design opportunities for further study and enrichment, either for the class or on an individual basis. You are now ready to teach the course.

In the next section we will briefly discuss the attitudes toward the death of children of various ages. Some teaching strategies, a few age appropriate books and a list of the teaching units that are available will round out the chapter.

---

[3]From *A Coney Island of the Mind* by Lawrence Ferlighetti (N.Y.: New Directions Books), pp. 88 and 89.

THE CHILD FROM 3 - 6

View of Death

At ages three to six, death is not understood by children as a final separation. They often believe they are responsible when a death occurs. If they are good, they think, death will not occur. Children of this age often mourn without showing it.

Teaching Strategies

1. Care for pets in the classroom. When pets die, reassure children that they are not responsible, that death just happens and that it is part of nature. Tell them we don't know why the animal dies — we can only guess. If they feel guilty about the death, reassure them that they can do better in the future. Don't replace the pet immediately. Offer sympathy and let the children grieve. Let them touch the dead bird or pet if they wish to do so.
2. Bury a dead pet. Make a marker for the grave, sing songs, plant flowers and encourage the children to talk about their feelings. Help them to do so by making such statements as, "I will miss our gerbil," "He was our friend," "Our gerbil will never come back — he is dead." "What are some good things you remember about our animal?"
3. Point out flowers that are dying. Touch them. Crumble dead leaves. Draw the leaves and flowers.
4. Grow and observe plants.
5. Draw pictures of animals alive and dead.
6. Use a flannelboard to tell stories of an animal's life.
7. Read books about animals that die, such as *The Dead Bird* and *The Tenth Good Thing About Barney*.
8. Show a filmstrip about a pet that dies, such as "The Dead Bird" (Oxford Films, Inc., 5451 Marathon St., Hollywood, CA 90038).

Age Appropriate Books

Abbott, Sarah. *The Old Dog*. N.Y.: Coward, McCann and Geoghegan, 1972.

Aliki. *Go Tell Aunt Rhody*. N.Y.: Macmillan Publishing Co., Inc., 1974.

Brown, Margery W. *The Dead Bird*. Reading, Massachusetts: Addison-Wesley Publishing Co., Inc., 1965.

Carrick, Carol. *The Accident.* N.Y.: Human Sciences Press, 1976.

Stein, Sara Bonnett. *About Dying: An Open Family Book for Parents and Children Together.* N.Y.: The Danbury Press, 1954.

Viorst, Judith. *The Tenth Good Thing About Barney.* N.Y.: Atheneum Publishers, Inc., 1971.

THE CHILD FROM 7 - 9

View of Death

Children of this age are aware that death is final for all living things. They associate death with the disintegration of the body, and are curious about what happens to the body. (When they ask, it is all right to say you don't know.) They also tend to personalize death as a ghost, bogeyman or skeleton. They begin to question the cause of death. Between seven and nine, children think of death as mostly for old people, but they are beginning to understand that it could happen to adults like their parents and possibly even to children as well.

Teaching Strategies

1. Caring for and observing pets is still one of the best ways to introduce the subject of death. Keep a pet in the classroom. See items 1 and 2 under the teaching strategies for ages 3 - 6 above for details.
2. Write an epitaph for a pet that died.
3. Discuss and tell stories about the cycles in nature — birth, death, the seasons.
4. Go on nature walks. Take photographs, then make bulletin boards and collages.
5. Do nature experiments — look at plants under a microscope.
6. Talk about the death of a public figure. Discuss the person's life and how he/she affected the children's lives.
7. Talk about grandparents. Invite them to class. Reminisce about those who have died.
8. Do art projects using various media.
9. Sing folk songs, such as "Go Tell Aunt Rhody."
10. Read and report on books about death (see below for titles).

Age Appropriate Books

Bernstein, Joanne E. and Gullo, Stephen V. *When People Die.* N.Y.: E.P. Dutton, 1977.

Brown, Margery W. *The Dead Bird.* Reading, Massachusetts: Addison-Wesley Publishing Co., Inc., 1965.

Corley, Elizabeth Adam. *Tell Me About Death: Tell Me About Funerals.* Santa Clara, California: Grammatical Sciences, 1973.

Dobrin, Arnold. *Scat!* N.Y.: Four Winds Press, 1971.

Grollman, Earl A. *Talking About Death.* Boston: Beacon Press, 1970.

Harris, Audrey. *Why Did He Die.* Minneapolis: Lerner Publications, Co., 1965.

Kantrowitz, Mildred. *When Violet Died.* N.Y.: Parents' Magazine Press, 1973.

LeShan, Eda. *Learning to Say Good-By: When a Parent Dies.* N.Y.: Macmillan Publishing Co., Inc., 1976.

Miles, Miska. *Annie and the Old One.* Boston: Little, Brown and Co., Inc., 1971.

Shechter, Ben. *Across the Meadow.* Garden City, New York: Doubleday & Co., Inc., 1973.

Warburg, Sandol. *Growing Time.* N.Y.: Houghton Mifflin, 1969.

Zolotow, Charlotte. *My Grandson Lew.* N.Y: Harper and Row, 1974.

Teaching Units

Joseph, Rabbi Samuel K. *A Time to Die: A Course on Death in 7 Units for Third and Fourth Grade Students.* N.Y.: UAHC Experimental Editions, June 1977.

The Inkling, Volume II, Number 3. Denver: Alternatives in Religious Education, Inc., 1975.

THE CHILD FROM 10 - 12

View of Death

By the age of ten, children have completed the basic development of their concepts of time, space, quantity and causality. Most understand death as final and inevitable, but they fantasize an alternative to death, such as an afterlife.

Teaching Strategies

1. Discuss death and decay as part of the natural life cycle. Study what happens to small animals when they die.
2. Do Rank Orders, such as the following: A favorite pet of yours has a very bad (and very painful) disease. Would you let it die naturally, have it put to sleep, or ask to have its body frozen in the hope of some medical breakthrough?
3. Identify with characters in stories (see below for titles).
4. Watch "The Day Grandpa Died," an excellent film about a boy of this age. A useful discussion guide for the film can be obtained from The Jewish Media Service, Jewish Welfare Board, 15 East 26th Street, New York, NY 10010.
5. Conduct an interview to find out what the Rabbi does when notified of the death of a member of the congregation.
6. Survey parents on such questions as: Should children attend funerals? Should they be allowed to visit cemeteries? Should flowers be permitted at a Jewish funeral? Should *Kaddish* be recited even if there has not been a death in the family?
7. Study the Hebrew terms associated with death — e.g., *aninut, avelut, avelim, alav hashalom, alehah hashalom, Chevrah Kaddisha, hesped, kaddish, keriah, matzevah, Seudat Havra-ah, shiva, Sh'loshim, vidui, yahrzeit, yizkor.*
8. Involve youngsters in role play. Do it in small groups so they will be comfortable.
9. Write stories and poetry about death, then illustrate them.
10. Do research and write a report on death.
11. Write a condolence letter, real or imaginary, to someone who has experienced a death.

Age Appropriate Books

Bernstein, Joanne E. *Loss and How to Cope With It.* N.Y.: Seabury Press, 1977.

Buck, Pearl S. *The Big Wave.* N.Y.: Day, 1948.

Gersh, Harry. *When a Jew Celebrates.* N.Y.: Behrman House, 1971.

Klein, Stanley. *The Final Mystery.* Garden City, New York: Doubleday & Co., Inc., 1974.

Krüss, James. *My Great-Grandfather, the Heroes and I.* N.Y.: Atheneum Publishers, Inc., 1973.

Smith, Doris Buchanon. *A Taste of Blackberies.* N.Y.: Thomas Y. Crowell, 1973.

White, E.B. *Charlotte's Web.* N.Y.: Harper and Row, 1952.

Teaching Units

Marcus, Audrey Friedman; Bissell, Sherry; and Lipschutz, Karen S. *Death, Burial & Mourning in the Jewish Tradition.* Denver: Alternatives in Religious Education, 1976.

Mersky, Rabbi David. "A Teaching Unit on Death." *Compass,* Number 27, New York: UAHC, March 1974.

THE CHILD FROM AGE 13 UP

View of Death

Young people of this age sense the personal meaning of death, this sense often leading to a fuller appreciation of life. They may have difficulty applying fears about death in a personal way. They long to talk about death, to share feelings and anxieties.

Teaching Strategies

1. Role play in small groups. Some excellent situations are found in *Death Out of the Closet,* page 60.
2. Write condolence letters to real or imaginary individuals who have experienced the death of a close family member.
3. Communicate an early childhood experience with death through writing or art.
4. Determine how attitudes have changed over the centuries in regard to death and immortality.
5. Have a dialogue with death.
6. Read Jewish fiction on the subject of death, such as the book of Job, *The Diary of Anne Frank, The Last of the Just,* books by Elie Wiesel, The novel *Exodus* and short stories, such as "Silent Bontche" by I.L. Peretz.
7. Compare the style and content of obituaries. Rewrite them more appropriately. Have each student write his/her own obituary as if he or she were to die suddenly, listing their unique accomplishments, those worthy of being remembered.
8. Have each student write his/her own epitaph, summarizing their life and expressing how they would like to be remembered.

This exercise can help students identify what is important to them and can serve as a stimulus for goal setting in their lives. (Students enjoy hearing W.C. Fields' epitaph: "On the whole I'd rather be in Philadelphia.")

9. Study death, burial and mourning customs in other cultures. View films on the subject, such as "The Parting."

10. Read poetry about death. (For good examples from secular literature, see *Death Out of the Closet*, pages 92-94.) Then have students write their own poems about death, either as a class or individually.

11. Look up secular and Jewish quotations about death. Collect these in a notebook. Then have students write their own pithy statements and add them to the collection.

12. Visit a cemetery. Make tombstone rubbings.

13. Interview clergy from various faiths about death.

14. Have students outline a *Magen David*. In each of the six points, have them make a drawing to represent their response to the following six questions or statements. (This can be a very heavy exercise and should be used only with older high school students and adults and only when you are sure the group can handle it.)

    a. If you were to die right now, what do you think your friends would miss most about you?

    b. Think of something about which you feel strongly, something for which you would be willing to give you life.

    c. What was the closest you ever came to losing your life?

    d. Think of someone who was close to you who died. What do you miss most about that person?

    e. What are you doing to help yourself to live a long, healthy life?

    f. Imagine that you have one year left to live. What would you do in that year? Share students' responses in small groups, then ask for volunteers to share with the whole class. Be sure to be supportive of the thoughts and feelings that emerge.

15. Analyze death as it is "described" in classical music. Listen to a Requiem by Mozart or Verdi, "Juliet's Death" from "Romeo and Juliet" by Prokofief, "Kaddish Symphony" by Leonard Bernstein.

16. Ask students to bring in the lyrics from popular songs which talk about death. Discuss and compare the songs.

17. Discuss the attitudes toward death found in such movies as "Easy Rider," "The Godfather," "Love Story," "Butch Cassidy," "Romeo and Juliet" and "West Side Story."

18. Study the funeral business. Interview a mortician, a salesperson, an embalmer. Visit a funeral home. Discuss the revival of the *Chevrah Kaddishah*. Read and discuss *The High Cost of Dying* by Ruth Harmer and *The American Way of Death* by Jessica Mitford.

19. Discuss preparing for death — wills, organ banks, life insurance, living wills.

20. Discuss and research related topics, such as the causes of death, suicide, aging, "small deaths" (separations like divorce, moving, breaking up), euthanasia, the right to life, cryogenics, cremation, autopsies and the legal issues surrounding death — brain death, the California Right to Die Law, living wills, etc.

Age Appropriate Books

Agee, James. *A Death in the Family*. N.Y.: Avon, 1959.

Beckman, Gunnel. *Admission to the Feast*. N.Y.: Holt, Rinehart and Winston, 1971.

Blinn, William. *Brian's Song*. N.Y.: Bantam, 1952.

Caine, Lynn. *Widow*. N.Y.: Bantam, 1952.

Craven, Margery. *I Heard the Owl Call My Name*. Garden City, New York: Doubleday & Co., Inc., 1973.

Farley, Carol. *The Garden is Doing Fine*. N.Y.: Harper and Brothers, 1949.

Gunther, John. *Death Be Not Proud*. N.Y.: Harper and Brothers, 1949.

Harmer, Ruth. *The High Cost of Dying*. N.Y.: Crowell-Collier Press, 1963.

Ish-Kishor, Sulamith. *Our Eddie*. N.Y.: Pantheon Books, 1969.

Klein, Isaac. *A Time To Be Born, A Time To Die*. N.Y.: Dept. of Youth Activities, United Synagogue of America, 1976.

Levin, Meyer. *Beginnings in Jewish Philosophy*. N.Y.: Behrman House, 1971.

Lifton, Robert Jay and Olson, Eric. *Living and Dying*. N.Y.: Bantam Books, 1974.

Segal, Eric. *Love Story*. N.Y.: Harper and Row, 1970.

Turner, Ann Warren. *House for the Dead: Burial Customs Through the Ages*. N.Y.: McKay, 1976.

Teaching Units

Marcus, Audrey Friedman; Bissell, Sherry; and Lipschutz, Karen S. *Death, Burial & Mourning in the Jewish Tradition*. Denver: Alternatives in Religious Education, Inc., 1976.

Keeping Posted, Vol. XVII, No. 6. N.Y.: UAHC, March 1972.

Conclusion

We are models for children in coping with painful experiences. Children can acquire a fear of death by observing the behavior of fearful adults. Thus it is vital that we deal with death realistically and that we answer our students' questions simply and factually, using the correct words. We must avoid comparing death with sleep or referring to a journey. Such comparisons may cause children to be afraid. Nor should we tell children that God wanted the person and that's why he/she died. Such a statement can lead to a resentment of God. In our attitudes — and even in the tone of voice we use — we must be calm, sympathetic and warm when discussing this sensitive subject.

Shielding children from the realities of death can stand in the way of emotional growth. The efforts we make to help the youngsters we teach understand and accept death as natural, inevitable and irreversible can have an important impact on their healthy adjustment to life.

BIBLIOGRAPHY

Books and Articles

"A Time to Be Born A Time To Die." *Keeping Posted.* XVII, No. 6, March 1972.

Aries, Philippe. *Western Attitudes Toward Death From the Middle Ages to the Present.* Baltimore and London: Johns Hopkins University Press, 1974.

Bender, David L. *Problems of Death,* Anoka, Minnesota: Greenhaven Press, 1974.

Bial, Morison David. *Liberal Judaism at Home.* N.Y.: UAHC, 1971.

Donin, Rabbi Hayim Halevy. *To Be A Jew.* N.Y.: Basic Books, 1972.

Dresner, Samuel H. *The Jew In American Life.* N.Y.: Crown, 1963.

"Films on Death and Dying." Educational Film Library Association, 17 West 60th St., New York, NY 10023.

Gaster, Theodor H. *Customs and Folkways of Jewish Life.* NY.: William Sloane, 1955.

Gersh, Harry. *When a Jew Celebrates.* N.Y.: Behrman House, 1971.

Gertman, Stuart A., Editor. *What is the Answer.* N.Y.: UAHC, 1971.

Gittelsohn, Roland. *Wings of the Morning.* N.Y.: UAHC, 1969.

Green, Betty and Irish, Donald P. *Death Education: Preparation for Living.* Cambridge: Schenkman, 1971.

Greenberg, Rabbi Sidney. *A Treasury of Comfort.* North Hollywood: Wilshire Book Co., 1954.

Green, Betty and Irish, Donald R. *Death Education: Preparation for Living.* Cambridge: Schenkman, 1971.

Greenberg, Robbi Sidney. *A Treasury of Comfort.* North Hollywood: Wilshire Book Co., 1954.

Grollman, Earl A. *Concerning Death.* Boston: Beacon Press, 1974.

——————— . *Explaining Death to Children.* Boston: Beacon Press, 1967.

——————— . *Talking About Death.* Boston: Beacon Press, 1970.

Habenstein, Robert and Lamers, William M. *Funeral Customs the World Over.* Milwaukee: Bultin Printers Inc., 1973.

Harlow, Jules, Editor. *The Bond of Life.* N.Y.: The Rabbinical Assembly, 1975.

The Inkling. Bert S. Gerard, Editor. Alternatives in Religious Education, Inc., Vol. II, No. 3.

Joseph, Rabbi Samuel K. *A Time to Die: A Course on Death in 7 Units for Third and Fourth Grade Students.* N.Y. : UAHC Experimental Education Educations, June, 1977.

Klein, Rabbi Isaac. *A Time To Be Born, A Time To Die.* N.Y.: Department of Youth Activities, United Synagogue of America, 1976.

Kübler-Ross, Elisabeth. *Questions and Answers on Death and Dying.* N.Y.: Collier, 1974.

Lamm, Maurice. *The Jewish Way in Death and Mourning.* N.Y.: Jonathan David, 1969.

Levin, Meyer. *Beginnings in Jewish Philosophy.* N.Y.: Behrman House, 1971.

Lifton, Robert Jay and Olson, Eric. *Living and Dying.* N.Y.: Bantam Books, 1974.

Marcus, Audrey Friedman; Bissell, Sherry; and Lipschutz, Karen S. *Death, Burial and Mourning in the Jewish Tradition.* Denver: Alternatives in Religious Education, 1976.

Medium. Jewish Media Service. Number 6, March-April 1975.

Millgram, Abraham, *Jewish Worship.* Philadelphia: Jewish Publication Society, 1971.

Mersky, Rabbi David. "A Teaching Unit on Death." *Compass,* Number 27, March 1974.

Mills, Gretchen C.; Reisler, R.; Robinson, A.E.; Vermilye, G. *Discussing Death: A Guide to Death Education.* Palm Springs: ETC, 1976.

Mitford, Jessica. *The American Way of Death.* N.Y: Simon and Shuster, 1963.

Perspectives on Death: A Thematic Teaching Unit. Perspectives on Death, P.O. Box 213, DeKalb, Illinois 60115.

Riemer, Jack. *Jewish Reflections on Death.* N.Y.: Schocken, 1974.

Roth, Cecil and Wigoder, Geoffrey, editors. *Encyclopaedia Judaica.* Jerusalem: Keter Publishing House, Ltd., 1971.

Schauss, Hayyim. *The Lifetime of a Jew.* N.Y.: UAHC, 1950.

Schrank, Jeffrey. *Teaching Human Beings: 101 Subversive Activities for the Classroom.* Boston: Beacon Press, 1972.

Stanford, Gene and Perry Deborah. *Death Out of the Closet.* N.Y.: Bantam Books, 1976.

Stein, Sara Bonnett. *About Dying: An Open Family Book for Parents and Children Together.* N.Y.: The Danbury Press, 1974.

"A Study of Death Through the Celebration of Life." *Learning,* March 1976.

"The Study of Death and Dying." *Media and Methods,* February 1977.

Yamamoto, Kaoru. *Death in the Life of Children.* West Lafayette, Indiana: Kappa Delta Pi, 1978.

"You and Death.": *Psychology Today,* August 1970.

Zwerin, Raymond A.; Friedman, Audrey; and Kramish, Leonard. *Medical Ethics.* Denver: Alternatives in Religious Education, Inc., 1973.

Films and Filmstrips

"Accident" Doubleday Media, P.O. Box 11607, Santa Ana, CA 92705.

Survivor of a plane crash explains his new attitudes toward life after the crash.

"After The First." Teleketics, 1229 S. Santee St., Los Angeles, CA 90015.

A boy's first hunting trip and his realization of the cruelty and finality of death.

"Bashert." Jewish Media Service, 15 E. 26th St., New York, NY 10010.

A pious old man, anticipating his own death, sees in his mind's eye time reversed, the events of his life played backward.

"Brian's Song." Learning Corporation of America, 1350 Avenue of the Americas, New York, NY 10019.

Feature film of true story of death of Brian Piccolo, 26 year old player for the Chicago Bears.

"The Day Grandpa Died." Jewish Media Service, 15 E. 26th St., New York, NY 10010 or BFA Educational Media, 2211 Michigan Ave., P.O. Box 1795, Santa Monica, CA 90406.

Young Jewish boy is plunged into shock and disbelief at the death of his beloved grandfather.

"Day of the Dead." Espousal Film Center, 554 Lexington St., Waltham, MA 02154.

Examines Mexican concept of death.

"Death." Parents Magazine Films, Inc., 52 Vanderbilt Ave., New York, NY 10017.

5 filmstrips and cassettes, dealing with the grieving process of children, the child's perception of death and how to explain death to youngsters. Good for teachers.

"Death and Dying: Closing the Circle." 5 filmstrips and cassettes with discussion guide. Guidance Associates, 757 Third Ave., New York, N.Y. 10017.

The meaning of death, terminal illness, dealing with grief, etc.

"Death Be Not Proud." Learning Corporation of America, 1350 Avenue of the Americas, New York, NY 10019.

Story of the death of John Gunther's son.

"Emily - The Story of a Mouse." Viewfinders, P.O. Box 1665, Evanston, IL 60204.

Brief trigger film that follows a mouse through her life span. Told simply, like a children's story.

"The Garden Party." Kent State University Audiovisual Services, Kent, OH 44242.

A story of an affluent adolescent girls' first encounter with death.

"I Heard The Owl Call My Name." Learning Corporation of America, 1350 Avenue of the Americas, New York, NY 10019.

Terminally ill young priest sent to small Indian village to learn the true meaning of life. Good for attitudes toward death of other cultures.

"A Journey." Wombat Productions, 77 Tarrytown Rd., White Plains, NY 10607.

The image of life as a journey on a train. Symbolic, mysterious, existential.

"Leo Beuerman." Centron Educational Films, 1621 West Ninth St., Lawrence, KS 66044.

Examination of a severely disabled man's courageous struggle to live.

"Living With Dying." Sunburst Communications, Pound Ridge, NY 10576.

2 filmstrips and records dealing with accepting death, the psychological and emotional stages of the terminally ill, immortality, death's place in the cycle of life.

"The Magic Moth." Centron Educational Films, 1621 West Ninth St., Lawrence, KS 66044.

Adaptation of a children's book which examines the death of a child and how family members react to their tragic loss.

"The Mortal Body." Filmakers Library, 290 West End Ave., New York, NY 10023.

Nonverbal visually powerful examination of the life cycle from birth to death and the transience of human existence.

"Occurrence at Owl Creek Bridge." Contemporary/ McGraw Hill Films, Princeton Rd., Hightstown, NJ 08520.

Ambrose Bierce's story of a man's feelings, perceptions, thoughts as he is hanged.

"The Parting." Wombat Productions, 77 Tarrytown Rd., White Plains, NY 10607.

Stylized, nonverbal depiction of the funeral of a peasant in a remote Yugoslavian hamlet.

"A Plain Pine Box." Committee on Congregational Standards, United Synagogue of America, 155 Fifth Avenue, New York, NY 10010.

About members of a Minneapolis congregation's *Chevra Kevod HaMet,* who wash, dress and watch over the body.

"The Right To Die." Macmillan Films, 34 MacQuesten Parkway South, Mt. Vernon, NY 10550.

Examines the right to die and the right to live using real life situations.

"Seige." JWB Lecture Bureau, 15 E. 26th St., New York, NY 10010.

Israeli feature film about the re-integration into normal life of a young woman widowed by the Six Day War.

"Soon There Will Be No More Me." Churchill Films, 662 N. Robertson Blvd., Los Angeles, CA 90069.

A young mother's feelings of fear and insecurity in the midst of death.

"Talking About Death With Children." Batesville Management Services, P.O. Drawer 90, Batesville, Indiana 47006.

Explains to children what death means, why it happens, what happens to the body and why we have a funeral.

"Those Who Mourn." Teleketics, 1229 S. Santee St., Los Angeles, CA 90015.

5 minute film of a woman's struggle to understand and accept the sudden death of her husband.

"To Die Today." University of Michigan, Audio Visual Education Center, 416 Fourth St., Ann Arbor, MI 48103.

Kübler-Ross presents the five emotional stages through which dying patients go.

"Understanding Death." Educational Perspectives Asso-

ciates, Box 213, DeKalb, IL 60115. 5 filmstrips.

Designed to help middle school children develop affectively as well as cognitively by exploring values and attitudes toward life and death.

"Where Is Dead?" Encyclopedia Britannica Educational Corporation, 425 North Michigan Ave., Chicago, IL 66061.

Response of a six year old child to the death of her brother.

"You See, I've Had a Life." Eccentric Circle Cinema Workshop, P.O. Box 4085, Greenwich, CT 06830.

Young boy's fight to deal with leukemia.

TEACHING HEBREW: INITIAL CONSIDERATIONS

by Yosi Gordon

ARE YOU SURE YOU *WANT* TO TEACH HEBREW?

We have all had the experience, as students and as teachers, of pouring over — or sitting through — Hebrew lessons, during which little or no learning takes place. Week in, week out, the same material (often the same page!), with no signs of progress. Year after year of the present tense, or of singulars and plurals, until — mercifully — along comes Bar/Bat Mitzvah and liberation. At that point, our students can recite intricate combinations of foreign-sounding syllables with the appropriate oriental chant, negotiate the choreography of the *bimah* and, when necessary, translate "Father comes, Mother comes" into Hebrew.

There *are* alternatives to trying to teach Hebrew as a *language*. Before you decide whether you really want to teach Hebrew, here are some options for consideration.

Sounding Hebrew

"Reading" means "translating written symbols into meaning." "Sounding" means "translating written symbols into sounds." When we say we are reading Hebrew, or teaching Hebrew reading, we usually mean we are teaching Hebrew sounding. (How quaint when parents say, "My child reads well but has trouble translating," as if half the task has already been accomplished!)

"Sounding" is not a noble skill. It is hard to imagine Rabbis Akiva, Meir and company sitting around the yeshiva and pouring over a text which reads: *ba, bi, beh, boo.*

But, sounding is a very necessary skill and holds an important place in the socializing of our students. It is not only the congregation, rabbi and parents preparing for the home *seder* who ask, "Why does little Stevey read (i.e., sound) so slowly?" If big Steve is someday to take his place as a congregant, able to participate in services and other rituals, he must know how to sound Hebrew. Otherwise, despite his philosopical sophistication, his profound sense of identity with *Am Yisrael* and his spiritual sensitivity, he will be lost, excluded, uninvolved in the most significant of Jewish communal-congregational activities: the religious service. The teaching of sounding will be dealt with later in this chapter.

Hebrew for Prayer

Hebrew for prayer is a few steps above sounding. Its goals include providing the learner with the tools for some experience of comprehension along with the ability to sound the Hebrew. It may even set as a goal the understanding, in Hebrew, of certain value concepts or central prayer words (*kadosh, baruch, hallel,* etc.). Behrman House's series *Baruch U-m'vorach* is designed to do exactly this.

Hebrew For Text Reading

If your school's main goal is to enable students to decipher ancient texts (Bible, *Siddur,* Rabbinic texts), then Melton is your system. The Melton Series of Hebrew materials, available through the Melton Foundation, 3080 Broadway, New York, NY 10027, is a meticulously developed program designed to prepare students to translate texts. It is probably the best prepared, best tested of all Hebrew programs. Remember, though: its goals are limited, and it requires better than average teaching from specially trained teachers in order to function optimally. It also requires a high level commitment from all involved parties (school boards, faculty, administrators, parents) to devote considerable time and effort, year after year, to this serious, demanding curriculum.

Hebrew To Help Us Find Mishpachat Doron

Audiolingual was the magic word in language instruction 20 years ago. *Sh'ma V'daber, Habet Ush'ma* and *B'yad Halashon* (the most scientific of the three) prepared students to order dinner, play soccer and find the Doron family in carefully memorized patterns of speech. Little Debbie can say an Israeli *"resh"!* Can the *mashiach* be far behind?

These materials have lost much of their popularity lately, and for several reasons. First of all, they become boring after the first lessons. They require numerous repetitions. Some of them require students to memorize dialogues as homework assignments, a very unmodern concept, alas. They deal with issues and topics which are of little concern to American synagogue-centered Jews (like naming the positions on a soccer team or finding the central bus station). Although students could repeat the dialogues, they could not personalize them. ("I can look for the home of the Doron family, but heaven help me if I should ever need to find the Goldberg's.") And, finally, they leave you high and dry: the series ended and the student had two or three more years of Hebrew school.

It Sounds Like Hebrew, It Looks Like Hebrew, But It's Really. . .

Ethics! *Mah Tov* is a charming series with some very substantial stories that deal with major ethical issues. Unfortunately, there seems to be little language-learning opportunity from the text. Hebrew, and Hebrew-teaching decisions, take a back seat to content. And the length and difficulty of the stories may convert your Hebrew class to a further chapter of *War and Peace*. The series is recommended, however, as supplementary reading.

To compensate for inadequacies in language instruction, the people who brought you *Mah Tov* came out with the Shmueli family series, a translation of a French textbook noted for its outstanding cartoons. But it takes more to create a good Hebrew text than a French translation. There is, of course, no logical development of language which is faithful to Hebrew structure. Even the pictures retain their French titles (hence the Introduction, which explains that the Shmuelis are a Jewish family living in France). Finally, this supplement to a Hebrew text which really teaches ethics contains many sexist stereotypes. *C'est la vie!*

Ulpan Hebrew

There is no such thing. An Ulpan means 30 hours/week of class time, 20 + hours/week homework, 6-12 months of study, a Hebrew-speaking environment and learn-Hebrew-or-starve motivation. Unless you can provide that, you cannot teach the "Ulpan Method." In fact, there is no "Ulpan method." Rather, there are long hours, no English and desperation. It works wonders, but not in your Hebrew school.

We Call It Ulpan, But It's Really Just Conversational Hebrew

A little bit of conversational Hebrew is good for several things:
1. Developing an interest and delight in the language, and also in Israel
2. Preparing students to go to Israel and have a few pleasant experiences
3. Providing an oral base for a complete language-learning experience which includes considerable reading, writing, grammar, etc.

But there is a danger. Few of us can provide the hours of instruction (1900 or so, according to Shlomoh Haramati) to enable our students to learn to express themselves in Hebrew. Consequently, a third year conversational Hebrew class sounds very much like a second year conversational Hebrew class, which in turn sounds like. . .

Hebrew For Literacy

For elementary students, this means the Lador, Oneg or other series, which teach Hebrew reading the "natural way," that is, by Hebrew reading. The stories are fairly good, but the Hebrew is hard, the selections are long and there is little systematic development of Hebrew skills. Vocabulary selection is usually determined solely by the story content, and especially difficult grammatical and syntactical structures are introduced at random and, often, unnecessarily. The same problem plagues the Israeli

Gesher series. Some of these books are appropriate for Day Schools, outstanding students or for excerpting as supplementary readers.

For Hebrew High School students, there is a very competent series, developed by Professor Arnold Band and the faculty of the Los Angeles Hebrew High: *Hebrew: A Language Course* (New York: Behrman House, 1982). It is systematic to a fault, contains some good, although longish, stories and some excellent grammar explanations and exercises, and — best of all — it can be taught fairly easily and can be individualized. But, it teaches only reading and understanding skills. Speaking goals must be dealt with separately by the resourceful teacher, or abandoned.

Maybe-It'll-Work-This-Time Hebrew

If you still want to teach Hebrew, the living language of the Jewish people, the language of its texts and literature, of its prayers and values, of its people in Israel and around the world, and if the above options are not to your liking, then you are ready for the rest of this chapter which is concerned with the how of teaching it.

HOW TO TEACH HEBREW

I know a student who could probably learn Hebrew by leaning on an Israeli phone book. I know a teacher who could probably teach Hebrew to a rock. For the rest of us, students and teachers, "how" is an important question. I regret that I cannot provide any easy formulas, nor can I suggest, at this time, a curriculum which works.[1] Rather, I will share some basic considerations which should increase your efficiency and efficacy in teaching Hebrew.

Time

Dr. Madeline Hunter calls time "the coin in education." That is what we have to spend in order to teach. Teaching Hebrew requires a lot of time. Unless you—and your school—are willing to devote a lot of time to teaching Hebrew, choose one of the above alternatives. It

is better to succeed small than to fail big. Some additional suggestions follow:

Start early. Can you open a program for first-graders? for kindergarteners? Explore all such opportunities.

Hours/week. Four. Better, five. Three, if necessary. No fewer, please.

Days/week. Do not consider teaching Hebrew once a week. If your Hebrew school is twice a week and children come on Sunday or Shabbat for other subjects, steal some time on that third day and add Hebrew. Open a four-day-a-week option for "accelerated" or "honors" or *"Chalutzim."* Add days.

Months/year. Summer classes? Winter vacation programs?

Additional activities. Drama. Hebrew sports program. *Shabbatonim.* Hebrew clubs. Summer camps. Hebrew recreational activities. Choirs. Biking. Camping. Swimming. Karate. Atari. *Ongei Shabbat.* Anything. (Ask your Rabbi to announce page numbers and stand-up-sit-down instructions at services in Hebrew.)

Year-to-year. Review the specific Hebrew skills (vocabulary, grammar, syntax, topics, oral-written skills, etc.) in your school. Pretest, test, post test. Much time is wasted in schools which don't coordinate the progression of Hebrew language skills from year to year, or in schools which arbitrarily determine what skills each grade should learn without evidence from testing and other diagnostic procedures. Build in reviews to reinforce the skills, but continue to grow at the rate the students can learn.

Minute-to-minute. Language learning rates differ so among students. I can think of no other subject which so demands 1)homogeneous classes (with adjustments made regularly) and 2) individualization. If you need to learn how to individualize your classes, consult your local experts (Jewish and non-Jewish) and read *Rx Improved Instruction,* by Dr. Madeline Hunter, TIP Publications, POB 514, El Segundo, CA 90245.

Years. A Hebrew school which stops at Bat/Bar Mitzvah is not a Hebrew school: it's a hospice. Until *"Abba ba"* becomes Agnon (or at least Chaim Pumpernickel), your students haven't learned enough Hebrew *not* to be insulted by the content of the stories. If your students, or enough of them, are going to continue into their

---

[1]I am currently directing the Capp Hebrew Curriculum Project, which is developing a complete four-year elementary Hebrew curriculum. Materials will not be available for several years.

high school years, teach them Hebrew. Otherwise select one of the options above. Consider a two-track system, if necessary. Don't promise them Hebrew in *Kitah Alef* and then send them packing after Bar/Bat Mitzvah with a shrug and a *"slicha."* It's not fair to them. If you can't teach them very much Hebrew in the elementary school (and you can't), make sure parents and children know that you have selected a less ambitious option. "Mrs. Schwartz, if you'd like Michael to learn Hebrew you'll have to prepare him for elementary *and* high school."

TEACHERS

Teachers must 1) know Hebrew, 2) know English, 3) know how to teach, 4) be *menschen,* 5) be committed to Hebrew, 6) cooperate with each other, 7) have a sense of humor, 8) like kids and enjoy helping them learn, and 9) have Jewish commitments beyond Berlitz-style language instruction (for Jews, Hebrew is a means to an end).

ENVIRONMENT

Pack your school with Hebrew:

Signs and posters	Services
Announcements	Dances
Books	Assemblies
Records	Activities
Contests	Titles (principal, library, etc.)
Songs	Plays
Films	Awards
Tapes	Jokes, stickers, labels,
Games	buttons, comics.
Teacher conversations	

Talk to your students in Hebrew. They will probably understand you, at least after a while. Praise them in Hebrew. Then, they'll certainly understand you. Scold them in Hebrew. They don't have to understand you.

Use natural Hebrew, in whole sentences, at normal speaking speed. Repeat (and repeat) if necessary. Don't talk in robot Hebrew ("Pencil, please."). Don't let kids wean you back to English. It's amazing how much they can more or less understand when they have to. (We converted our before school snack program to

Hebrew, and in five minutes every child in the school knew how to ask for chocolate chip cookies!)

Create needs. We all learn things we need to learn. Every time you create a need to learn, your students will learn Hebrew.

Use verbs, adjectives, adverbs, prepositions. We have a tendency to speak "noun-Hebrew" (I'm going to the *bet-shimush."* "When is *hafsakah?").* That's not Hebrew, as I learned from Professor Jonathan Paradise; that's Yiddish (i.e., nouns in Hebrew, everything else in the vernacular).

Recruit help. Get as many people as possible to speak, or in some way use, Hebrew as much as possible, at synagogue meetings, services, programs, JCC activities, sermons, on library bookplates, in bulletins, whatever. Start a movement, a campaign, a cause.

WHAT HEBREW TO TEACH

Not everything in Hebrew is worth learning. I spent many years learning to identify the parts of my body in Hebrew. ("This is my nose." "This is my ear.") *Nobody ever says that, except in Hebrew School!* It is useless, and time spent learning that is time wasted. As I have learned from Professor Dale Lange, language must be functional. It must perform the function of communication. If it communicates nothing, or nothing you'd like to communicate, it is pointless.

Therefore, begin by asking yourself: What do my students need to communicate (say, understand, write, respond to. . .)? Do they need to function with
"I need a pencil."
"Praised are You, Lord our God. . ."
"One who entrusts to another person an animal or utensils. . ."
"Hear, O Israel, . . . "
"If you will it, it is no dream."

So, you determine what communication is necessary (STEP ONE).

Then you determine what form the communication must take (STEP TWO). By this I mean, does the student have to speak, to answer, to read and understand, to "sound," to write, to respond in action? Teach the appropriate form. (Your students may need to learn how to read Rashi script; they will probably not need to learn how to write it.)

THE TEXTBOOK AND OTHER PLAGUES

Most beginning Hebrew textbooks are fairly adequate for *Kitah Alef. Dan V'Dina, Ivrit, Shalom Y'ladim, Hebrew and Heritage* (and all the other David Bridger materials) and most of the others do a pretty good job of beginning from scratch and teaching something. In several cases, there is no connection between the *Alef* and the *Bet* textbooks. (Did their authors assume that the students spend the intervening summer in an Ulpan?) Many books stop after *Bet*, probably because many Hebrew schools stop real Hebrew language instruction after *Kitah Bet*. You will probably do fairly well with any of these books for the first year or two. (Approach Israeli Hebrew texts with extreme caution. Some are written for Hebrew instruction in Israel, with appropriate pace and topic selection. Others are written as if the students really knew Hebrew, then forgot it and need to be reminded. This concept, Platonic, produces a Hebrew text which introduces dozens of new language patterns per page — frustrating and unteachable.)

Beginning with *Kitah Gimel*, language instruction becomes very difficult and texts become much worse. Some proceed much too quickly. Others ramble around with no direction. What is the teacher to do?

Some of our colleagues teach entirely from dittos which they prepare. It is a demanding solution; it makes continuity difficult (not only from grade-to-grade, but from day-to-day); it is often monotonous and unproductive. Others resort to other texts (oral-lingual, Bible texts, high school texts such as *Modern Hebrew,* even college texts) for these grades. I have found that *Modern Hebrew,* by Blumberg and Lewittes, is a helpful tool in these grades. Granted, it is heavily grammar oriented, its stories are out of date and its Hebrew is very peculiar. (It's New York Hebrew of the 1920's.) But it all depends on *what you do with it,* and that applies to any textbook for *Gimel* and *Daled* (or for *Alef* and *Bet,* for that matter).

What You Do With It

First: Read the unit to determine what it tries to teach, in terms of vocabulary, grammar, syntax, communication skills, topics, functions of communication (e.g., showing agreement: "I think so, too"/making requests: "Please tell me how to find the Doron family"/apologizing: "I'm sorry I set off the fire alarm.").

Second: You decide which of the items you would like your students to know, and how they should know them (be able to say them, understand them, write them. . .).

Third: Figure out what approaches and materials you will need in order to teach those items. The textbook will probably be only one of the materials. You supply the rest.

Fourth: Make your approaches and materials as functional as possible. Teach what your students need to know. If you want them to know a prayer, for example, create a need for knowing that prayer.

Fifth: Test, check up, diagnose, find out when your class has learned those items. Then, stop teaching them. Endless repetition doesn't teach. We don't learn what we hear overandoverandover. We learn what we need, what we can use. Create a need, a use, and provide sufficient repetition for it to be learned. Then stop teaching it and go on to something else. But, provide for occasional review/reinforcement of those items. (I use a diary of language items and check it as part of my lesson preparation to see which items need to "come around again.")

Sixth: Look for new ways of using familiar items or of recombining them. Students can learn to say more with less.

Seventh: Teach everything at least two ways. Some students learn through examples, others through explanations. Some learn by hearing, some by reading, some by speaking or by writing. Watch how each of your students learns and teach accordingly.

Eighth: Use games to get kids to do the same thing over and over again in order to have sufficient repetitions for mastery. Those enjoyable, ritualized, highly repetitive activities, which automatically provide "functionality" to your language instruction, are among our most effective language-teaching tools. For games:

1) "Translate" English games into Hebrew.

2) See any one of several collections of Hebrew games. (My favorite is *Hebrew Games,* Parts I and II, by Nachama Skolnik (Moskowitz), published by the

Union of American Hebrew Congregations as part of their Experimental Education Editions. Order through U.A.H.C. Publications Dept., 838 Fifth Avenue, New York, NY 10021.)

3) Hold a game sharing seminar for Hebrew teachers. Remember to test the games you use to see if they really teach anything.

HOW TO TEACH SOUNDING, OR DOWN WITH *BA BI BEH BOO*

The very best graduates of twelve years of Hebrew Day Schools probably cannot read the *Akdamut* with sufficient accuracy and speed to keep up with a *minyan* at full gallop. Since it is impossible to teach speed-sounding, let's see what *is* possible: Select the prayers and songs you want your students to be able to do pretty well. Then, do them — often, aloud, with a melody if at all possible. No one ever taught me the *Ashrey,* and I've probably never actually read it. But I know it and can recite it. I heard it, and later said it, every morning at Camp Ramah. That is the best way to learn how to

sound well enough, and fast enough, to participate in a service. (When students need to learn how to lead services, that is, to pronounce every word correctly, then they can practice the fine points of sounding.)

It is amazing how well students can learn to sound prayers by making group-sounding (or group-praying) a very regular activity. So, do not ask Sarah to claw her way through the *Sh'ma;* rather, have your class pray (or sing or recite) the *Sh'ma* together every day. For other practice, read, don't sound — i.e., read something that has meaning for the students, not obscure verses or nonsense syllables.

TEACH SOMETHING TERRIFIC!

Each student should feel that Hebrew provides him/her with an opportunity to enjoy something which would otherwise be inaccessible. Therefore, even at the earliest stages, teach something terrific: a wonderful epigram from *Pirke Avot,* a beautiful verse from *Tanach* or *Siddur,* a song or poem: something to remind them, although it's a lot of work, that it's really all worthwhile.

OF PRAYER AND PROCESS— ONE MODEL FOR TEACHING JEWISH PRAYER

by Stuart Kelman and Joel Lurie Grishaver

For more than ten years, each of us independently has been working on ways to teach Jewish prayer. About six years ago, each of us independently began an article which tried to correlate the "content" of the liturgy with the "process" of prayer: the "what" with the "how." At that time, an ongoing discussion between the two of us began. In this chapter, we hope to share the beginning of our tangible results.

Fear of Praying/Fears of Teaching Prayer

For some of us, there is something scary about teaching prayer. We tend to fear it more than most other areas in the Jewish curriculum. Some of that fear stems from our own insecurity regarding our "liturgical performance," and much of the fear anticipates our students' probable reaction to having to study prayer — boring! Yet, the prayers themselves are probably the most frequently taught piece of Jewish content. For years, they have been the classic battleground and training field for the skill of mechanical Hebrew reading. They are well known as places for identifying the roots of Hebrew verbs and they provide an endless supply of Hebrew one-liners for song leaders. We sing prayers. We read prayers. We go through prayers — but we rarely talk about praying. We discuss the tension between *Keva* (the fixed regimen of prayer) and *Kavanah* (prayer with intention)—but we don't get involved in what one actually does. We avoid the "how you do it," because we are either unsure ourselves or we are convinced that it is personal, "something you can't really talk about."

Our own insecurity with prayer is only part of the problem. There are some other difficulties:

1. Prayers as found in the *Siddur* are Hebrew literature—a genre often foreign to us. Frequently, we are forced to encounter them in translation, sometimes with "thee's" and "thou's," "whenceforths" and "harkens." Even for those of us fairly familiar with Hebrew, the prayers are a technical literature which conforms to formal and stylistic conventions. The literature is subtle. It is permeated with illusions, allusion and nuances, many of these drawn from Rabbinic literature (the *Talmud* and the *Midrash)* — also areas in which we may not feel particularly comfortable. Often, when we read the *Siddur,* we know that the text is doing something, but we aren't sure what.

2. Prayers talk about God. Sometimes, prayers even ask us to talk *to* God. And God is a problem for many modern individuals. There seems to be a direct connection between "God-concept" and "ability to pray." Both we and our students feel that we need a cosmic setting— a theological blueprint of what we are "actually doing" when we pray, before we can risk praying. The "try it—you might like it" popular mystical approach to prayer has lost some of its effectiveness in the face of the pragmatic hedonism of most "preppie" kids.

3. Prayer has "bad press." Prayers are used in "services." Most of our students have had negative (boring) experiences with services. When our students have had positive

worship experiences (usually in summer camps or youth programs), these are attributed to special people, or special places, and not to the process of praying. Meaningful prayer is seen as having nothing to do with real (or even weekly) life.

4. Prayer seems difficult. Most of the student texts are just not adequate. The secondary literature (which seems to be filled with endless Hebrew terms in transliteration) can be hard to master, especially without a good basic knowledge. Prayer seems like a hard thing to really learn, unless you grew up in a circle of people who actually pray regularly (and who seem to understand what they are saying).

5. Deep down, both teachers and students intuitively know that prayer is a process, not just a content area. At some point, though, we have to get past the structure, history and order of the prayers and into the process of praying. Because prayer seems to be a dynamic-intra-psychic-communicative-evocative-associative-*personal* process, we don't know how to teach it.

Ironically, the prayers themselves *do* teach us how to pray — once we learn how to read them. Reading them successfully has as much to do with an attitudinal awakening as it does with a series of fact and skill learnings. To understand this abstraction, consider the following analogy, a common occurrence in many family rooms throughout the country.

The parent is listening to Gershwin on the FM radio. Enter the child, a typical 12 to 14 year old. Disliking "classical music," the child puts a Led Zeppelin album on the turntable. The parent quickly complains about the noisy "disco" music. Neither has any insight into the other's music. The child is unable to distinguish between Bach and Gershwin — both are long pieces of orchestral music without any discernible melody. For the parent, both Billy Joel and Led Zeppelin present short, loud pieces of music which the child plays too loudly. These usually employ distorted guitars and a driving (annoying) electric bass. In facing the *Siddur,* we are like both parent and child. We lack the combination of technical insight and experiential enrichment to involve ourselves in the art form. We need to learn how to perceive the melody, the themes and variations, the jargon, the feeling and even the dance steps. We need to know the contextual setting of prayers, and

to add to our own experiences some moments of closeness to prayers and some moments when praying creates a sense of closeness.

In this chaper, we will 1) consider the liturgical material itself and make explicit the process of praying which it suggests, 2) look at one prescriptive model of providing students with both a cognitive background and an experiential resource for internalizing the liturgy, and 3) provide the teacher with realistic tools to comprehend #1 and #2.

TOWARD A WORKABLE MODEL OF JEWISH PRAYER

Most models of praying assume that a true prayer conforms to Newtonian physics — e.g., that "every action has an equal and opposite reaction." A "reaction," though, is not a reasonable expectation. Jewish worship is a mundane, ongoing process. Rather than seeking a single special moment, a "religious experience," a sudden insight into the "other," Jewish prayer attempts to create a regular community process through which the individual can evaluate and plan for *new* moments. Traditionally, the Jew prays three times a day, and uses the same basic text continually. The Jewish worship experience is rooted in the regular application of an intricate, multi-leveled framework of questions, images and symbols to each new day of living. Jews pray by gathering in groups and participating in a fixed process. Jewish worship is a structured attempt to evolve a community lifestyle and to evoke self-evaluation. It seeks both a sense of community and the development of the individual. In this way, it evolves—rather than reveals— a "sense of the holy."

The *Siddur* is a text which was designed for constant reuse. The Rabbis who shaped and crafted the *Siddur* didn't know the word "gestalt," but they did understand its impact. They didn't see the endless renditions of the liturgical cycle as merely a "holding action," a waiting for a time of need or for a moment of breakthrough or insight. Rather, they saw the daily passage through the regimen of prayer much the way a weight-lifter/body builder looks upon his/her endless exercise "reps," or the way a jogger justifies the continuous laps or the way a singer practices arpeggios. The effect of any single "training experience" is hard to identify, but the total impact of *all* "training experiences" is manifest in the present state of the person.

Philo, an ancient Jewish philosopher living in a Greek sphere of influence, used this image when he described the Jew as being an "athlete of virtue."[1] While he didn't specifically delineate the role of praying in the "ethical-athlete's" training, he does describe the Jewish lifestyle as one which is constantly in preparation for doing right (in classical terms: doing *mitzvot*).

Max Kadushin, a 20th century American Jewish scholar, did draw this connection. In *Worship and Ethics* he describes the constant ethical underpinning of the liturgy. He sees the regimen of the *Siddur* (as well as *brachot* such as *Birkat Hamazon)* as reinforcing and developing ethical insights and sensitivities.[2] He makes explicit the "training process" which Philo implies. Kadushin's work was the foundation of our own. We started with his insights into the pedagogic nature of the *Siddur* and then began exploring. We thought that if the prayer process was indeed a "learning experience," then perhaps the use of various learning models might help us to understand its nature. Ironically, or perhaps self-evidently, the most fruitful analogy to the process of prayer was a Rabbinic model of Jewish learning.

Paradise and Prayer

The Middle Eastern mind saw paradise as a rich, lush orchard. In many Semitic languages (including Hebrew) the root *PaRDaiS,* which means "orchard," also came to mean paradise. Jewish biblical commentators used the word *PaRDaiS* as the basis of a model of Torah study. They believed that studying the biblical text was in a way like modern archaeology; that to discover truth one must dig through layers. For them, each layer brought one deeper into the text and deeper into oneself. They defined these four layers as 1) *P'shat* - the literal/plain meaning of the text, 2) *Remez* - hints or allusions found in the text, especially about political events (in a future spiritual history), 3) *D'rash* - interpretations of the text (related to *Midrash)* and 4) *Sod* - secret or mystical meanings. The nature of these four can best be clarified through an example. First, we take half a biblical verse. This one comes from the story of Jacob's dream about

the ladder reaching from earth to heaven. It says:
"And behold the angels of God *ascending* and *descending* on it" (Genesis 28:12).

P'shat

It is hard to study *P'shat* — the plain meaning in English — because the translation has already told us what the words mean. The Hebrew text is far richer. The word *hiney* which was translated as "behold," could also have been rendered as "and here," "and there was" or even skipped. The word "*Malachim*" which was rended as "angels" could also have been translated as "messengers."

The text, however, contains a problem. It states that angels were *ascending* and *descending*. If we assume that angels begin in heaven and come to earth, the order seems backwards. To solve this problem in the *"P'shat"* of the text, the Rabbis moved through the other levels.

D'rash

D'rash is an explanation which is to be given within the context of other biblical material. Jacob was about to leave the land of Israel. What is happening is a changing of the guard. The Israel angels *ascend* and the diaspora angels *descend*. The moral: life in Israel is different from life elsewhere.

Remez

Remez is a hint of a future spiritual history. Each individual angel went up and then down. Each angel represented the rise and fall of earthly kingdoms. Specially Assyria, Babylonia, Rome and then the Messianic rule of David — which has not yet come. The moral: the future of the world is redemption through Israel.

Sod

Sod represents mystical insight. Like the angels, each of our spiritual ascents also contains descents. As we move up the ladder (toward union with the Deity), we will make progress and slip back, but the overall direction of our growth should be upward.

According to the Rabbis, a person did not have to choose between these explanations of the text. There was truth in each of them singly and in all of them collectively. A text has a *P'shat*, a *D'rash*, a *Remez* and a *Sod* — a PaRDaiS. There is literally a little piece of

[1]Hans Lewy, Alexander Altman, and Isaak Heinemann, *Three Jewish Philosophers* (Cleveland: World Publishing Co., 1960).
[2]Max Kadushin. *Worship and Ethics* (Chicago: Northwestern University Press, 1964).

heaven in every verse. Notice, however, that the learning wasn't necessarily linear. The reader could start anywhere and proceed everywhere. For the fullest understanding, though, all the levels needed to be touched individually and put together collectively.

Of the four layers of interpretation, *Sod* was the most difficult to reach, for *Sod* was found not *in* the text but *through* the text. *Sod* was the personal, private path of association: our version of what the prayers said to us at that moment. Collectively, like a jogger, the weight lifter, the singer, each experience served as preparation for the next.

The text, for the Rabbis, was not merely a listing of ethical precepts, but rather a complex puzzle which forced the reader to guess and compare, to associate and intuit, to ferret out the meaning(s). In making life a conscious, careful search for meaning, the medium mirrored the message. How the text was to be learned was a reflection of what the text had to teach. It is this process of study and learning which we believe defines a model for decoding the liturgy, and which ultimately establishes the vectors for Jewish worship.

TOWARD THE TEACHING OF PRAYING: DECODING AND ENCODING

Facility with the *Siddur* is only *one* prerequisite for successfully praying. If prayer is both a drawing together of previous Jewish learning and an interweaving of personal metaphors with traditional images, students of prayer must be able to "associate" on two levels: analytical and personal. In an analytical association, connections are made relative to specific contextual connections. In a personal association, an "emotional" free association is required in order to link images. To reach these two associative processes, we need to add a facility with the prayer book: a general Jewish literacy, a working "Judaism"- concept, and personal experiences which give emotional depth to concepts.

P'shat utilizes formal analysis. It concerns itself with the structure of the prayers. We want to know the format of each prayer and the sequence which all prayers follow. We are interested in the words which form the prayers. We are concerned with their meaning and the possible ambiguity in their meaning. The *P'shat* level is the development of basic competency at

using the *Siddur*. It is having the student reach the point where he/she can open the book, find the right place, know what's there, feel comfortable with what's there (including knowing the names of most of the parts and pieces), and be able to function as a participant in services (reading, chanting, doing the appropriate movements, etc.).

D'rash applies content analysis. It concerns itself with basic Jewish literacy. We have established that Jewish liturgy is a literature of allusion. *D'rash* provides the students with the background to recognize and appreciate the images which are referenced in the *Siddur*. That means that he/she can read "who by His word brings on the evening" and recognize it as a reference to the first story of creation; or when reading "God of Abraham, God of Isaac and God of Jacob", the student knows that the Patriarchs each had a unique relationship with God. *D'rash* provides the background to appreciate from where the prayers have emerged.

Remez uses conceptual analysis. It involves identifying and correlating the themes in the *Siddur*. We recognized the fact that Rabbinic "spiritual-history" underpins the structure of the liturgy, and that it emerges as we probe the prayers. In order to appreciate this, and formulate their own insights, students have to be able to weave the Jewish knowledge they have amassed into "Judaism" concepts. We are used to talking about "God-concepts," but these form only part of an understanding of being a Jew. To apply Jewish knowledge to real life (which is indeed one of the key functions of prayer), one has to have an understanding of key Jewish concepts. *Remez,* therefore, involves the study of Jewish thought and evolution of working "Judaism" concepts.

Sod is experiential. It is the process of connecting the conceptual to the actual. In *Remez,* biblical stories and Rabbinic legends have coalesced into "creation," "revelation," "redemption," "covenant," *"mitzvah,"* etc. The *Sod* level is where we move from the intellectual to the real. Prayer is concerned with human connection to the Divine. Part of the challenge is to demonstrate the experiential reality of the Divine. A quick example: Rabbi Lawrence Kushner reported the following interaction with a group of young students. He asked, "How many of you believe in God? He was shocked to find that the majority of the class didn't believe in God. He later asked the class, "How many of you have ever felt close to God?" The response was a classroom full of stories. While the concept of God was difficult, the experience of God was real.[3] In a secular society, the role of *Sod* is to conjure the Divine which is present in ordinary life, and to acknowledge its presence. It is the experience of being created, of connecting to revelation, of expecting redemption, etc. *Sod* is both the mystical level and the real connection of the prayer process.

While these four levels provide a background for praying, they don't guarantee that the learner will choose to apply them toward prayer. They are sort of a "praying readiness" process. While nothing will insure the production of students who readily gravitate to services, the combination of these four levels of insight, coupled with regular chances to participate in "good" services and the availability of appropriate adult and peer models, may give someone a chance to become a praying person. While the classroom can prepare a student to worship, the sanctuary is the place where the background and training coalesce into prayer. If you are teaching prayer, you must also provide settings for praying. Reciprocally, services are places to pray, the needs of the liturgy are complex enough to warrant classroom time.

To better understand this *PaRDaiS* model of praying and prayer instruction, let us examine a single prayer (*Ma Tovu*), reveal the layers of insight and then move into some instructional designs. *Ma Tovu* is an opening prayer or meditation traditionally said quietly as one enters a sanctuary. This prayer deals with the relationship between an individual and God. It explores the nature of Jewish prayer which takes place in specific locations, at fixed times and through a proscribed ritual.[4] Let's see how the prayer develops these themes. To begin, let's read the text of the prayer.

[3] Lawrence Kushner. "Holier Worlds Than This." *Keeping Posted*. Volume 25, No. 3. (N.Y.: UAHC, 1979.)

[4] We are grateful to Dr. Reuven Kimmelman of Brandeis University for his illuminating insights into the understanding of this prayer.

מַה־טֹּבוּ אֹהָלֶיךָ, יַעֲקֹב,
מִשְׁכְּנֹתֶיךָ, יִשְׂרָאֵל!
וַאֲנִי, בְּרֹב חַסְדְּךָ אָבֹא בֵיתֶךָ,
אֶשְׁתַּחֲוֶה אֶל־הֵיכַל קָדְשְׁךָ
בְּיִרְאָתֶךָ.
יְיָ, אָהַבְתִּי מְעוֹן בֵּיתֶךָ,
וּמְקוֹם מִשְׁכַּן כְּבוֹדֶךָ.
וַאֲנִי אֶשְׁתַּחֲוֶה וְאֶכְרָעָה,
אֶבְרְכָה לִפְנֵי־יְיָ עֹשִׂי.
וַאֲנִי תְפִלָּתִי לְךָ, יְיָ, עֵת רָצוֹן.
אֱלֹהִים, בְּרָב־חַסְדֶּךָ,
עֲנֵנִי בֶּאֱמֶת יִשְׁעֶךָ.

1. How goodly are your tents, Jacob,
   your dwelling place (Tabernacle), Israel.

   Numbers 24:5

2. As for *me*, through Your abundant kindness
   I will enter Your House (Temple)
   I will incline toward Your Holy Sanctuary
   (Temple) in awe of you.   Psalms 5:8

3. Lord, I love the refuge of Your House
   (Temple)
   and the place where Your glory dwells
   (Tabernacle).   Psalms 26:8

4. *I* will incline, and
   I will bow,
   I will kneel before the Lord my Maker.

   Psalms 95:6

5. May *my* prayer to You, Lord,
   be at a favorable time;
   God, in the abundance of Your kindness
   answer me with the truth of
   Your deliverance.   Psalms 69:14

The P'shat

1. *Ma Tovu* is made up of five biblical verses. Four of them are taken directly from the Bible, and the fifth is reworked (Psalm 95:6) from first person plural (we) to first person singular (I) to fit with the prayer's syntax. Four of the verses are in poetic-parallel, a literary device in which both halves of a sentence say the same thing in different words.

2. If we look at the way words are used and reused, we will learn something about the message of this prayer. The following terms are repeated:

Me-I-My (italics)	ואני	- 3 times
Lord	יי	- 3 times
Abundant kindness	ברב חסדך	- 2 times
I will incline	אשתחוה	- 2 times
House (Temple)	בית	- 2 times
Dwelling (Tabernacle)	משכן	- 2 times

This kind of word count can be a key to understanding a Hebrew text. In this case we learn the number of times the word ואני (Me-I-My) is used, equals the number of time the word יי The Lord is used. This helps to define the prayer, showing us that it deals with *My* relationship to *God*.

3. When we look at the nouns used by this prayer, we discover a second insight. Looking closely, we find a progression of nouns: tents, dwelling place, Your House and Your Holy Sanctuary. Each of these represents a specific place the Jewish people set aside for communicating with God. They are: The Tent of Meeting, The Tabernacle, and the Temple (twice). The repetition of משכן (Tabernacle) and ביתך (Temple) in the third line seems to reemphasize this progression.

4. Finally, if we look at the "active" verbs, we discover one more factor:

(a) I will enter	אבא
(b) I will incline	אשתחוה
(c) I will incline	אשתחוה
(d) I will bow	אכרעה
(e) I will kneel	אברכה
(f) (You) answer	ענני

The middle three verbs — incline, bow, kneel — describe three specific physical postures for worship, each a bit harder, lower and more complex. These three actions are introduced by a verb denoting entry תבא and a foreshadowing of the first gesture אשתחוה They are followed by the single verb which requests Divine rather than human action. All of these actions have been performed by *me,* except for the final request that *God* answer me. Thus the text describes worship as a progression of actions which become harder, deeper and more complex.

5. By examining segments of the prayer, we have seen that *Ma Tovu* concerns itself with 1) the relationship between God and an individual, 2) specific places of worship, and 3) the fixed process of worship. If we look at the whole prayer, we will see their interrelationship. Verse #1 is an external description of the place of worship. Verse #2 describes the entry into the place of worship. Verse #3 verbalizes the feelings generated by being in the place of worship. All of these are states of preparation. Verse #4 describes the threefold postures of prayer and culminates with "before the Lord my Maker." This is not a casual or distant description of God, but rather an acknowledgment of the most intimate and essential kind of relationship between God and people. The last verse has a shift in focus from I the subject to the impact of my feelings, perceptions and actions on God. In essence, I am asking God to move from being my Maker — a fact which has been accomplished — to becoming my Redeemer, a truth which yet needs to be revealed.

The D'rash

We have seen that this prayer is drawn from five biblical verses. To further understand their impact, we need to look at their context.

1. Numbers 24:5 - This verse is the culmination of the story of Balaam. It is the focal line in the blessing which he gives to Israel, rather than the curse which he intended. Dr. Reuven Kimmelman points out that this is an example of energy transformation: Balaam sets out to do one thing (curse) and ends up doing something different (blessing).

2. Psalm 5:8 - This Psalm is introduced as a "Psalm of David." It begins with the "prayer-relationship," but essentially focuses on God's desire for ethical actions — "For Thou dost bless the righteous" (verse 13).

3. Psalm 26:8 - This also is "of David." It begins "Judge me, O Lord" . . . "Examine me. . .Test my reins." The middle of this Psalm describes David's strivings for ethical action, and it ends: "Redeem me, and be gracious unto me." This Psalm echoes the concerns of the first, but adds the themes of judgment and redemption.

4. Psalm 95:6 - This Psalm is not specifically assigned to David. It begins with a general description of "praising the Lord," and then moves into 1) a description of God as creator, and 2) the historical relationship between God and Israel, particularly the conflicts in

the wilderness. This is the verse which was changed from plural to singular, and it makes no specific reference to a "place of worship."

5. Psalm 69:14 - This is also a "Psalm of David." It begins: "Save me. . ." and then lists a) the dangers which David feels surround him, and b) the remorse he feels for the evil he has done. The middle of the Psalm contains our verse — "let my prayer. . .answer me with the truth of your deliverance." It is followed with deliver me, answer me, draw my soul near, ransom me, etc. It then moves through repentance to a description of the establishment of God's Kingdom. The Psalm ends:

> For God will save Zion and build cities for Judah . . .
> The seed also of His servants shall inherit it;
> And they that love His name shall dwell therein.

When *Ma Tovu* was assembled, the Jewish people knew their sources via an oral tradition. Much the same way in which we identify a strand of a popular song and know the whole tune and lyrics, they could be given a single line of a Psalm and know its entirety. Thus, our searching the context of these verses merely reestablishes the initial impact of this composition. While it has a rhetorical meaning (that which we found in the *P'shat*), it also has a contextual meaning. We know that the prayer concerns itself with human relationship to God within the context of worship. To that concern we have added 1) ethical behavior, 2) Divine judgment, 3) a God of creation and of history, and 4) a God who will redeem, via 5) the process of repentance. In addition, we know that much of this prayer represents the personal artistry of King David. The more we know of his life and struggles, the more we can appreciate his statements of need and faith. Finally, we realize that the sources used to assemble this prayer overtly connect David and the "Sanctuary." We are thus drawn towards the story (II Chronicles 22:6-16) in which God refused to allow David to build the Temple because "you have spilled much blood on the earth before me." David is instructed that Temple building will be the task and honor of his son, whose name will mean peace — Solomon.

The Remez

Our entry into the *Remez* of a text comes via Rabbinic literature. That literature comes in two forms: *halachah* (legal material) and *aggadah* (exegetical and homiletic material). To understand the *Remez* of this prayer, we will need to look at the passage in terms of both of these categories.

1. We know that it is the Jewish custom to recite *Ma Tovu* as one enters a synagogue. The second line of *Ma Tovu* contains ten words and serves a particular function. Jewish superstition prohibits the counting of people by numbers, so counting was accomplished by reciting verses — matching words with objects. The second line of *Ma Tovu* became the formula through which the *minyan* was established. Thus while the prayer contextually connects the individual with God through personal prayer, it functionally connects the individual with the other members of the community.

2. Near the end of this prayer, the pray-er asks: "May *my* prayer to you, Lord, be at a favorable time." The notion of an appropriate time for prayer is an important Jewish concept. Jews have set time periods for worship, and the legal literature is extensively concerned with defining the parameters of favorable, or appropriate time.

3. This concept of acceptable worship time provides another connection. Balaam is the soothsayer who is employed to curse Israel and who finally issues the blessing which forms the first line of the *Ma Tovu*. In *Talmud, Berachot* 2b, the Rabbis suggest that even though Balaam was a non-Jew, his invocations could greatly influence God because he knew the proper times to pray.

4. *Ma Tovu* concerns itself with "places of worship." In the *P'shat* we recognized the progression from Tent of Meeting, to Tabernacle, to Temple. The Temple mount is an important location in Rabbinic "salvation history." In various *midrashim*[5] the Temple Mount is the center of the universe, the foundation stone of creation, the place where Adam was created, the corner of the Garden of Eden, the place where Noah sacrificed after the flood, the location where Abraham bound Isaac, the bottom of the ladder in Jacob's dream, the source of the Ten Commandments (where the stones came from), the

---

[5]Zev Vilnay. *Legends of Jerusalem* (Philadelphia: Jewish Publication Society, 1973).

place David bought for the Temple (because of the love demonstrated there by two brothers) and the spot from which the Messiah is to begin his campaign.

5. Jewish concepts of "holy space" are defined by the introduction God gives Moses at the burning bush: "Take off your shoes, because the ground on which you stand is holy ground" (Exodus 3:5). The legal literature sets down a whole number of conditions regarding the proper treatment of a place of worship (*Babylonian Talmud, Megillah* 29b). As one enters the sanctuary, the legal obligations of being in Temple come into play (head coverings, saying *Ma Tovu, minyan*, etc.). These activities set the tone and begin a process of association.

The Sod

Ma Tovu is a journey. It is a pilgrimage. That is the motif which has underpinned each of the previous layers. On the *P'shat* level we 1) moved through a series of verbs into a state of worship, and 2) followed a historical progression from the desert Tent of Meeting to our own sanctuary. In *D'rash* we recognized the "Davidic" connection and saw worship expanded to include a number of Jewish themes moving from creation to redemption. Following David's own struggle with faith and ethical living, we are

led into the dialogue with the Divine. In *Remez* these connections were made more explicit. From a *halachic* standpoint, a number of required physical tasks bring the intellectual process of the words into the real world — symbolic sanctuaries connect to real synagogues. We touch the *mezzuzah* upon leaving the house and quicken our pace as we come near the synagogue. In the *aggadah* the real synagogue is connected to historical events, both actual and yet to be actualized. In all of these there is a movement. The person praying follows the *Ma Tovu's* paths and matches the "guided imagery" with his/her own. Among the issues the individual must consider are:

1. The nature of "sanctuary." What is a holy/special place?

2. What is prayer? I am about to engage in a process which has a long historical tradition. How do I relate to it?

3. *Ma Tovu* is a prayer about relating to God in prayer. What is my sense of that relationship? Most of all, the person praying must define his/her own journey. As he/she enters the sanctuary and recites the words of *Ma Tovu,* the individual struggles with the meaning of entering the synagogue at that given moment of life.

The matrix below summarizes the layers of insight into the *Ma Tovu* prayer which have been revealed by using the PaRDaiS model:

P'SHAT	**D'RASH**
1. 5 Biblical verses: Num. 24:5, Ps. 5:8, 26:8, 95:6 and 69:14	1. Numbers 24:5 - Balaam's story
2. The progression of nouns: Tent, Tabernacle, house, Temple	2. Psalm 5:8 - Psalm of David, Ethics
3. The progression of verbs: enter, prostrate, bow, kneel, answer	3. Psalm 26:8 - Psalm of David, Judgment and Redemption
4. Prayer process - from external viewing to anticipating God's answer	4. Psalm 95:6 - God of creation, God of history
	5. Psalm 69:14 - Psalm of David, Redemption
	6. The David Saga - including the refusal to let him build the Temple.
REMEZ	**SOD**
1. *Ma Tovu* and *minyan*	1. Making a pilgrimage
2. Fixed time for worship	2. "Sanctuaries" - holy places
3. History of Temple Mount	3. "Holy times"
4. Regulations of holy space	4. Relationship with God/Prayer

PLANNING LESSONS

While all of these biblical-Rabbinic pyro-technics seem a little scholarly, they do provide us with a number of instructional possibilities. The above matrix shows the vast variety of knowledge, conceptualization and experience a student should have. All of these may not need to be covered by the "prayer" teacher. Some may come from earlier learning, some may come in later schooling and some may never be formally transmitted. That kind of decision is made by the teacher in concert with the school curriculum. What this concept matrix does show us is that there are a number of good starting places for getting into the *Ma Tovu*.

From *P'shat*, we can begin with the way words are used, and establish a) my relationship with God, b) the history of Jewish worship places, c) the physical component to praying, and d) the overall movement of the prayer. We can also start with the four basic places for Jewish prayer: The Tent, The Tabernacle, The Temple and the synagogue and compare the ways of worshiping in each.

From *D'rash* we can study two personalities: Balaam, a professional soothsayer who felt no concern over using his ability to pray successfully and King David, who was hypersensitive to his human weaknesses and used prayer to try to overcome them. From these "contexts," these biblical verses take on added life.

From *Remez* we can draw on the history of the Temple Mount, and see in that one location a connection between the act of prayer, and the process of history from creation through revelation to a final redemption. We can also examine the legal literature, finding out how required and prohibited actions shape spaces and times, generating certain kinds of processes within them.

From *Sod*, we can enter into the student's own quest. We can lead the student to define and connect with his/her own sense of pilgrimage, and use it to define sacred space, sacred time, prayer and the relationship between people and God.

What this means is that a number of possible lessons present themselves to us. From the standpoint of goal statements, the following are objectives that a person teaching the *Ma Tovu* (completely) should want his/her student to accomplish:

1. That the student can identify the basic patterns in the prayer. These include: a) the overall structure, b) the progression of nouns and verbs, c) the number of times certain words are used, and d) the change of perspective and movement.
2. That the student is familiar with the basic places and ways Jews have worshiped and feels some connection to them.
3. That students know the stories of Balaam and King David, and can see how the verses used in assembling this prayer (and perhaps the large literary sources from which they are drawn) reflect their personal struggle with the meaning of prayer.
4. That the students know some of the events which the *midrash* locates at the Temple Mount, and can explain why the Rabbis want to find that sense of connection between a place and world history.
5. That the students study some of the rules regarding behavior and entry into the synagogue and connect the actions to the text through the meaning/process they embody.
6. That the students explore their own view of holy space and time through a connection to the concept of pilgrimage/quest. (The current emphasis on "Dungeons and Dragons," *The Lord of the Rings* and the King Arthur legends should make this one easy. Quest is a popular notion among young people.)

From this point on the teacher should have no problem in developing lesson plans. Once an achievable set of goals for the lesson has been isolated, all a teacher needs to do is apply the whole menu of instructional devices and styles. All of the trade secrets, from ditto worksheets to multimedia, from role play to computer programs, can be applied. The hard part is in deciding which things about the prayers (the content) you will select to teach.

Starting With P'shat

In our presentation of the *Ma Tovu*, we demonstrated the sequential approach by which a teacher can, layer by layer, reveal the meanings of this prayer. The following represents other potential instructional sequences.

Starting With D'rash

The class spends several sessions studying the history of King David. They understand the basic struggles David has gone through in his life: his rise to power, the conflicts with Saul, his friendship with Jonathan, his marital problems, the struggles against Achitophel and Absalom, his desire to build a Temple. They know that he has high points and low points in his life: King and fugitive, lover and sinner, poet and participant in numerous power struggles. The students then sit down with 1) an outline of the major events in David's life, and 2) a number of verses from Psalms 69, 26 and 5. They are asked to try to determine what personal event David was thinking of when he wrote each verse. Here are several examples:

> Thou destroyest them that speak falsehood;
> The Lord abhorreth the man of blood and
>   deceit.
> But as for me, in the abundance of Your loving
>   kindness will I come into Thy house.
>
> (Psalm 5:7-8)

> Gather not my soul with sinners,
> Nor my life with men of blood.
>
> (Psalm 26:9)

> I am become a stranger to my brother,
> And an alien to my mother's children . . .
> Thou knowest my reproach, and my shame,
>   and my confusion:
> My adversaries are all before Thee.
>
> (Psalms 69:9 and 20)

As the students look at these verses, some may think the "evil person" in the first verse is Saul; others might think that it is Abner. Some may decide that David didn't want to be a sinner after Nathan reproached him for taking Bathsheba; others will think it was when God refused to let him build the Temple. Some might suggest that the third verse referred to the time when David hid from Saul. Others may argue that it was when Absalom drove him out of Jerusalem. The discussion will be intense. But more than deciding that a specific moment was behind each verse, the class (with the teacher's direction) can realize that the poetry which forms these Psalms (and consequently *Ma Tovu*) came from a real person (*davka*, a soldier, warrior, lover, King) and was generated out of real critical moments in his life.

In the next step, the students are asked to describe David's concept of prayer. Slowly a model emerges: 1) prayer can affect God, 2) praying can affect people, 3) *t'shuva* (repentance and real change) is possible, and 4) faith and praying make a difference in a person's life. Then the teacher can ask, "Did David really believe in 'all this stuff' or was he simply a King putting on a good show?" The argument will again be intense, but the class will probably

agree that 1) David really did listen to Nathan when confronted, and 2) he really did devote a lot of effort toward establishing a Temple.

In the following session the class stages a debate between Balaam who believes that anyone's prayers can work (if they pray at the right time and aren't against God's will) and David, who believes that people really have to be sincere. Finally, the teacher passes out a copy of *Ma Tovu*, and the class does the word counts and form analysis. They recognize the verses as coming from stories and texts they have already studied, and discover that the debate they had on the meaning of prayer is contained in this prayer. When they come to the prayer's text, it is already infused with meaning from their insights into David and Balaam.

Starting With Remez

In this classroom, the teacher has pushed back the desks and taped a 4' x 4' square in the middle of the floor. After the class has entered and commented on the square, the teacher asks them to imagine that this square is a piece of sidewalk. The teacher picks pairs of students, asks them to "meet on this square" and create any scene regardless of content. After the whole class has participated, the teacher begins to "mix and match" scenes, bringing characters and situations from one into another. In the course of fifteen minutes, the improvisations have been woven into a play. The teacher then asks the students to work in small groups and diagram the play. In sharing the diagrams and discussing them, the question is raised: "Is the location of the square important, or is it merely coincidental that all these things happened here?" As they begin to discuss this, the teacher clarifies by asking: "What thing *caused* all the other things in our story to happen?"

The teacher then shifts the focus, and asks the students to imagine that this square was the most important location in all of Jewish history. The teacher asks every student to pick a partner and act out, in the square, the event which makes the location important. As the students act out the scenes, the teacher lists them on the board. The list will include such items as receiving the Ten Commandments, Adam and Eve, crossing the Red Sea, etc. Looking at the list, the teacher asks which of them happened in the same place. Very few of them seem to have a geographic connection.

The teacher then passes out a page of texts which describe the various activities which took place on the Temple Mount. (If the class is in the right mood, the teacher may have them dramatize each of the events to make sure that all the students know what happened in each.) Then the teacher asks: "Why did the Rabbis want to have one spot connect so many events?" The class comes up with lots of answers: the ground is holy, they wanted the events to be connected, something else about the place connected the other events. The teacher establishes that all of these are correct, and then introduces the significance of the Temple in Jewish life. Among other things the teacher quotes, "For from Zion shall go forth the Law, and the word of the Lord from Jerusalem." Through a combination of lecture and discussion, the class learns that the Temple was a place which 1) unified the Jewish people, 2) connected the Jew to God, and 3) was the center of the Jew's becoming a "light to the nations." Then the question is asked: "So why connect the Temple to creation, Adam and Eve, Noah, the Messiah, etc.?" With the teacher's help, the class comes to understand the connection the Rabbis want to make between prayer and history. They also understand that the Rabbis believed that history had a direction.

When the teacher distributes the text of *Ma Tovu,* the class is able to find many connections between the events listed in the *midrash* and the things mentioned in the prayer. Once the class understands that this prayer is really the history of a relationship between God and people, and that the Temple is the place where the two regularly meet, someone is able to conclude that these events represent the major moments which shaped the relationship. Some one else might suggest: "It's like going to see grandparents you don't see all the time. On the way there, you remember lots of other visits — it helps you to get ready."

Starting from Sod

In this session, the teacher has asked the students to relax, close their eyes and concentrate:

Imagine that you can see a very special location. It is a place you have never been, but it is a place which feels wonderful. It is a place which is full of peace and beauty . . . it is a place which is hard to reach. Walk around the place, and get to know it.

The teacher pauses for a minute or so.

I want you to imagine that a number of things are hidden in this special spot. In this spot there is a secret message written just for you. In this spot there is a mirror which can let you know who you are, and who you can be. In this spot is a crystal ball which can answer many of your questions. In this spot is a clue to your past — something which belonged to your family for generations, but which has been lost for a long time. Hidden in this spot are things which can make you wiser, things which can make you rich, sayings which can make you feel connected, things which can help you to become happy. Look at all the things and find them hidden in this secret spot.

The teacher pauses after each of these sentences, and then waits for a minute after the last before going on.

This spot is a very special place, but it is hard to get to. There are many struggles and obstacles in getting there. Some people don't even really believe that this place exists. Imagine all the things you would have to do to come to this place, and find the special things which are hidden there.

The teacher has the students look around this special place, hear its sounds one more time (so as never to forget it) and then "wake up back in the classroom." Without letting them talk, the teacher asks the students to write a story about leading an expedition to their special place. After the stories are written, the group begins to share some of their adventures. As they do so, the teacher notes some of the key elements from each story on the blackboard.

Having gone through all of these stories, the teacher then asks the class to compare these stories to other stories they know. The class responds with various fantasy stories and fairy tales. The teacher establishes the idea that most people have dreams of a quest hidden inside of them.

The teacher explains that Jews have long had dreams of a return to the Temple — the place which held those kinds of treasures. The teacher then compares the list of things which could be found in this special place to things Jews expected to find in the Temple. The class then goes back and studies the layers of *P'shat, D'rash* and *Remez* and sees how each is a quest for the treasures which can be found in the Temple.

FINDING BACKGROUND MATERIAL ON PRAYER

There is no one volume which contains an adequate analysis of the prayers in the *Siddur*. While it would be simpler to study from one reference text, were that book to exist, you would probably miss some of the richness found in other sources. Our suggestions, therefore, should be taken as starting points only.

P'shat

Annotated *Siddurim* such as:

Hertz, Joseph. *The Authorized Daily Prayer Book.* N.Y.: Bloch, 1955.

Davis, Rabbi Avroham. *The Metsudah Siddur.* N.Y.: Metsudah Publications, 1981.

Other useful works:

Arzt, Max. *Justice and Mercy.* N.Y.: Holt, Rinehart and Winston, 1963.

Donin, Hayim Halevy. *To Pray As A Jew.* N.Y.: Basic Books, 1980.

Idelsohn, A.Z. *Jewish Liturgy.* N.Y.: Schocken, 1932.

Jacobson, B.S. *The Weekday Siddur.* Tel Aviv: Sinai, 1973.

D'rash

The best place to begin is the *Tanach* itself. Look up the quotations and establish the context. Probably the best and most easily accessible commentary is the one published by Soncino Press.

Remez

Bialik, C. And Rabinitzky, Y. *Sefer Haggadah.* Tel Aviv: Dvir, 1960.

Braude, William G. *The Midrash on Psalms.* New Haven: Yale University Press, 1959.

Ginzberg, Louis. *Legends of the Bible.* N.Y.: Simon and Schuster, 1956.

Klein, Isaac. *A Guide to Jewish Religious Practice.* N.Y.: Jewish Theological Seminary, 1979.

Kushner, Lawrence. *The Book of Letters.* N.Y.: Harper and Row, 1975.

Kushner, Lawrence. *The River of Light.* Chappaqua, New York: Rossel Books, 1981.

Kushner, Lawrence. *Honey From the Rock.* N.Y.: Harper and Row, 1975.

Midrash Rabbah. 5 Volumes. London, Soncino Press: 1959.

Mindel, Nisson. *As For Me, My People — A Commentary on the Daily Prayers.* N.Y.: Merkos L'inyonei Chinuch, 1972.

Montefiore, Claude and Loewe, H. *A Rabbinic Anthology.* London: Macmillan, 1938.

Munk, Elie. *The World of Prayer.* N.Y.: Feldheim, 1961.

Sod

Blasser, Elissa; Cutter, William; and Kadosh, Mary Ann. "Searching for Hametz." *Alternatives Magazine,* Winter, 1976.

Brown, George I. *Human Teaching for Human Learning.* N.Y.: Viking Press, 1971.

Brown, George I. *The Live Classroom.* N.Y.: Viking Press, 1975.

Reisman, Bernard. *The Jewish Experiential Book.* N.Y.: KTAV, 1979.

Waskow, Arthur I. *Godwrestling.* N.Y.: Schocken, 1978.

THE EPILOGUE

Our students are the products of visual rather than verbal imagery. Walt Disney has implanted within most of us the image of a mirror which can reflect back to us our deepest thoughts and aspirations. Via the "Wicked Witch of the West," we understand the workings of a crystal ball which can reveal happenings from other places. And, six dwarfs and a kid gave us the feeling that a map can lead us back and forth through our history. These fantasies have a very powerful reality.

The prayer book is indeed a mirror, a crystal ball and a map. Through it we can see reflections of our own thoughts and aspirations *(Sod)*, things happening at other places (our ethical responsibilities), lost civilizations *(D'rash)*, and a map which leads us from creation towards redemption *(Remez)*.

And what of the teacher? It would seem that to teach a prayer, a teacher must be a biblical scholar, a *Talmudic* expert, well versed in *midrash* and able to lead students safely into their own dreams and hopes. Teachers, however, can join the ranks of Merlin, Gandalf, Yoda and the Rabbis. None of those mentors had all the answers. If they had, there would have been no need for Arthur, Frodo and Bilbo, Luke

Skywalker and us. The teacher of prayers need only share a few secrets with his/her students: 1) that each student is a hero or heroine engaged in a struggle to let good overcome evil, to bring peace, prosperity, completion and redemption to creation, 2) that the *Siddur* is indeed a magical tool which can open many pathways within and between us, and 3) that there are ways to decode the *Siddur* and find its meanings, both private and communal. From these starting points, teachers and students can start their quest through the *Siddur* and beyond.

APPENDIX A

A TAXONOMY OF BEHAVIORAL OBJECTIVES FOR THE MASTERY OF JEWISH LITURGY

P'SHAT — Literal Meaning

Prayer Level:

1. That for each prayer in the service the learner can:
   A. State the name
   B. Describe the structure
   C. State the theme
   D. Translate
      1. From Hebrew to English
      2. From "English" to his/her own language
   E. Read-Sing-*Daven*- etc. (e.g., congregational participation)

Structural Level:

2. That the learner can:
   A. Identify the major sections of a service
   B. State which sections make up each service
   C. State the sequence of prayers in each section

D'RASH — Biblical Interpretation

Prayer Level:

3. That the learner can explain the denotative meanings of the images/metaphors of the prayers:
   A. Find and trace the biblical allusions
   B. Find and trace the historical background
4. That the learner can accept the Prayer-Theme as a Jewish category of significance:
   A. That the learner can organize and correlate material to the theme
   B. That the learner can correlate personal experiences to the theme

Structural Level:

5. That the learner can describe the structure of the service and:
   A. Trace the interaction of imagery between prayers
   B. Describe the "flow" of the structure of the service
      1. as a progression of images
      2. as a progression of themes

REMEZ — Clues/Salvation History

Prayer Level:

6. That the learner can explain the connotative meanings of the images/metaphors or the prayers:
   A. Find and trace the *midrashic* allusions
   B. Synthesize the *midrashic* allusions with the Prayer-Theme.

Structural Level:

7. That the learner can describe the structure of the service

   A. Trace the interaction of *midrashic* imagery between prayers
   B. Describe the "flow" of the structure of the service
      1. as a progression of *midrashic* images
      2. as a progression of *midrashic* themes

SOD — Secret/Internal/Meanings

8. That the learner can integrate learned material with personal experience
   A. That the learner can integrate his/her own symbol system into his/her perceptions of the liturgy and its structure.
   B. That the learner can integrate the structure and symbol system of the service into his/her own life and perception of reality.
9. That the learner can use the liturgy as a tool to shape, direct and evaluate his/her own actions, feelings, beliefs and lifestyle.

APPENDIX B

CONTENT ANALYSIS OF BASIC PRAYERS

THE PRAYERS	P'SHAT	D'RASH	REMEZ	SOD
BIRKOT HA-SHA-CHAR These are a string of "one-line" *brachot* which were originally designed to be said individually as one woke up each morning. They were later moved to part of the introductory ritual in the synagogue.	The following are the sequence of blessings and issues: (All present tense excepting #1.)	These Biblical verses are in some cases clear sources for these blessings, and in others merely image-linked.	This sequence of blessings is described in the *Talmud*, (*Brachot* 60b). Each blessing is connected to an action.	This series of blessings correlates the process of physically waking up to a spiritual awakening.
	1. rooster (or heart) power to distinguish	Job. 38:36	hearing rooster crow	
	2. not a heathen	Deuteronomy 10:19	(not in *Talmud*)	
	3. not a slave (or made me Israel)	Leviticus 25:55	(not in *Talmud*)	
	4. not a woman (or made me according to will)		(not in *Talmud*)	
	5. sight to blind	Psalm 146:9 / Lev. 19:14 Gen. 3:5	opening eyes	continued . . .
	6. frees prisoners	Psalm 146:7	stretches and sits up	
	7. clothes naked	Genesis 3:21	dressing	
	8. raises the bowed	Psalm 145:14/146:8	getting out of bed	
	9. spreads earth on the waters	Psalm 136:6	feet on ground	
	10. directs people's steps	Psalm 37:31	first steps	continued . . .
	11. all my needs		tying shoes	
	12. girds Israel with strength	Jeremiah 13 Psalm 65:7 / Job. 38:3	tying belt	
	13. crowns Israel with glory	*Pirke Avot* 2:1 / 4:1 Psalm 103:4 / Is. 49:3	covers head	
	14. strength to weary	Isaiah 40:28-31	(not in *Talmud*)	
	15. removes sleep from my eyes		washes face	

THE PRAYERS	P'SHAT	D'RASH	REMEZ	SOD
			Most of these can be sorted into Creation, Revelation (Ethics) and Redemption.	
P'SUKAI D'ZIMRA Verses of Song:	This is a string of biblical verses — essentially songs of praise — which are woven into an introduction to the morning service. It has an opening blessing (*Baruch She-Amar*), and a closing blessing (*Yish-ta-bach*). We will focus on 4 of the 15 prayers.			
1. *BARUCH SHE-AMAR* — This is the introductory *bracha*. It begins the first third of these "hymns."	This is a string of God names preceded by "*Baruch*," introducing a long blessing. 1. He who spoke and the world was	These diverse God names are drawn from diverse (and non-specific) biblical verses. The Bible expands on the idea of God's names: Exodus 3:1-5 (Burning Bush) Exodus 6:2-4 (History of God's names)	David creates Psalms: At midnight the strings of his harp, which were made of the gut of the ram sacrificed instead of Isaac, began to vibrate in the wind. David would awaken, study Torah and write Psalms. (*Ginzberg*, 545)	Personal associations: 1. Attributes of God 2. Role of names 3. Identity
	2. The do-er of creation.		"Why does Israel pray in this world without being heard? Because it doesn't know the Holy name of God. (*Midrash Psalms* 91)	
2. David's song - (I Chronicles 16:8ff)	3. He who says and does.			
	4. He who decrees and fulfills.		*Montefiore*: pp. 10-12 also, index note - 822	
3. *Hodu* - collection of verses	5. He who has mercy on the earth.		Notice structure - 1-6 Creation 3-8 Revelation 7-10 Redemption	Continued . . .
	6. He who has mercy on the creatures.			
4. Psalm 100	7. He who grants fair reward . . .			
	8. He who lives forever.			
	9. He who redeems . . .			
	10. He whose name is blessed.			
	The second half of this prayer is the long blessing. It contrasts two words: (a) *Hillul* and (b) *She-vach* - both of which are related to "praising."	Many biblical verses in Psalms. It may be good to fore-shadow the *Hallel* Psalms.	Rabbinic literature is full of images of the angels being involved in praising God . . . See *Montefiore* - p. 642	Associations with: 1. Praising 2. Learning from giving praise.

THE PRAYERS	P'SHAT	D'RASH	REMEZ	SOD
5. *ASHREI* - Psalm 145 The Psalm most frequently used in the liturgy. 6. Psalm 146 7. Psalm 147 8. Psalm 148 9. Psalm 149	Ashrei is made up of Psalm 145, with 2 verses (Psalm 84:5, 144:15) added at the beginning, and 1 verse (Psalm 115:8) added at the end. The Psalm is an acrostic—the sequence of verses are alphabetical (with the letter *Nun* missing). They are in poetic parallel. All the Psalms in this series begin and end with *Halleluyah* (excepting *Ashrei*) which only ends with it.	The structure of the prayer asks these three questions: 1. Why the two introductory verses? 2. Why is the *nun* missing? 3. Why is the verse added at the end? Part of the answer is to link *Halleluyah*. Also, notice the use of *Bless* - beginning, middle and end of piece. And, the word *all* - 10 times.	Importance of the Alphabet: *Ginzberg* - pp. 2 - 3 Ben Shahn - *Alphabet of Creation* Kushner - *Book of Letters* *Ashrei* in *Talmud - Ber.* 4b. *Midrash - Nun* is missing because it stands for *naphelah* - fallen (cf. Amos 5:2), but it is lifted up in the *Samach* verse.	Progressions, orders and sequences in our lives. Poetic parallel in our lives - two things which mean the same thing which happen differently. Exceptions from our orders. Lifting up the fallen - (*Tzedakah*, etc.) the needs and effects.
10. *Halleluyah* - Psalm 150 This is the last Psalm; it is also the last in this series of 6 Psalms.	This Psalm is built around the word *Hallelu* - praise. It appears 13 times. It appears 15 times when the last line is repeated (as is the custom).	This Psalm is present without modification. It is worth noting it's role as the culmination of the Book of Psalms. Look at how it echoes the previous 5 Psalms.	The number 13 is equated with the 13 articles of faith - by Maimonides. The *Zohar* identifies it with 13 attributes of God.	Use of music in praise - celebration. Non-verbal (instrumental praise). Relating to *all* life praising.
11. *Baruch Ha-Shem*... verses from: Psalms 89:53, 135:21 and 72:18-9 12. I Chron. 29:10-3 13. Nehemiah 9:6-11 14. Exodus 14:50-15:18	The repetition is attributed to it being the last verse of a biblical book.	The context of the Psalm is the Levitical rites in the Temple.	Investigation of the Temple ritual.	Personal articles of faith and attributes.
15. *Yishtabach*	This is the closing blessing in *P'sukai D'Zimra*. It is a short blessing. It contains a list of 15 verbs reflecting praise.	The Bible describes the Temple as having 15 steps. The Levites worked their way up the steps, singing one Psalm at each step.	The number 15 is associated with God, because (*Yud - Hey*) the core of Divine name (The Lord) adds up to 15. The *midrash* describes God's throne as having 15 steps - *Ginzberg*, **pp. 566-8 (Under parallel of Solomon's throne).**	Create your own list of 15 steps of ascent.

THE PRAYERS	P'SHAT	D'RASH	REMEZ	SOD
BARECHU The call to worship - *Brachah* which introduces the *Shema* and it's blessings.	Consists of two lines: A command to bless in the plural, followed by an individual statement of blessing.	Compare to Psalm 149:18 the next to last Psalm in *P'sukai D'Zimra*.	*Montefiore:* On "*Minyan*" - 97, 107 348 On "Blessing" - 375-8	Individual/community.

BIBLIOGRAPHY

The instructional materials listed below have been selected from a much larger and more complete bibliography of materials prepared by Diane Fishman Landau. These works were chosen because they are readily available and they are compatible with the model for teaching prayer outlined in this chapter.

Arian, Philip; and Eisenberg, Azriel. *The Story of the Prayer Book*. Connecticut: Prayer Book Press, 1968.

Barish, Shirley. "Encounter with Prayer." In *Six Kallot: Retreats for Jewish Settings*. Denver: Alternatives in Religious Education, Inc., 1978, pp. 69-91.

Bnei Akiba of North America. *Tochnit Gurim: Tefilot U'Brachot*, Unit 1. Bnei Akiba of North America, 1954.

Borovetz, Frances. *Hebrew Blessings Ditto Pak*. Denver: Alternatives in Religious Education, Inc., 1980.

Borovetz, Frances. *Hebrew Prayers Ditto Pak*. Denver: Alternatives in Religious Education, Inc., 1980.

Brown, Steven M. *Higher and Higher: Making Jewish Prayer Part of Us*. New York: United Synagogue of America, Department of Youth Activities, 1979.

Cone, Molly. *Hear O'Israel*. 4 books. New York: Union of American Hebrew Congregations, 1972. Book 1: *First I Say the Shema*. Book 2: *About Learning*. Book 3: *About Belonging*. Book 4: *About God*.

Davis, Ralph; Schoolman, Rabbi Leonard A.; and Syme, Rabbi Daniel B., editorial committee. *Why Pray?* Film-strip, cassette tape, and leader's guide (by Bennett F. Miller). New York: Union of American Hebrew Congregations, 1979.

Dorph, Gail Zaiman; and Kelman, Victoria Koltun. *Teaching Holidays/Mitzvot/Prayer. Level Alef. Volumes 1-6.* N.Y.: The Melton Research Center of the Jewish Theological Seminary of America, 1979. Prepublication edition. Section on prayer in Vol 2 - pp. 143-185.

Teaching Holidays/Mitzvot/Prayer for the second grade (nine-year olds). N.Y.: Melton Research Center, forthcoming.

Fields, Harvey J. *Bechol Lavavcha. With All Your Heart.* N.Y.: Union of American Hebrew Congregations, 1976.

Grishaver, Joel. *Shema is For Real: A Book on Prayer and Other Tangents, The Prayerbook Board Game Book.* Chicago: Olin-Sang-Ruby Institute, 1973.

Grishaver, Joel. *Teachers' Guide, Shema is For Real.* Chicago: Olin-Sang-Ruby Union Institute, 1974.

Jacobson, Rabbi Burt. *The Bar/Bat Mitzvah Program.* Oakland, California: Kehila, the Bay Area Community Synagogue Without Walls, 1979, 1980.

Jacobson, Rabbi Burt. *The Teaching of the Traditional Liturgy.* N.Y.: Melton Research Center, 1971.

Karp, Laura. *Students' Encounter Book for When A Jew Prays.* N.Y.: Behrman House, Inc., 1975.

Kelman, Stuart. *Prayer Transparencies.* Milwaukee: Arbit Books, 1982.

Keeping Posted, Vol. 22, No. 6. N.Y.: Union of American Hebrew Congregations, March 1977.

Medium. No. 17. Massachusetts: The Jewish Media Service, Spring 1978.

Response, Special Issue on Prayer. Vol. XIII, Nos. 1, 2, Fall-Winter, 1982.

Rossel, Karen Trager and Mason, Patrice Goldstein. *Hebrew Through Prayer, Book 1 and 2.* N.Y.: Behrman House, Inc., 1980.

Rossel Seymour. *When A Jew Prays.* N.Y.: Behrman House, Inc., 1973.

Segal, Seymour and Bamberger, David. *Teachers' Guides for When A Jew Prays.* A Conceptual Guide by Seymour Segal. A Functional Guide by David Bamberger. N.Y.: Behrman House, Inc., 1974.

Siegal, Richard; Strassfeld, Sharon and Strassfeld, Michael. *The Jewish Catalog.* Vol. 1-3. Philadelphia: The Jewish Publication Society, Vol. 1 - 1973, Vol. 2 - 1976, Vol. 3 - 1980. Index to all three volumes in Vol. 3.

ENCOURAGING MORAL DEVELOPMENT

Earl Schwartz

One Sunday morning, a few years back, I told a group of nine and ten year olds the famous story of how Hillel, unable to pay for his daily Torah lesson, listened to the lecture through a skylight *(Yoma 35b)*. I chose the story because I felt that Hillel's actions were a wonderful expression of devotion to *talmud Torah.* I assumed that Hillel's behavior could not help but evoke each listener's empathy. You can therefore imagine my surprise when on this particular morning the empathy I evoked was rather tepid. In fact, I soon found myself scrambling to defend Hillel against a volley of accusations. Instead of seeing Hillel as a model of piety, several students derided him as a cheat and a coward who had ripped off a lesson via the skylight. In their eyes Hillel was no better than someone who sneaks into a movie theater through the exit. I left class quite befuddled. How could I have so grossly miscalculated my students' reaction to the story?

About a year before giving this lesson on Hillel I had begun work on a dilemma-discussion moral development curriculum for use in Jewish schools. The curriculum is in large part based upon the research of Lawrence Kohlberg, a professor of education and social psychology at Harvard. Kohlberg's theory of moral development proposes that:

1. "... there is a natural sense of justice intuitively known by the child."[1]
2. "... moral judgement develops through

... (a) culturally universal invariant sequence of stages."[2]
3. "... the existence of moral stages ... provide(s) a universal or non-relative and non-arbitrary approach to moral education. They define the aim of moral education as that of stimulating movement to the next stage of moral development ... the process for doing this ... rests on having students discuss moral dilemmas in such a way that they confront the limits of their reasoning and that of their fellow students."[3]
4. "One important stimulus to moral development is. . . the sense of uncertainty which arises when one's easy judgements lead to contradiction or uncertainty when facing difficult decisions. A second stimulus is exposure to the next stage of reasoning above one's own."[4]

On the basis of these four principles Kohlberg maintains that moral development should be understood as a process whereby a person's moral judgement develops through a set series of stages. Each of these stages is typical of a particular period in one's overall maturation, but they are not strictly correlated with specific ranges of age. This is because moral development is also a learning process:

---

[1]Lawrence Kohlberg, "Education, Moral Development, and Faith," *Journal of Moral Education,* 4:5, January, 1975.

[2]Moshe M. Blatt and Lawrence Kohlberg, "The Effects of Classroom Moral Discussion Upon Children's Level of Moral Judgement," *Journal of Moral Education,* 4:129, February, 1975.

[3]Lawrence Kohlberg, "Education, Moral Development, and Faith," p. 9.

[4]Ibid.

one must acquire, stage by stage, ever more adequate structures of moral logic. Kohlberg's research suggests that this type of learning is achieved by the thoughtful consideration of moral dilemmas.

Through the first year of my curriculum's development I had yet to witness a dramatic confirmation of Kohlberg's findings. But in mulling over what might have been behind the lack of empathy for Hillel on the part of my class, it occurred to me that perhaps the confirmation I was looking for was now staring me in the face. The lesson on Hillel had, in fact, turned into a discussion of a moral dilemma, the question being: is simple egalitarianism always an adequate measure of justice? Perhaps I had expected of my students a moral judgement for which they were cognitively unprepared.

To test this hypothesis, the story about Hillel was transformed into a dilemma about a child who is confined to a wheelchair and is thus barred from attending school by *architectural* rather than financial barriers. I wanted to see if my class would empathize with such a child any more than they had with Hillel. Specifically, I asked the class whether money which had been set aside for use by the student body as a whole should be used to make the necessary architectural changes for this one new child. At first the discussion of this "new" story followed the same line of reasoning with which poor Hillel had been "done in," but at a crucial point in the discussion two concepts were introduced that turned the whole thing around.

First, one student was unable to maintain his argument against making the architectural changes when I asked him whether the child in the wheelchair had a *right* to attend the school. Immediately following this, another student wondered aloud whether the *brit* at Sinai, which mandated that *talmud Torah* be made available to *all* Jewish children, was more important than simple "fairness." The second child was actually struggling to apply the concept of rights to this dilemma. With this concept at their disposal several of the students began to see the dilemma in a very different light. Before the idea of rights was introduced, most of the students did not have the conceptual tools necessary to understand the virtue of Hillel's behavior. When these tools were provided, those who were prepared to do so quickly scampered up a step in moral judgement. At the end of the

discussion I was convinced that I had witnessed what Kohlberg's cognitive-developmental theory predicts: the development of moral judgement through guided exploration of a moral dilemma.

The Dilemma-Discussion Model In Traditional Jewish Sources

Examples of teaching ethical principles through discussion of moral dilemmas are found throughout Jewish literature. Rabbinic sources make frequent use of the dilemma-discussion model *(Baba Metzia* 1a, 60b; *Ketuvot* 17a). In the Torah such discussions often flow from a dilemma over which God and a prophet meet in dialogue. Abraham's attempt to save Sodom (Genesis 13), the case of the daughters of Zelophehad (Numbers 27, 36), and chapter four of the book of Jonah (note how it ends with a question) are all examples of this process.

In many of these dialogues the participants' lines of reasoning are quite explicit. In the discussion between God and Abraham about the fate of Sodom, for instance, Abraham uses a *kal va-homer* argument ("Will the Judge of all the earth not do justice?!") to secure God's commitment to spare the innocent. Another such discussion in which a *kal va-homer* argument plays a significant role comes in the wake of Miriam's bout with leprosy (Numbers 12). Here Miriam is punished with leprosy for showing disrespect towards her brother Moses. Moses, being the most humble of all people (Numbers 12:3), is *mohel al k'vodo* and thus prays for Miriam's immediate recovery. The Lord, however, suggests to Moses that if he were to be successful in his intercession it would seem as though Moses could be taunted with impunity. This, in turn, would undermine the just authority of both God and Moses. God nails down the point with a *kal va-homer* argument: if a similar act of disrespect towards a parent deserves punishment, how much more so when it is directed towards "My servant Moses" (Numbers 12:7, 8).

But the most dramatic and complete example of the dilemma-discussion method found in Jewish sources is the confrontation between Nathan and David in II Samuel, chapter 12. Here we have it all — an actual dilemma (David murders Uriah and takes Bathsheba as his wife) transformed into a hypothetical problem (the poor man and his lamb), an initial reaction to the dilemma (David's exclamation: "Someone who would do that deserves death!"), guidance from a morally superior source (Nathan's reply: "You are that man!") and moral advancement (David's admission: "I have sinned against the Lord.").

Three Possible Problems

We have seen how the dilemma-discussion model is frequently found in the classic Jewish sources, but three important questions remain to be considered before the method can be prescribed for use in our schools:

1. Does the dilemma-discussion method threaten the norm-setting authority of the traditional sources?
2. To what extent do the stages of moral development which Kohlberg has derived from his cross-cultural research correspond with a classic Jewish hierarchy of values?
3. Does this method fail to connect *knowing* what is right with *doing* what is right?

Let us consider item #1 first. Does the dilemma-discussion method threaten the norm-setting authority of the traditional sources?

In this regard, Saadia Gaon commented, ". . . we inquire and speculate in matters of our religion for two reasons: 1) in order that we may actualize (*bi-l-fi'l* in Arabic) what we know in the way of imparted knowledge from the prophets of God; 2) in order that we may be able to refute those who attack us on matters connected with our religion. For our Lord (be He blessed and exalted) instructed us in everything that we require in the way of religion, through the intermediacy of prophets . . . . He also informed us that by speculation and inquiry we shall attain to certainty on every point in accordance with the truth revealed through the words of His messenger."[5]

Saadia presages modern cognitivists like Kohlberg when he maintains that a concept is not fully "actualized" unless it is rationally integrated into one's existing thought structure. He can therefore confidently assert that teachers of Torah have nothing to fear from rational inquiry. On the contrary, the speculations that pass between teacher and student are the heartbeat of the living Torah, as in the Rabbinic

dictum "Even what an advanced student points out to his teacher sometime in the future has already been told to Moses at Sinai."[6]

The central element of each unit of my moral development curriculum is a dilemma story, but each unit also includes a collection of references from traditional sources which touch upon the particular value concept at stake in the dilemma. These traditional sources are not meant to be used simultaneously with the dilemma-discussion portion of the unit, as this might cut short the process of inquiry which we seek to encourage. Rather, the sources are meant to be used by teachers at some time after the initial discussion to guide and reinforce the students' own judgement. The curriculm *does* presuppose a set hierarchy of Jewish values (as is expressed in the traditional sources), but is built on the assumption that it is preferable for students to develop an understanding of the function and need for these values (in Saadia's terms, to "actualize" them) rather than simply to present Jewish values as a "bag of virtues."[7]

Point #2 deals with the extent to which the stages of moral development which Kohlberg has derived from his cross-cultural research correspond with a classic Jewish hierarchy of values.

On the next page are Kolberg's six stages of moral reasoning. Note that each stage has a distinct cognitive basis for moral judgements. Following Kohlberg's stages is a selection from Maimonides' *Mishnah Commentary*. Here, too, we have a series of cognitive-developmental stages, with each stage characterized by a particular type of rationale for doing *mitzvot*. In comparing these two sets of stages we see that Maimonides and Kohlberg agree that:

1. Reasoning is an essential part of moral behavior.
2. Human beings pass through stages of moral development.
3. There is *some* correspondence between *age* and *stage*.
4. The thrust of moral development is *from* physical rewards, *through* "good roles" *to* principled behavior.

(Continued on page 137)

---

[5]Saadia Gaon, introduction to *Emunot V'Deot.*

[6]*Jerusalem Talmud, Peah* 2:6

[7]"Bag of virtues" is Kohlberg's term for the inculcation of a given set of arbitrarily chosen, non-developmentally structured values.

Kohlberg's Six Stages of Moral Reasoning[8]
TABLE 1
Classification of Moral Judgement into Levels and Stages of Development

Levels	Basis of Moral Judgement	Stages of Development
I	Moral value resides in external, quasi-physical happenings, in bad acts, or in quasi-physical needs rather than in persons and standards.	Stage 1: Obedience and punishment orientation. Egocentric deference to superior power or prestige, or a trouble-avoiding set. Objective responsibility. Stage 2: Naively egoistic orientation. Right action is that instrumentally satisfying the self's needs and occasionally others'. Awareness of relativism of value to each actor's needs and perspective. Naive egalitarianism and orientation to exchange and reciprocity.
II	Moral value resides in performing good or right roles, in maintaining the conventional order and the expectancies of others.	Stage 3: Good-boy orientation. Orientation to approval and to pleasing and helping others. Conformity to stereotypical images of majority or natural role behaviour, and judgment by intentions. Stage 4: Authority and social-order maintaining orientation. Orientation to 'doing duty' and to showing respect for authority and maintaining the given social order for its own sake. Regard for earned expectations of others.
III	Moral value resides in conformity by the self to shared or shareable standards, rights or duties.	Stage 5: Contractual legalistic orientation. Recognition of an arbitrary element or starting point in rules or expectations for the sake of agreement. Duty defined in terms of contract, general avoidance of violation of the will or rights of others, and majority will and welfare. Stage 6: Conscience or principle orientation. Orientation not only to actually ordained social rules but to principles of choice involving appeal to logical universality and consistency. Orientation to conscience as a directing agent and to mutually respect and trust.

Cognitive - Developmental Stages in Maimonides[9]

Imagine a child who is brought to a teacher to teach him Torah. This is actually the most important element in his development but because he is young and intellectually weak he doesn't understand its value and how it will contribute to his development. Therefore, the teacher (who is more developed than he) is forced to motivate him to study through things which he does find desirable, as befits his young age. So he [the teacher] says, "Read, and I'll give you some nuts and dates, and I'll give you a little honey," and for this he reads and makes an effort — not for the sake of the reading itself, because he doesn't appreciate its value, but rather, so that he can get the food. Eating these sweets is more valuable to him than reading, and certainly much superior to it, so he considers studying a burdensome chore which he's willing to put up with in order to get the desired result: a nut or a little honey.

[8]Lawrence Kohlberg, "Education, Moral Development and Faith," *Journal of Moral Education,* January, 1975, pg. 7.

[9]*Mishnah Commentary, Perek Helek.*

When he grows and his intellect becomes stronger and he thus loses interest in the thing which had previously been important to him and is no longer obsessed with it, you have to motivate him through something that he *does* find desirable. So his teacher says to him, "Read, and I'll get you some nice shoes or some attractive clothes," and for this he'll try to read — not for the sake of the study itself, but for the clothing, which is more important to him than the Torah, and which is therefore his reason for reading.

When he's more intellectually developed he'll come to think lightly of this as well and will then set his heart on something superior to it, and thus his teacher will say, "Learn this passage or chapter and I will give you a dinar or two," and for that he'll read and make the effort — to get the money. That money is more important to him than the study, because the purpose of studying is to get the money that was promised to him for it.

When he becomes quite knowledgeable and he doesn't think much of this (the money) because he knows that it's really of little value, he will desire something more worthwhile, and so his teacher will say to him, "Learn this so that you can become a head of the community and a judge. People will respect you and stand up when you go by, like so and so." So he'll read and make the effort, so that he might reach this rank. His purpose will be to gain respect and praise from others.

But all of this is unbecoming . . . our sages have warned us that one should not have some ulterior motive in serving God and doing a *mitzvah* . . . . Antigonos of Socho said, "Don't be like servants who serve the master so that they might receive a reward, but rather, like servants who serve the master even though they don't receive a reward." What I mean to say is that one should believe the truth for the sake of its truth, and this is what is called "service out of love."

(Continued from page 135)

Maimonides is only one authority on the matter, but he is an exceedingly important one. The striking similarity between these two taxonomies suggests that Kohlberg's hierarchy of values is essentially compatible with a classic Jewish value structure.

Item #3 above has to do with whether or not the dilemma-discussion method fails to connect knowing what is right with doing what is right. In an address to the National Catholic Education Association in 1975, Kohlberg made the rather daring assertion that the gap between having moral principles and acting upon them is bridged by "faith." The fact that people who had reached the highest stage of moral development also tended to be people who were "deeply religious" led him to concur with James Fowler's hypothesis that there exists a series of "faith stages" running roughly parallel to his own set of moral stages. Kohlberg concluded that these two sets of stages complement one another: "Moral principles . . . do not require faith for their formulation or for their justification. In some sense, however, to ultimately live up to moral principles requires faith. For this reason, we believe, the ultimate exemplars of stage 6 morality also appear to be men of faith."[10]

This formulation of faith, as that which empowers us to act on our principles, is very close to the biblical notion of *emunah*. Here, "faith" is not the substance of our values, but rather, the state of mind and spirit that allows for their fulfillment, developing parallel to the values we may hold at any given stage. A teacher of moral principles must therefore not only be concerned with a student's *cognitive* moral development, but must also nourish that student's existential sense of *emunah*. The teacher of Torah should strive to be a model of faithfulness to persons and principles: *ne'eman*, as was Moses *our* teacher. In this way we may help to enlarge our students' range of *emunah*.

The paradigm, then, is: *talmud + emunah* ⟶ *ma'aseh* (learning + faith lead to deeds). Which brings to mind the famous *baraita*: "When Rabbi Tarfon and the sages were dining in the upper chamber of the house of Nitzah in Lydda, this question was asked of them: 'What is greater, study or practice?' Rabbi Tarfon answered, 'Practice is greater.' Rabbi Akiba answered, 'Study is greater.' Then all the sages said, 'Study is greater because study leads to practice.'"[11]

[10]Lawrence Kohlberg, "Education, Moral Development and Faith," *Journal of Moral Education* 4 (January 1975) :14.

[11]*Kiddushin,* 40b.

How to Choose or Compose a Dilemma Story

Kohlberg's taxonomy identifies six basic stages of moral development. Each stage is characterized by a particular sort of moral reasoning, and movement through these stages is understood as both a maturational and a learning process. In stage one, for instance, moral judgements tend to be made on the basis of obedience vs. punishment, whereas in stage two they are oriented towards "satisfying the self's needs."

This taxonomy is often misunderstood as describing types of people. Not so. Kohlberg's stages describe moral premises and lines of reasoning, not types of people. A second common misunderstanding is the assumption that a person's moral reasoning must fit into precisely one stage at any given time. In fact, Kohlberg's findings tend to suggest that one's moral judgement is a *composite* of *previous, pre-dominant* and *anticipated* stages.

Knowing this, then, Kohlberg's categorization of types of moral reasoning is educationally valuable to the extent that it suggests what type of reasoning a given student will find most developmentally challenging. The taxonomy helps teachers ask the questions which are within "walking distance" of the students' present cognitive structure. You can parachute a stage 5 line of reasoning into a stage 2 argument, but it will leave no permanent structural tracks for the student to trace back to stage 5. Moral challenges are most effective when they are "local," i.e., from the next highest stage, and the taxonomy can serve as a road map in this regard.

From ages seven through fourteen most children reason in ways which are characteristic of the middle stages: 2, 3 and 4 (5 and 6 are mostly post-adolescent stages; stage 1 is typical of early childhood). There are formal tests available for ascertaining levels of moral reasoning, but informed observations of a few preliminary dilemma-discussions should give a teacher a very good sense of the class members' predominant stages of reasoning. With this information teachers can then decide which sorts of dilemmas are most appropriate for their classes. For instance, a dilemma which simply poses the question of whether pure accidents and intentional acts are morally equal will not be developmentally challenging for a child who usually reasons at stage 4, since a moral appreciation of intentionality is achieved at

stage 3. Likewise, the use of a dilemma which can *only* be understood as centering on a conflict between contract and conscience would be developmentally premature, and therefore ineffective, for students who are most at home in a stage 3 values structure.

Dilemma stories can be obtained from a variety of sources. On occasion Kohlberg has used selections from the Bible. Other researchers have taken stories from basal readers and literature texts. Sets of dilemmas have been published which are specifically designed for use as part of a moral development curriculum. Kohlberg has helped to produce one such set of dilemmas in the form of filmstrips (see Bibliography).

You may also choose to compose your own dilemmas. Writing your own dilemmas allows you to tailor the stories to the specific needs and experiences of your class. I have already mentioned how the story of Hillel was transformed into a dilemma about a child in a wheelchair. That dilemma is now part of a unit in my moral development curriculum.

Whether you choose to use dilemmas which have been written by others or decide to compose your own, you may find the following suggestions helpful:

1. Try to avoid characterizations which the students might understand stereotypically. Characters engaged in questionable activities should not be gratuitously stigmatized. Once, in the course of evaluating a dilemma that I had written, the reviewer noticed that I had managed to choose Teutonic names for every dubious character in the story, names which might sound particularly harsh to Jewish ears. One researcher who used filmstrips to present her dilemmas found that a particular group of students were seriously distracted from the actual dilemma by the color of one of the characters (although this, of course, is a moral dilemma in its own right).

2. Try to avoid characterizations which strongly suggest individuals with whom the students are personally acquainted. *Recognizing* a character makes it much more difficult to be objective about that character's role in the dilemma.

3. A well crafted narrative makes for an easier presentation of the dilemma. Too many extraneous details can be distracting. Unless such details are an integral part of the story, or the material is also being

considered from a literary point of view, it is probably best to skip them.

4. The dilemma should end with a clear and relatively specific question concerning one of the character's actions, e.g., "Should David take the money?", "Did Sandra do the right thing?", etc.

Leading a Discussion of a Dilemma

Earlier it was stated that it is preferable for a class which is discussing a moral dilemma to be made up of members who are *not* all at the exact same level of moral reasoning. This is because exposure to reasoning one step higher than one's own is a crucial element in the development of moral judgement. If a few articulate class members come up with a solution to a dilemma which is one step above the position of the majority, the discussion will contain the type of cognitive tension which Kohlberg has identified as a highly significant factor in moral development. Thus, if you find that your students all tend to employ the same line of reasoning in solving a particular dilemma it becomes *your* responsibility to introduce this tension into the discussion. It is clearly preferable that this process be the product of differences between peers, but when students are all in agreement, the task of suggesting a higher stage solution to the dilemma falls to the teacher. However, we should be careful in this regard not simply to bulldoze the discussion towards a higher stage solution. The dilemma-discussion method emphasizes growth in reasoning and this takes time and tact. It is important that a dilemma be looked at from many different angles so that no one leaps to artificial, unreasoned solutions. During this process of fully sizing up the dilemma there should be adequate opportunity for the teacher to hint at, probe for, or, as a last resort, suggest a higher stage solution. The first and most important principle in the procedure is simply to challenge every conclusion with "Why?" — *mai tama?*

One other important point about dilemma-discussions: it's very easy to get sidetracked. One suggestion I have in this regard is that you may sometimes wish to provide your students with a limited number of solutions to the dilemma. This might seem to be an unwarranted restriction on the free exercise of their reasoning skills, but it can help to prevent them from inventing ways of slipping out of the dilemma without really confronting the prob-lem. Try to provide at least one choice which is typical of the stage of reasoning of the majority of your students and one choice which is typical of the stage that comes after that one.

Evaluation of a Dilemma-Discussion Unit

In evaluating a dilemma-discussion moral development unit, keep in mind that the focal point of the approach is the development of moral reasoning. This means that it is not the students' immediate expression of appreciation for a particular value which validates the approach but, rather, long-term development in the way students think about moral questions. This sort of development can only be spotted in the context of subsequent discussions: traditional sources, whether biblical, *aggadic* or *halachic,* can be very useful in this regard. A discussion of a point of *halachah* which is related to a previous dilemma may provide the teacher with a sense of how well students have integrated the new moral schema into their own thought structures. For instance, an important stage 3 concept is "intentionality." Following up a dilemma on intentionality with a discussion of the Rabbinic dictum: *"Mitzvot* must be intended" *(Berachot 13a),* may give a teacher a good idea of how deeply the dilemma has "sunk in." Remember, however, that this type of evaluation will be most revealing if the passage of several intervening lessons obscures the connection between the initial dilemma and the follow-up discussion.

Summary

Moral education is not simply another item on the already cluttered agenda of Jewish education — it is of its essence. Our values define us as a people: "Anyone who has compassion upon creatures is certainly a descendant of Abraham our father, and anyone who does not have compassion upon creatures is certainly not a descendant of Abraham our father."[12]

Lawrence Kohlberg's work has been the subject of an enormous amount of criticism. His theory of developmental stages has been attacked as inflexible and arbitrary, but the fact that both the form and content of the approach is sound from a Jewish point of view renders much of this criticism irrelevant to Jewish education. It seems clear that discussions of dilemmas, in and of themselves, cannot trans-

---

[12]*Betzah* 32b.

form people into paradigms of virtue. Even after acquiring a rational appreciation of a certain value, a person must be sustained by "good faith" if he/she is to act in accord with that understanding. This is especially the case when there are strong influences to act to the contrary. But the need for *emunah* does not cancel out the need for understanding. In a *talmid chacham, emunah* and *havanah* (understanding) work hand in hand.

APPENDIX

The following is the dilemma which was composed as a result of the criticism by my students' of Hillel's "eavesdropping" on a Torah lesson through a skylight. Also included is a section on how to use the dilemma.

Dilemma:

The Talmud Torah is run on a budget. This means that each year a certain amount of money is available for operating the school. The Talmud Torah can spend only as much money as is in the budget.

In the spring the Board of Directors meets to decide on a budget for the coming year. One spring the Board finds that it will be able to meet all expected costs for the following year and still have a considerable amount of money left over. The Board decides to poll the student body on what they would most like to see done with the extra money.

*At this point solicit a few suggestions from the class as to what **they** would want done for the school with surplus funds. Have the class choose the suggestion they like best. The class' choice can then stand for the result of the "poll."*

The Board of Directors decides that *(whatever the class has chosen)* is a worthwhile use of the extra money, and directs the appropriate committee to go ahead with its use for that purpose.

Over the summer Susan signs up to attend the Talmud Torah. Susan's legs are paralyzed and she can only get around by using a wheelchair. She's a proud child who likes to do things for herself, but this sometimes requires special equipment — ramps or elevators instead of steps, support railings in the bathroom, a desk that can fit her wheelchair, etc. Until this year Susan had been studying with a private tutor, hired by her parents, but she now wants to attend Talmud Torah classes like everyone else.

At its summer meeting the Board of Directors is informed of Susan's application. The question is raised as to how the Talmud Torah could pay for special equipment for Susan, since the coming year's budget had already been allocated. At this point the Board member who was overseeing the "extra money" for _____ states that it had not yet been spent and was still in the bank. Perhaps this money could be used to make the accommodations for Susan. Another Board member responds: But is it right to deprive all of the other students of something which is valuable to the school for the benefit of one child? The Board decides to poll the students again.

Here's the question they asked:

A child has applied to the Talmud Torah who is confined to a wheelchair. If she is to attend classes here several items must be purchased to meet her special needs. It has been suggested that the money which you had decided should go for _____ could be used to make these purchases. Do you think this money should be used for this new purpose?

Poll the class on this new question.

Discuss their respective positions on the issue.

Re-poll the class at the end of the period to see if anyone's position has changed, and if so, why.

Suggested Procedure:

I. Read the dilemma-story to the class. Follow the instructions in italics as each comes up in the story.

II. During the discussion at the end of the story listen for an implicit or explicit suggestion that Susan has "rights." If the students don't bring it up themselves you might want to say something like: "Does Susan have a right to come to Talmud Torah? If so, what are the consequences of that right?"

III. Interject the following "what-ifs" into the discussion:

A) What if Susan's parents could themselves pay for the necessary adaptations but are not willing to do so?

B) What if no other children (unless they were also confined to a wheelchair) would be allowed to use Susan's special equipment (the elevator, for example)?

BIBLIOGRAPHY

Fowler, James W. *Stages of Faith*. New York: Harper and Row, 1981.

Fowler is the leading theorist of faith development. Kohlberg has embraced Fowler's work.

Galbraith, Ronald E. and Jones, Thomas M. *Moral Reasoning: A Teaching Handbook for Adapting Kohlberg to the Classroom*. St. Paul: Greenhaven Press, 1976.

A good practical guide to the dilemma-discussion method. Includes practical methods for constructing dilemmas and a collection of dilemmas.

Hass, Glen, Editor. *Curriculum Planning: A New Approach*. Boston: Allyn and Bacon, Inc., 1974.

A fine collection of articles on curriculum planning, including several articles on the cognitive development approach.

Kohlberg, Lawrence. *Moral Stages and the Idea of Justice, Vol. 1, Essays on Moral Development*. San Francisco: Harper and Row, 1981.

This is the first in a projected three volume anthology of Kohlberg's writings. Includes a complete bibliography of Kohlberg's writings.

Articles

Adams, Dennis. "Building Moral Dilemma Activities." *Learning*, March 1977, pp. 44-46.

Some good practical suggestions on presenting and discussing moral dilemmas. Also includes several sample dilemmas with accompanying "probe questions."

Blatt, Moshe M. and Kohlberg, Lawrence. "The Effects of Classroom Moral Discussion Upon Children's Level of Moral Judgement." *Journal of Moral Education* 4 (February 1975): 129-161.

This research report includes a brief description of a pilot moral development program in a Jewish Sunday School.

Galbraith, Ronald and Jones, Thomas M. "Teaching Strategies for Moral Dilemmas: An Application of Kohlberg's Theory of Moral Evelopment to the Social Studies Classroom." *Social Education*, Vol. 39, No.1 (January 1975), pp. 16-22.

Kohlberg, Lawrence. "The Child as Moral Philospher." *Psychology Today*, September 1968, pp. 25-30.

A good basic overview of Kohlberg's moral levels and stages.

Kohlberg, Lawrence. "Collected Papers on Moral Development and Moral Education." Center for Moral Education, 3rd floor, Larsen Hall, Harvard University, Cambridge, MA 02138.

Many of the essays in this early collection of articles (1973) have been published again in the first volume of Kohlberg's collected essays (see Books.)

Kohlberg, Lawrence. "Education, Moral Development, and Faith." *Journal of Moral Education* 4 (January 1975): 5-16.

An edited version of an address to the National Catholic Education Association in which Kohlberg discusses the relationship between faith and moral development.

Rest, James. "Developmental Psychology as a Guide to Value Education: A Review of Kohlbergian Programs. *Review of Educational Research 44* (No. 2, 1974): 241-258.

Rosenzweig, Linda W. "Toward Universal Justice: Some Inplications of Lawrence Kohlberg's Research for Jewish Education." *Jewish Education*, Vol. 45, No. 3 (Summer-Fall 1977): 13-19.

An overview of Kohlberg's levels and stages of moral development with recommendations for awareness of his theories in relationship to Jewish learning, specifically in the areas of ethics and history.

Rossel, Seymour. "Lawrence Kohlberg and the Teaching of Jewish Ethics." *Jewish Education*, Vol. 45, No. 3 (Summer-Fall 1977): 20-23.

An excellent article which punctures holes in Kohlberg's theories as they pertain to Jewish education. Rossel charges Kohlberg with secularizing morality.

Schein, Jeff. "Lawrence Kohlberg's Theory of Moral Development: Some Implications for Jewish Schools." *Alternatives*, Winter 1978.

Briefly reviews Kohlberg's theory and suggests how it might be applicable to Jewish education.

Schnaidman, Mordecai. "Values in Orthodox Yeshivot and Day Schools." *Pedagogic Reporter* 32: 16-19, Fall, 1980.

Briefly analyzes some of the more prominent needs and resources in Jewish moral education.

Social Education, Vol. 40, No. 4 (April 1976): 213-215. This issue contains a special section on the cognitive developmental approach to moral education, including an introduction by Kohlberg and an extensive bibliography.

Sosevsky, Moshe Chaim. "Kohlberg Moral Dilemmas and Jewish Moral Education." *Jewish Education*, Vol. 48, No.4 (Winter 1980): 10-13.

The author suggests adapting Kohlberg's theories to Jewish education by presenting *midrashic* and *Halachic* data along with the dilemmas.

Dissertations

Glosser, Joanne Katz. "Moral Development in Jewish Education: In Search of a Synthesis." Masters Degree Thesis, Hebrew Union College-Jewish Institute of Religion, Los Angeles, 1977.

Menitoff, Michael. "A Comparative Study of Moral Development in Jewish Religious School Settings. Ph.D. dissertation, U.C.L.A., 1977.

Rosenzweig, Linda W. "Moral Dilemmas in Jewish History." Ph.D. dissertation, Carnegie Mellon University, 1975.

Schein, Jeffrey. "Genesis and In Their Footsteps: An Evaluation of Two Programs in Moral Education Designed for Jewish Schools." Ph.D. dissertation, Temple University, 1981.

Sosevsky, Moshe Chaim. "Incorporating Moral Education Into the Jewish Secondary School Curriculum." Ph.D. dissertation, Ferkauf Graduate School, Yeshiva University, 1980.

Ury, Zalman F. "The Ethics of Salanter and Moral Education in the Jewish School." Ed.D dissertation, University of California, 1966.

Journal

Journal of Moral Education. For subscription information, write:

> NFER - Nelson Publishing Co., Ltd.
> Darville House 2 Oxford Road E.
> Windsor, Berks SL4 IDF
> England

Kohlberg is an associate editor of this journal. It is an excellent source of information on many topics related to moral education.

Audiovisual Materials

"Teacher Training in Values Education: A Workshop." Filmstrip Series. Guidance Associates, 757 Third Ave., New York, NY 10017, 1976.

Kohlberg and Edwin Fenton helped produce this series of four sound filmstrips, which also includes an audio-tape, worksheets and a teacher's guide.

PROVIDING FOR THE JEWISH GIFTED

Zena W. Sulkes

In our continuing effort to be part of the successful middle class of American society, Jews have typically stressed school, learning and achievement. Along the way, we have perpetuated the image of all of our children as high achieving, talented students. How many times have we heard the statement "All Jewish children are gifted"?

The fact that there has been a growing trend in our country to recognize special and individual needs of students has brought about increased study, funding, programs and literature about the gifted. "We Americans are justly proud of our egalitarianism . . . but we are equally proud of our goal of individualization to fit the program to the child's needs."[1] Jewish educators need to be aware of the direction that secular education is taking in this area, its implications and applications to the Jewish educational setting.

Defining the Gifted

Before we deal with the needs of the gifted students in our religious schools, we need to have some understanding of the population about whom we are concerned. Educational reseachers, teachers and governmental agencies have recommended many methods of identification. Although religious school administrators do not have the responsibility for identifying exceptional children, they have traditionally asked parents to share information about their child's school performances. Religious school parents have frequently been reluctant to share with us information about school related prob-

lems and labels attached to their children such as "learning disabled," "emotionally disturbed," etc. However, they have usually been most eager to share the label "gifted" and/or "talented" and to tell us proudly about accelerated or enriched secular school programming.

In 1972, the United States Office of Education report to Congress created a National Office of Gifted and Talented and delineated six general areas of gifted and talented abilities. This report suggested that any person who possessed superior ability in any of these general categories, or any combination of them, should be considered gifted.[2] These categories are:

1. General Intellectual Ability: This kind of giftedness corresponds roughly to I.Q. Any child in your classroom who performs very well in almost every academic area falls into this category.
2. Specific Academic Ability: A child fits this category who does outstanding work in math, language arts or other areas and yet is an average pupil in other subjects.
3. Creative Thinking: This category refers to the divergent thinker — the child who comes up with extraordinary responses even to the very ordinary questions.
4. Leadership Ability: You know the kind of student who is gifted in this area — the child who naturally and consistently assumes a positive leadership role.
5. Visual and Performing Arts Ability: This gifted child is consistently outstanding in aesthetic production in one or more such

[1] James J. Gallagher, *Teaching the Gifted Child* (Boston: Allyn & Bacon, 1975), p. 9

[2] S.P. Marland, *Education of the Gifted and Talented* (Washington, D.C.: U.S. Office of Education, 1972), p. 261.

areas as the graphic arts, sculpture, music and dance.

6. Psychomotor Ability: A child fits this category who displays mechanical skills or athletic ability superior to other children in the school.

In 1978, Congress redefined gifted and talented students in Public Law 95-561. It stated:

"For the purpose of this part, the term gifted and talented children means children and, whenever applicable, youth, who are identified at the preschool, elementary or secondary level as possessing demonstrated or potential abilities that give evidence of high performance in capability in areas such as intellectual, creative, specific academic, or leadership ability, or in the performing and visual arts, and who by reason thereof require service or activities not ordinarily provided by the school."

The application of these definitions to students to determine which students require special services, is not, of course, the responsibility of the religious school. However, the many models available which enable us to recognize these children are varied and often confusing. The major procedures recommended in the 1972 U.S. Office of Education report are:

1. Teacher observation and appointment
2. Group school achievement test scores
3. Group school intelligence test scores
4. Previously demonstrated accomplishments (including school grades and cummulative records)
5. Individual intelligence test scores
6. Scores on tests of creativity

In addition, behavior rating scales, parent recommendations and peer recommendations are sometimes utilized.

Standardized group tests of intelligence and achievement are easy to use, but have several drawbacks. Tests such as these are basically designed for the average student, and their objectivity is based on limiting responses to a selection of "correct" answers. Gifted students tend to see beyond these answers. Pegnato and Birch found that group I.Q. tests failed to identify nearly fifty percent of the students who scored about 125 on individual I.Q. tests.[3] Although they focus on general

intellectual ability, individual I.Q. tests such as the Stanford-Binet or the WISC-R, are usually the final screening in most schools.

In the area of creativity, the most widely used instruments are the Torrance Tests of Creative Thinking. These tests look for fluency, flexibility, originality and elaborated skills. Test items are usually open-ended questions and task completion exercises. These tests are usually administered by a school psychologist or specially trained teachers of the gifted and the results of these evaluations help the secular school design appropriate educational programs. A release form signed by parents can provide information to the religious school which can aid in designing appropriate programs of Jewish education. Teachers should ask the religious school principal or administrator to secure such information and a consultant should help with the interpretation if necessary. Characteristics of the gifted and talented students are almost as numerous as the number of students themselves. Most descriptions of the gifted refer to the characteristics found most often among them. Gifted individuals, however, do not necessarily possess all characteristics. The gifted child is likely to possess the following abilities:[4]

1. Reads earlier and with greater comprehension of nuances in the language.
2. Learns basic skills better, faster and needs less practice. Overlearning can lead to boredom.
3. Makes abstractions when other children at the same age level cannot.
4. Delves into some interests beyond the usual limitations of childhood.
5. Comprehends, with almost nonverbal cues, implications which other children need to have "spelled out" for them.
6. Takes direction independently at an earlier stage in life and assumes responsibility more naturally.
7. Maintains much longer concentration periods.
8. Expresses thought readily and communicates with clarity in one or more areas of talent, whether verbal, numerical, aptitudinal or affective.
9. Reads widely, quickly and intensely in one subject or in many areas.
10. Expends seemingly limitless energy.
11. Manifests creative and original verbal or

[3]Carol W. Pegnato and Jack W. Birch, "Locating Gifted Children in the Junior High Schools: A Comparison of Methods," *Exceptional Children* 25 (March 1959):300-304.

[4]Paul, Plowman and others, California State Department of Education, 1971.

motor responses.

12. Demonstrates a more complex processing of information than the average child of the same age.

13. Responds and relates well to peers, parents, teachers and adults who likewise function easily in the higher level thinking processes.

14. Has many projects going, particularly at home, so that he or she is either busily occupied or looking for something to do.

15. Assumes leadership roles because the innate sense of justice gives them strengths to which other young people respond.

Undoubtedly you have taught students who have demonstrated these characteristics. On first reading, these traits may appear to be totally positive. Yet there are problems inherent in each. For instance, a student who learned to read very early and is far advanced in that skill (characteristic #1) may find the usual religious school textbook for his/her grade level too simple and be bored by its approach. In this case, teachers should find a book with similar content at a higher reading level.

Similar problems exist in others of the categories. A student who displays characteristic #7, and is thus able to maintain concentration on a specific content area for a long period of time, might be reluctant to move on to another activity with the majority of the class. The child who exhibits characteristic #10 and expends seemingly limitless energy requires firm and consistent handling and many positive learning outlets for his/her energy.

Jewish Identity and Giftedness

In an age where cultural pluralism and ethnic identity seem to be at odds with one another, studies often examine the differences in racial and ethnic groups. While we find that gifted and talented students come from all different types of homes and all racial and ethnic groups, they are more likely to be found in some groups than others. Groups with the highest percentages of gifted students are those that place a great emphasis on intellectual areas and values. These families tend to have more extensive opportunities to develop those talents and skills that are already present in the child.[5]

Adler (1967), in a review of studies designed to relate intelligence to ethnic groups, found that high ability students can be found in every racial and ethnic group. However, there are clear differences in the proportion of students that are identified as gifted in different racial and ethnic groups. According to Adler, the highest ranking in terms of gifted students identified were: Jewish, German, English and Scottish origins. Terman and Oden noted a very high incidence of Jewish children in their now classic longitudinal study conducted from 1920 - 1960. Their research indicated that over ten percent of the sample was Jewish which is far larger than population incidence would indicate. Terman and Oden state:

> "The conclusion suggested by these detailed comparisons is that the Jewish subjects in the study differ little from the non-Jewish except in their greater drive for vocational success, their tendency toward liberalism in political attitudes and somewhat lower divorce rate."[6]

While it is precisely in the area of motivation that we may find the key difference between groups, updated studies are clearly needed. Current trends which point to a rapidly increasing Jewish divorce rate and a turning away by Jews from the liberalism of the past make Terman and Oden's conclusions somewhat suspicious for the 80's.

While genetic factors may be considered as a source for the different ethnic proportions found in identifying the gifted, the genetic pluralism of European society and the nature of intelligence indicate that it is more likely that cultural influences are the determining factor. Strodbeck (1953) compared family and cultural values and found that Jewish families doubled their numbers in the professional classes in one generation. He concluded that Jewish family values produce more achievers because they stress:

a. A belief that the world is orderly and amenable to rational mastery

b. A willingness to leave home to make one's way in life

c. A preference for individual rather than collective credit for work done

d. The belief that individuals can improve themselves through education and that one should not readily submit to fate

---

[5]M.A. Adler, "A Study of the Effect of Ethnic Origin on Giftedness," *Gifted Child Quarterly* 7 (1963) :98-101.

[6]L. Terman and M. Oden, *Genetic Studies of Genius,* Vol. 5 in *The Gifted Group at Mid Life* (Stanford, California: Stanford University Press, 1960), p. 310.

e. A greater equality in the power structure between the mother and the father in the family.[7]

Programming for the Gifted

Assuming that we are able to identify the gifted and talented students in our religious schools, the next step is determining how we can best provide for their special needs within that setting. Gallagher states that there are three types of changes a school can make: 1) the content; 2) the method of presentation; and 3) the learning environment.[8] These changes are particularly appropriate in a religious school setting. Yet, we need to remember that all students can benefit from an approach which considers their best learning style, includes involvement and provides flexibility for individual interests and needs.

Programs for the gifted in religious school are: alternate classes, honors sections, enrichment classes, in-class independent study, self-contained classes, special enrichment in classes, tracking, tutors and aides and resource people. In the remainder of this chapter these alternatives will be discussed with particular emphasis on school and on specific appropriate methodologies.

Alternative classes provide a different setting and curriculum which complement the regular religious school classroom. Such classes may be optional or required and should have a specially trained, knowledgeable instructor. Take for example, a sixth or seventh grade class whose major curriculum area is Jewish History and which utilizes Abba Eban's *My People* adapted by David Bamberger (Behrman House). An alternate class on Jewish history could be offered to bright and identified gifted students. This class could provide an expanded view of the subject and perhaps even use a variety of textual approaches using the original Abba Eban text from which the younger version is drawn.

This model is limited to a larger religious school where space, funding and the number of students is large enough to accomodate such a plan. The group might consist of an honors class of students who have demonstrated excellence in academic studies and express an interest in a more challenging class of the same curriculum. In an enrichment class, cross-grade groups for three grade levels meet on a regularly scheduled basis as part of the school. For example, a group of fourth, fifth and sixth grade students, clearly identified as gifted, can switch for a thirty to forty-five minute segment of the regular class to enrichment activities. This program can include curricular areas from all three of the grades that are part of the class. It can involve a specialist in gifted who works with the entire school on a rotating basis, dealing with bright students, grouped by approximate ages, and involved in the special enrichment class for a regularly scheduled time.

The drawback to cross-grade groups is the time absent from the regular classroom. It is also necessary to decide whether students are responsible for the regular class program as well as the enrichment class. Is there opportunity for the teachers of both groups to meet, share and discuss what will benefit the students most? Any type of additional programming for gifted students should include specialized staff, additional planning time, involvement of all teachers and staff working with a given child.

Kough has listed requirements that he feels should be met if an enrichment model for the regular classroom is to be implemented.[9] Questions to be answered are:

1. Has the classroom teacher identified students who are gifted?
2. Can the classroom teacher describe specific curriculum modifications?
3. Does some specific person have responsibility for the entire program?
4. Are students, Rabbi, parents, teacher, education director and the religious school committee in support of the plan? Do they know what is involved?
5. Are the parents of the students involved in the program involved in its process of creation and are they aware of the specifics of the program?

Any program worth doing is worth doing well; this involves planning, specifics and evaluation.

Tracking can allow students who are gifted in a specific area to be grouped together for part of their religious school educational program, but remain with their own age group

---

[7]F. Strodbeck, "Family Interaction, Values and Achievement," in *Talent and Society,* edited by B. McClelland (Princeton: Van Nostrand, 1958), pp. 186-190.
[8]Gallagher, *Teaching the Gifted Child,* p. 72.

[9]J. Kough, "Administrative Provision for the Gifted," in *Working with Superior Students: Theory and Practices,* edited by B. Shertzer (Chicago: Science Research Associates, 1960), p. 147.

for other areas. This is the most commonly utilized method for Hebrew instruction which, as a skill, can be assessed. Students can then be grouped by achievement levels. These same students may quite possibly be grouped by grade level for Judaic studies.

Strategies for Teaching the Gifted

Many religious school settings do not afford us the opportunity for special programs for the gifted. When this is the case it then becomes the responsibility of the classroom teacher to help his or her own gifted students. Religious school teachers can effectively use traditional techniques with gifted children in a heterogeneous classroom and still meet their needs through a differentiated curriculum.

Religious school teachers who want to help their gifted students can: 1) make it a point to use open-ended, divergent questions and activities; 2) get out of the gifted pupil's way, so he or she can learn things that are truly new and not a rehash of previously learned material; 3) pay attention to gifted students (they need you — your touch, your approval, your interest); and 4) examine your attitudes toward the gifted student. Learn to relax and enjoy the challenge they provide.

It is possible for a gifted student to participate with the classroom teacher in designing, executing and evaluating curricular modifications appropriate to his or her needs and still be an active classroom participant. Programs devised can involve a wide range of sensory experiences such as trips, films, books, records, pictures, charts, maps, art, etc. Students who find a particularly exciting learning experience can make this an area for independent study.

Independent study is one of the best models for the gifted because it builds on the gifted student's desire for self-initiated learning. The teacher's role is limited to that of encouraging gifted students to initiate projects of their own, to supervise and monitor the process and share in the product. A sample contract form for monitoring independent study follows:

CONTRACT FORM

Name of student or students involved in this activity:

_____

What I want to find out: (content to be studied)

_____

What I need to do: (resources to be used)

_____

_____

_____

What I will do with what I have learned: (method of sharing)

_____

_____

_____

_____

Date begun: _____

Anticipated date of completion: _____

_____

Teacher's Signature

_____

Student Signatures

Perhaps the greatest advantage to independent study is that the gifted student can acquire motivation and skills which will help him or her become a continuous Jewish learner throughout life.

Games have long been recognized as a valuable tool for educators. Particularly useful for gifted students are activities that simulate real life. Simulations have high motivational value because students see an immediately useful reason to learn — to succeed and win. Such games afford the gifted: 1) opportunities for high level thinking (critical, creative and logical thinking); 2) opportunities for teaching social values because although competition is present, cooperation is the common goal; 3) opportunities for gifted children to act and interact. While students become involved in the facts, the process and the key concepts to be learned in the game, they are engaged in exciting and satisfying play.

The key features of a simulation are:

1. It must clearly be focused on selected concepts and processes.
2. It should involve the students in a simulation of a reality based situation.

3. It must involve the dramatic qualities of a game.

4. Rules should be divided into several of the following kinds:

   a) procedural rules that tell how a game is to be played

   b) behavioral rules which tell what one player can do and the role specifications for each player

   c) goal rules that clearly delineate the goals and means of achieving the goals

   d) rules that specify consequences to a player when any of the game's rules are broken.

A format for designing your own simulation games for gifted and other students follows:[10]

Name of the Game _____

Statement of the Problem _____

Objectives of the Game _____

Scenario: Include past events, background information, the present time and setting, the conditions that may affect the game.

Characters and Their Goals: Give a brief description of the physical characteristics, the personality, and the player's goals for the game:

_____

A Point in Time: The exact place and time when the game begins.

_____

Resources: Props for the game — physical, social, economic, political, or personal.

_____

Rules and Their Administration: To govern players, the game pattern and scoring and how they are implemented.

_____

Evaluation and Feedback: Were objectives reached; can the game be improved?

_____

Inquiry is another strategy appropriate for teachers in regular classrooms for gifted and other students. The best lesson will not reach the student and create a commitment to learning until he/she has become personally involved in the learning process. Learning is an active process requiring a personal commitment

through the inquiry oriented strategy of teaching as endorsed by Arthur Combs.[11] This engages the pupil in decision making regarding his or her own instruction. It sees the student as seeking, probing and processing data from his or her own environment.

The process of inquiry involves first identifying and narrowing a problem of some kind to be studied. Then hypotheses are proposed by the gifted students to help guide their investigation. This is followed by proposals for the gathering of data. These processes are evaluated and then data are gathered and summarized about the hypotheses. The role of the teacher is that of guide, counselor or consultant. The teacher helps by providing situations and materials that create questions in the minds of students. An example of inquiry for middle school students might be to investigate whether there were really "righteous Christians" during the Holocaust. What methods would they employ, what processes for gathering data, what do they think the data would show? For more information on inquiry, see Chapter 5.

Another strategy appropriate for gifted students helps them to develop strategies to facilitate more effective problem solving. Synectics is a technique devised by W.J.J. Gordon.[12] The term denotes a process to stimulate creativity through analysis. Synectics can be thought of as specific stages or as skills. The first stage requires active listening skills and is characterized by feedback. A typical Synectic session might be: 1) problem formulation — one person defines a problem and indicates what has been tried and the type of ideas wanted; 2) group ideation — group members share the essence of ideas, and these are collected; and 3) potential goals identified — potential valuable goals are identified by the problem giver. The teacher may introduce speculation or creative ideas which might help spur on the process. This is known as excursion, and the students may be asked to think of analogies in a different environment. For example; religious school students attempting to gain a better understanding of ancestors and anti-Semitism might be asked to pretend

---

10 Dorothy, Sisk *Teaching Gifted Children,* Federal Grant Title V., The State of South Carolina, 1978.

11 Arthur Combs, *Perceiving, Behaving and Becoming* (Washington, D.C.: Association for Supervision and Curriculum, 1962).

12 W.J.J. Gordon, *Synectics* (New York: Harper and Row, 1961).

that they are a pair of J.C. Penney "plain pocket jeans" hanging on a rack with Sassoon, Jordache and other designer blue jeans. Their reactions as to how this might feel takes them away from the reality of the problem of being different and they may return to it shortly, refreshed and with new insights.

Enrichment activities can include individualized encounter lessons, bonus tables, "Super Heroes" and working as tutors and aides.

Encounter lessons are activities that stimulate creativity and utilize gifted students' inner strengths and their perceptions of these inner strengths to aid in the further development of their feelings and values. An encounter lesson is based on four principles which can be expressed in terms of teacher behavior.[13] The teacher will:

1. Help student think about who he or she is and what he or she can and ought to do.
2. Help the student feel valuable and worthwhile.
3. Help the student to see learning as relevant to his or her individual needs.
4. Help the student to develop and maintain a learning atmosphere that reflects psychological safety and freedom.

Encounter lessons are short in duration, lasting from twenty to thirty minutes. They are made up of an "involving" activity in which the students, usually in small groups, actively see, hear, taste, touch, smell and react to ideas and others. The activities should be as open-ended as possible, thus providing each student an opportunity to bring his or her uniqueness to task.

Encounter experiences are particularly suited to the religious school setting as part of a lesson used to introduce or to motivate, or as a culmination. They can be adapted to all levels, preschool through seniors. A specific example:

Lesson: The Torah

Objectives: To foster understanding
To implement self-awareness
To identify with the Torah and experience it in a unique way.

Procedure: Introduce the idea of the Ark as a resting place for the Torah. The scene is set and five students are selected at random and asked to stand next to each other facing the remainder of the group. They are then asked to imagine themselves as Torahs in an Ark. Each student should respond to the following sample questions:

1. The Ark door is closed, it is dark and the sanctuary is quiet. How do you feel? What are your thoughts?
2. It is Shabbat morning. The Rabbi and Synagogue President approach the Ark to open it and remove one Torah for the reading of this week's portion. Why should they pick you?
3. Tonight is Simchat Torah. The congregation is in attendance and eager to celebrate. You are about to be taken from the Ark and placed in the arms of one of the members. What do you want to tell this person who will carry you?

Evaluation: This is an important part of any encounter lesson. Discuss such questions as: To what extent did you become involved in this exercise? Did your awareness level change?

Bonus tables can be used to keep bright students who finish assignments very quickly involved in meaningful activites. A section can be set up for "Super Heroes," (students desiring more difficult, creative and innovative activities). For example; in connection with a unit of study, "The American Jew: Past-Present-Future!" (Eisenberg and Sulkes), "Super Heroes" could choose one of the following activities:

1) Research about Sephardic Jews (*Keeping Posted,* November, 1974). Create a pamphlet of the famous Sephardic Jews of our history such as Aaron Lopez, Judah Touro, Solomon Nunes Carvello, etc.
2) Investigate the traditions of Sephardic Jews (*Encyclopaedia Judaica, The Jewish Catalog*). Prepare a playlet depicting a Sephardic family and some of their traditions.
3) How did Jews respond to the question of slavery? Describe both positions as though you were their advocate and prepare a debate between the followers of Abraham Lincoln, such as David Einhorn, and those in favor of slavery, such Judah P. Benjamin (Karp, *Heroes of American History,* KTAV, 1972).

Another suggestion for a bonus table activity is a "Thing To Do Box." This is usually developed around a central stimulus material such as a book, a record, a play or filmstrip.

---

[13]Sisk, *Teaching Gifted Children,* p. 6.

The box lends itself to both elementary, middle and high school levels. It can be used as an extender and as enrichment for the regular classroom curriculum or to allow students to pursue an interest in a given subject.

Prepared ditto sheets, flash or task cards, records or tapes with headsets, books, etc. are appropriate for these individualized, enriching activities.

Conclusion

A number of different methods and ideas have been presented in this chapter. It is up to the individual teacher to incorporate into the curriculum those with which he or she is comfortable. In the past, education of gifted children in our religious schools may have been hampered by criticisms of elitism. Our gifted students need a better Jewish education so that they will provide future leadership for our communities and because education that has been adapted to their needs will mean that they can lead happier and more satisfying Jewish lives. If we can accept the premise that the purpose of Jewish education is to promote excellence and ensure the preservation of Judasim, then an educational system that is appropriate takes into account individual needs and differences.

BIBLIOGRAPHY

Books and Articles

Adler, M.A. "A Study of the Effect of Ethnic Origin on Giftedness." *Gifted Child Quarterly, 1963, 7, pp. 98-101.*

Abraham, W. *Common Sense About Gifted Children.* New York: Harper & Brothers, 1958.

Barbe, W.B., Ed. *Psychology and Education of the Gifted: Selected Readings.* New York: Appleton-Century-Crofts, 1965.

Combs, Arthur., *Perceiving, Behaving, and Becoming.* Washington, D.C.: Association for Supervision and Curriculum, 1962.

Cox, Ann. "The Gifted Student; A Neglected Presence." *Teacher,* November/December, 1979, pp. 75-76.

Education of the Gifted and Talented. Volume 1: Report to the Congress of the United State by the U.S. Commissioner of Education, August, 1971.

Gordon, W.J.J. *Synectics.* New York: Harper and Row, 1961.

Gowan J.C., and Demos, G.D. *The Education and Guidance of the Ablest.* Springfield, Ill.: Charles C. Thomas Publishers, 1964.

Guilford, J.P. *Intelligence, Creativity, and their Educational Implications.* San Diego: Knapp, 1968.

Isaacs, Ann Fabe, National Association for Creative Children and Adults, 1976.

Kough, J. "Administrative Provison for the Gifted." In *Working with Superior Students: Theory and Practices.,* edited by B. Shertzer. Chicago: Science Research Assoc., 1960.

Lamkins, Ann, "A Model: Planning, Designing, and Evaluating. Identification and Instructional Program for Gifted, Talented, and/or Potentially Gifted Children." Albany, New York: University of New York, State Department of Education, 1977.

Pegnato, C.W. and Birch, J.W. "Locating Gifted Children in Junior High Schools: A Comparison of Methods." *Exceptional Children* 25, (1959) pp. 300-301.

Plowman, P.D. and Rice, Jr., J.P. *Final Report: California Project Talent.* Sacramento: California Department of Public Instruction, 1969.

Renzulli, J. *The Enrichment Triad Model.* Connecticut: Creative Learning Process, 1977.

Sanderlin, O. *Teaching Gifted Children.* New York: A.S. Barnes, 1973.

Sisk, Dorothy, *Teaching Gifted Children.* Federal Grant Title V., The State of South Carolina, 1978.

Strodbeck. F. "Family Interaction Values and Achievement." In *Talent and Society,* edited by D. McClelland, Princeton, N.J.: Van Nostrand, 1958.

Terman, L.M. et al. *Genetic Studies of Genius.*I--V. Stanford, California: Stanford University Press, 1925, 1926, 1930, 1947, 1959.

Tuttle, Frederick B., Jr., and Becker, Laurence A. *Characteristics and Identification of Gifted and Talented Students,* Washington, D.C.: National Education Association, 1980.

National and State Resources, Organizations

Office of the Gifted and Talented
U.S. Office of Education
Washington, D.C. 20202

National Association for Gifted Children
8080 Springvalley Drive
Cincinnati, OH 45236

The Association for the Gifted
The Council for Exceptional Children
1411 S. Jefferson Davis Highway, Suite 900
Arlington, VA 22202

The Gifted Child Research Institute
300 West 55th Street
New York, NY 10019

Journals:

Exceptional Children
Council for Exceptional Children
1920 Association Drive
Reston, VA 22091

Gifted Child Quarterly
National Association for Gifted Children
217 Gregory Drive
Hot Springs, AK

G/C/T
Box 6654
Mobile, AL 36606

Journal for the Education of the Gifted
Ruffner Hall
University of Virginia
Charlottesville, VA 22903

EVALUATING AND CHOOSING LEARNING MATERIALS

Ronald Wolfson

On any given day in a Jewish educator's office, dozens of pieces of mail come across the desk. Among this onslaught of material are catalogues, brochures, and circulars announcing the latest filmstrip or textbook that is, according to its publisher, *guaranteed* to revolutionize Jewish teaching forever.

Not too long ago, Jewish educators bemoaned the fact that there was precious little to choose from in the way of classroom instructional materials on Jewish subjects. There were the two major private publishers of Jewish textbooks, the three ideological commissions on Jewish education and assorted large and small Jewish organizations which put out materials for "Jewish education" in its broadest sense.

As of this writing, a recent survey lists some 67 publishers of Jewish educational materials, ranging from large, well-established houses to small "kitchen table" publishers with something unique to offer. This tremendous growth in sources of instructional materials is in evidence at national teacher and educator conventions, in Jewish bookstores and in the large number of publicity circulars which are mailed to Jewish schools and teachers. Never in the history of Jewish education has there been such a wealth of instructional material for teaching the subject matter of Jewish schools.

Moreover, the variety and breadth of these new materials are quite impressive. The traditional text books are perhaps still the bedrock of published curriculum offerings. Yet, more innovative forms of instructional materials, including many "teacher-made" materials are available through the emerging network of Jewish teacher centers and libraries. In a word, the Jewish educator of the 80's has a new flexibility to be eclectic in the choice of instructional materials to bring to students.

However, with this new flexibility comes a new challenge — *how to evaluate and select the best materials*. How are Jewish teachers, principals and school board members to sift through the brochures and catalogues? How are they to make comparisons between various materials designed to reach the same objectives? How are they to judge the quality and effectiveness of expensive media programs? In other words, how do those responsible for selecting instructional materials become enlightened consumers of these products? There are three steps to making informed choices about which materials to use in a classroom or school. First, identifying and locating what currently exists in any specific area of curriculum — "What's available and how do I get it?" Second, once located, evaluating the material against some objective criteria — "Does the material meet our standards?" Finally, after evaluating what's available, comparing competing materials and reaching a decision regarding which material to use — "What shall we buy?"

Step I: Identifying and Locating Learning Materials

The most obvious source for identifying and locating what materials exist is the publishers themselves. Most companies mail brochures and catalogues on a regular basis to lists of Jewish schools provided by mailing houses or national agencies. If you or your school are missing catalogues, it is a good idea to prepare a short letter asking to be put on the mailing list of publishers from which you want to hear. The most current source of publishers active in Jewish materials development appears in *The Jewish Teachers Handbook, Volumes I and II* edited by Audrey Friedman Marcus[1] and *The New Jewish Yellow Pages,* edited by Mae Shafter Rockland.[2]

In addition to the Jewish publishers of curriculum material, there are many sources of learning materials that may be appropriate for your school or classroom available from publishers and distributors of general educational materials. For example, a company called Miller-Brody Productions[3] offers a series of filmstrips on famous authors which include the Isaac Bashevis Singer story *"Why Noah Chose the Dove."* A national distributor of Social Studies materials, Social Studies School Service,[4] offers a catalogue of materials dealing with religious and values education which includes many items of possible use in Jewish schools published by these general education companies. A local teacher center, library or university instructional materials center will usually have catalogues from these publishers.

Other resources for identifying learning materials are magazines, newsletters and professional journals published by educational organizations. Sometimes publishers will advertise in these journals. Some journals carry columns highlighting new products. Recently, two newsletters have appeared which publish critical reviews of materials —*The Center Review,* published by the Clejan Educational Resources Center of the University of Judaism[5] and SAFRA, A Quarterly Review of Jewish School Materials.[6] In the area of "teacher-

made" materials, *The Pedagogic Reporter*[7] publishes an annual round-up of innovative programs and the Jewish Education Service of North America offers a search service out of its National Curriculum Research Institute.[8]

Beyond catalogues, actual collections and displays of materials are certainly an important way to locate materials of possible interest. The first collection to consider is your own school office or library. You may be surprised at what you discover. Next look at collections of fellow teachers; many colleagues will gladly share resources. The third place to look is other schools and libraries in the area, especially those with teacher resource centers. At local Bureaus of Jewish Education, there is usually a collection of material which can be perused. In larger Jewish communities, Jewish teacher training institutions, universities and independent teacher centers often have extensive collections of published and unpublished learning materials. In some communities, Jewish bookstores carry publishers' lines, especially those which supply the local religious schools with texts.

One of the major attractions of national conferences of Jewish teachers and educators is the display of instructional materials offered by publishers. Not only are the materials available for inspection, but often a representative of the publisher or even the author of a particular item will be there to discuss materials of interest. Moreover, it is sometimes possible to arrange for a publisher's representative to visit your community to explain the company's products or to conduct a workshop on how to use certain materials. Of course, remember that publishers are trying to sell a product; although most want to be honest about their materials, their claims do reflect a biased opinion.

Step II: A Guide for Evaluating and Choosing Learning Materials

Once the search for materials has been completed, the next task is to subject the product to close scrutiny, preferably by using a set of objective criteria for evaluation.

Using established criteria for evaluating learning materials ensures that the evaluator

[1] Audrey Friedman Marcus, editor. *The Jewish Teachers Handbook, Volume 1.* Denver: Alternatives in Religious Education, Inc., 1980, pages 191-193 and Resource section, Volume II, 1981.

[2] Mae Shafter Rockland, editor. *The New Jewish Yellow Pages.* N.Y.: SBS Publishing Inc., 1980.

[3] Miller-Brody Productions, Inc., 342 Madison Avenue, New York, New York 10017.

[4] Social Studies School Service, 10,000 Culver Boulevard, Culver City, CA 90230.

[5] *The Center Review,* published by the Clejan Educational Resources Center of the University of Judaism, 15600 Mulholland Drive, Los Angeles, CA 90077.

[6] *SAFRA, Jewish School Materials Review,* Jewish Education Service of North America and the Board of Jewish Education of Metropolitan Chicago, 114 Fifth Avenue, New York, New York 10011.

[7] *The Pedagogic Reporter,* Jewish Education Service of North America, 114 Fifth Avenue, New York, New York 10011.

[8] Write the National Curriculum Research Institute, 114 Fifth Avenue, New York, New York 10011.

approaches the task with some guidance and that the results of the evaluation are based on a comprehensive examination of the product. It is so easy simply to "eyeball" material and make quick judgments about its worth. And yet, time and again in workshops on evaluating materials, participants have changed their opinions after examining materials using the criteria.

The following Guide for Evaluating Instructional Programs and Materials has emerged over the past six years of courses and workshops with teachers and educators interested in refining their evaluation skills.[9] It will be presented in outline form, with explanatory comments where necessary. Following the outline, some suggestions for use will be offered.

GUIDE FOR EVALUATING INSTRUCTIONAL PROGRAMS AND MATERIALS

NAME _____

DATE _____

1.0 Description

    1.1 Title

    1.2 Author(s)

    1.3 Author's qualifications
    Does the publisher detail the background and experience of the author? How much confidence do you have in the author's abilities?

    1.4 Publisher
    What do you know about the publisher? Have you used other products from them?

    1.5 Copyright Date
    How recent is the material? Beware of Social Studies texts with outdated information or pictures — particularly material on Israel.

    1.6 Cost
    Many times you will find the cost only in publicity brochures or catalogues.

    1.7 Components
    What's in the package?

    1.8 Type of material
    Is it a text, teacher's guide, film, filmstrip, map, transparency, game, videotape, record, cassette, slide program, learning center, etc.?

    1.9 Technical characteristics

    Number of pages _____ Size _____ Speed _____ Length _____

    Black and white _____ Color _____ Sound _____

2.0 Appropriateness

    2.1 Is the target population specified?
    Does the producer tell you for which learners this material is intended?

        2.1.1 Age

[9]The field of product evaluation in general education has itself emerged only in the last decade. Major references are:
a. Bank, James A., "Evaluating and Selecting Ethnic Studies Materials." *Educational Leadership* 31. (April 1974), p. 593-96.
b. *EPIEgram, the Educational Consumers Newsletter.* Educational Products Information Exchange Institute, 475 Riverside Drive, New York, New York 10027.
c. *Instructional Materials: Selection and Purchase.* Washington, D.C.: National Educational Association, 1976.
d. Klein, M. Frances. *About Learning Materials.* Washington, D.C.: Association for Supervision and Curriculum Development, 1978.
e. Tyler, Louise L., M. Frances Klein, and associates. *Evaluating and Choosing Curriculum and Instructional Materials.* Educational Resource Associates, P.O. Box 415, Glenville, California 93226, 1976.

2.1.2 Grade level

2.1.3 Special characteristics of learners
Do the learners need to be bilingual? Is it intended for students with special needs?

2.2 Is the product appropriate regarding:

2.2.1 Grade Level
In your best judgment, will this product be usable in the grade level indicated by the producer? If not, what grade level do you suggest?

2.2.2 Language
Will the vocabulary and terminology used in the product be understandable to learners in the grade level indicated? Look at both English and Hebrew words. Are Sephardic or Ashkenazic transliterations used? Are the instructions clear to students?

2.2.3 Freedom from bias, sexist language and prejudiced attitudes or concepts. Look carefully at materials from the various ideological movements. Can a Reform school use materials published by Orthodox groups or vice versa?

3.0 Objectives

3.1 Are the objectives clearly and specifically stated?
What is the product intended to do? Are there behavioral objectives? Attitudinal objectives? Affective objectives? Social objectives?

3.2 Is the value of the objectives substantiated?
Does the publisher/author state why students should learn this material? Of what value will it be to them?

3.3 What outcomes are anticipated by the author if the program is used?
How much will be learned? What does the author state will happen after students finish the material?

3.4 Are there implicit objectives which may lead to unintended outcomes?
Beware of hidden curricula! Is there anything in the presentation of material which might result in outcomes *not* anticipated?

4.0 Learning Activities

4.1 What are the learning activities?

4.1.1 Types of activity
Projects, lectures, listening/viewing media, discussions, etc.?

4.1.2 Content areas
What content is presented? What is included? What is left out?

4.2 Are the learning activities directly related to the objectives?

4.2.1 Are the learning activities presented sequentially so as to develop student behavior, skills, attitudes?

4.3 Will the material and activities be of interest to students?
Is there sufficient motivation to activate student involvement with the material? Will the material be meaningful to the students?

4.4 Does the product communicate information which is accurate?

4.5 Are a variety of alternative learning experiences or activities suggested ?

4.6 Can the product be used in a variety of curricular contexts? Where in the school curriculum can the product be used?

5.0 Utilization

5.1 Is there a teacher's guide?   Does it:

5.1.1 Specify role(s) of the teacher?

Is the teacher a lecturer, discussion leader, facilitator, etc.?

5.1.2 Describe special skills necessary for the teacher and provide instruction in those skills? If the teacher is to lead a discussion, does the guide offer tips for leading discussions?

5.1.3 Describe special equipment conditions or materials that are necessary. Do you need a special film projector, craft supplies, etc.?

5.1.4 Is there a bibliography?

5.2 Is the material durable and reusable? Will the product stand up to the wear and tear of classroom use? Are any components of the product consumable, necessitating replacement?

5.3 Does the price reflect the full cost of the program? Do you need to buy or rent special equipment to use the product?

6.0 Technical quality

Rate on a four point scale: **Excellent**   **Good**   **Fair**   **Poor**

6.1 Photography

6.2 Graphics

6.3 Color

6.4 Sound

6.5 Music

6.6 Narration

6.7 Script

6.8 Sequence/layout

6.9 Type size

7.0 Evaluation

7.1 Was the program evaluated before publication? It is rare for publishers to document any field-testing of materials before publication. Nevertheless, write and ask.

7.1.1 If yes, in what different situations and what kinds of evaluations were done? If the field-testing was done at camp, why do you think it will work in school? Was it tested in "average" classrooms with "average" teachers?

7.2 Has the material ever been revised?

7.3 Can the effectiveness of the program be evaluated by means provided in the material? Are student tests provided? Other forms of evaluation?

8.0 Personal Preference

8.1 Does the overall plan, appearance and content of the product elicit in the educator feelings of

8.1.1 Worth Is it worthwhile?

8.1.2 Trust Do I trust it to do what it says it will do?

8.1.3 Reliability Will it continue to deliver what it promises for a long time (particularly when considering adopting texts or investing in media)?

8.1.4 Potential for approval/disapproval by others Will the product be controversial if used?

8.1.5 Does the material fit your philosophy of Jewish education? (If you're a "humanist," can you use programmed Hebrew material?)

9.0 General Summary Comments

_____

10.0 Would you purchase it?   _____

        use it?   _____

        not use it?   _____

Step III: Decision Making Among Alternatives

There is a variety of approaches to making decisions about curriculum in Jewish schools. In some schools, the school board decides on the curriculum to be used; in others, this decision is left totally to the professional educator. There are even instances when teachers are able to decide what materials to use.

In any case, the criteria suggested above should help whoever is charged with the task of evaluating learning materials for use in the school. This Guide is just that — a guide which should be adapted to each user's needs and situation. For some, the Guide is very thorough; for others, the Guide may demand more time than is available. The shorter Quick Checklist which follows is offered as an alternative for those unable to study a piece of material in depth:

A QUICK CHECKLIST

1. Is the product appropriate for the grade level specified?

2. Are the objectives clearly and specifically stated?

3. Are the learning activities directly related to the objectives?

5. Will the material and activities be of interest to students?

5. Are a variety of alternate learning experiences or activities suggested?

6. Is there a teacher's guide which provides teacher instruction?

7. Is the material durable and reusable?

8. Is the technical quality satisfactory?

9. Was the program evaluated before publication?

10. Can the effectiveness of the product be evaluated by means provided in the material?

I would purchase it _____

use it _____ not use it _____ .

The most comprehensive approach to evaluating and selecting learning materials might take the following form. Appoint a subcommittee of the school board to take on the responsibility of evaluating material before purchase. Include on this committee the principal and teacher representatives. Acquire copies of the material to be evaluated or, in the case of media, arrange a preview showing to the committee. Ask each committee member to fill out a "Guide for Evaluating and Choosing Learning Materials" for each product under consideration. If many products are being considered for one slot in the curriculum, assign one product to each committee member, asking each individual to prepare a summary report to the entire group. When all evaluations have been completed, share the results with the group and come to a consensus on which products should be purchased.

A note of caution. The evaluation of learning materials through the use of criteria is an important step, but even the most thorough examination of materials from an armchair will not substitute for tryout and evaluation in the field. It is entirely possible to rate a particular product high in quality, content and appropriateness, purchase it and introduce it into the classroom, only to find that it doesn't work. There is no substitute for experience. That is why reports of field-testing are so important. If the publisher cannot furnish evaluations of the material, ask for the names and addresses of other schools or teachers who have purchased and used the material. Contact them directly and ask them about their experience with the product. Beware! Just as asking someone else how they liked a movie carries the risk that your tastes may be different, so, too, asking colleagues their opinion about materials is somewhat risky. Yet, the more information you can gather about the product, the better the chances of making the right choice.

One further idea. Some instructional products, especially media, can be previewed before purchase. Or, if the publisher does not offer preview privileges, you might be able to borrow or rent the material from a library, learning center or neighboring school. As the cost of filmstrips, films and other media climbs higher and higher it behooves anyone assigned the task of evaluating and choosing instructional products to preview and try out *before* purchase.

Jewish educators today are indeed fortunate to have an ever increasing variety of learning materials from which to choose for their instructional purposes. Evaluating these learning materials requires an investment of time and energy. Yet, to invest this effort enables the educator to be a skilled and informed consumer and user of educational products. Our field demands no less.

The author is indebted to dozens of teachers, students, and colleagues who have used and commented on this Guide. A special thanks is due M. Frances Klein, a pioneer in this area of research in public education, whose work has been basic to my own.

INDEX

Index